MENTAL HEALTH ANI
WELLBEING THROUG
SCHOOLS

Ment(
variou
devel

Tl
some
in scl
propc

- (
  t
  a
- ~
  s
- ~
  a
  t
- ~
  a
)

Ment(
reseai
schoc
healtl
work
have
expei

Rosa
Fedei
psych
enced
psych

Phillip T. Slee is Professor in Human Development at the School of Education at Flinders University, Adelaide, Australia. He is a trained teacher and registered psychologist. His main areas of interest include childhood bullying/aggression, mental health and wellbeing, stress and teacher education. He has a particular interest in the practical and policy implications of his research. He and Shute recently co-authored *Child Development: Theories and Critical Perspectives* (second edition).

'Many guides focus on the prevention of school bullying. Few have been designed to take the challenge the other way round, that is to promote mental health for children through schools. *Mental Health and Wellbeing through Schools* is THE indispensable guide to improve the school experience and beyond of students and to implement interventions effectively. It provides a sound analysis of what works and most importantly under which conditions. Prompted by the Student Wellbeing and Prevention of Violence Centre (SWAPv) at Flinders University, this book is an invaluable contribution to a sensible evidence-based approach for intervention in schools and will no doubt be a source of inspiration and effectiveness for policy makers, school staff and researchers towards children's wellbeing.' – *Professor Catherine Blaya, Chair of the International Observatory of Violence in Schools.*

'Now that schools are taking a more central role in the promotion of mental health and wellbeing of children and young people, this book is a timely invaluable resource for educational authorities, teacher educators, school leaders, teachers and other educators and researchers. Through the varied contributions of key researchers and practitioners in the field, this book discusses the various challenges faced by those working in this area and suggests how such challenges may be turned into opportunities for the promotion of mental health and wellbeing through schools.' – *Professor Carmel Cefai PhD (Lond.), CPsychol FBPsS Head, Department of Psychology, Director, Centre for Resilience & Socio-Emotional Health, University of Malta*

'A growing number of children and young people struggle with a range of mental health issues in today's complex and changing world. This book provides compelling evidence for the value of programmes that promote emotional health and wellbeing on a large scale in schools. The international team of authors, each one widely-respected in the field, explores critical aspects involved in the implementation of such programmes across nations and addresses the many challenges that face educators and healthcare professionals in the task. This timely book is essential reading for researchers, practitioners, managers and policy-makers.' – *Helen Cowie, Emeritus Professor, Faculty of Health and Medical Sciences, University of Surrey*

MENTAL HEALTH AND WELLBEING THROUGH SCHOOLS

The way forward

Edited by
Rosalyn H. Shute and
Phillip T. Slee

Routledge
Taylor & Francis Group

LONDON AND NEW YORK

First published 2016
by Routledge
2 Park Square, Milton Park, Abingdon, Oxon, OX14 4RN

and by Routledge
711 Third Avenue, New York, NY 10017

Routledge is an imprint of the Taylor & Francis Group, an informa business

British Library Cataloguing in Publication Data
A catalogue record for this book is available from the British Library

Library of Congress Cataloging in Publication Data
Names: Shute, Rosalyn H., editor of compilation. | Slee, Phillip T., editor of compilation.
Title: Mental health and wellbeing through schools : the way forward / edited by Rosalyn H. Shute and Phillip T. Slee.
Description: Abingdon, Oxon ; New York, NY : Routledge, 2016. Identifiers: LCCN 2015036554| ISBN 9780415745185 (hbk) | ISBN 9780415745277 (pbk) | ISBN 9781315764696 (ebk)
Subjects: LCSH: Students--Mental health. | School children--Mental health. | Students--Mental health services. | School children--Mental health services. | School mental health services.
Classification: LCC LB3430 .M456 2016 | DDC 371.7/13--dc23
LC record available at http://lccn.loc.gov/2015036554

ISBN: 978-0-415-74518-5 (hbk)
ISBN: 978-0-415-74527-7 (pbk)
ISBN: 978-1-315-76469-6 (ebk)

Typeset in Bembo and Stone Sans
by Florence Production Ltd, Stoodleigh, Devon, UK

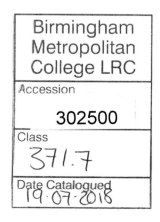

CONTENTS

FIGURES AND TABLES

Figures

Table

CONTRIBUTORS

ASKELL-WILLIAMS, Helen, BA, Grad.Dip.App.Psych, A.Mus.A, BEd (Spec. Ed. Hons), PhD. Associate Dean of Research, School of Education, Flinders University, South Australia. Director of the Flinders Educational Futures Research Institute. Her research and teaching interests are in cognitive psychology and mental health promotion in educational settings. She has recently edited the volume *Transforming the Future of Learning with Educational Research* (IGI Global). helen.askell-williams@flinders.edu.au

ASTOR, Ron Avi, PhD. Richard M. and Ann L. Thor Professor of Urban Social Development, School of Social Work and Rossier School of Education, University of Southern California. He has examined the role of the physical, social-organisational and cultural contexts in schools related to different kinds of school violence (e.g., sexual harassment, bullying, school fights, emotional abuse, weapon use, teacher/child violence). His recent research examines supportive school climates in military-connected schools. rastor@usc.edu

BARNES, Amy, BA (Hons), MPH. Research Support Officer at the Telethon Kids Institute, University of Western Australia. Her research interests include the social and psychological bases of health behaviour, gendered aspects of young people's wellbeing and prevention of bullying and cyberbullying behaviour in primary and secondary Australian schools. amy.barnes@telethonkids.org.au

BEINECKE, Richard H., DPA, ACSW. Professor, Suffolk University Institute for Public Service and Suffolk University Healthcare Department, Boston. He teaches US health policy, global health and leadership, is studying mental health responses to the Boston bombings and co-editing three books on change leadership (Sage). Former roles include: principal evaluator of the Massachusetts Behavioral Health

Program; co-principal evaluator of Boston HIV/AIDS programs; clinical/management positions in community mental health centres and at Harvard Community Health Plan. rickhbeinecke@comcast.net

BENBENISHTY, Rami, BSW, MSW, PhD. Professor of Social Work, Bar-Ilan University, Israel. He is interested in the welfare of children. His past work includes research on school violence and climate, and on children and youth at risk, with a focus on children in out of home care. ramibenben@gmail.com

BOTTROFF, Verity, Dip. T, Ad. Dip. T. (Sp. Ed.), BEd, MEd, PhD. Adjunct Associate Professor, Disability and Community Inclusion, Flinders University, Australia. Professional history includes: Head and Associate Dean School of Special Ed. and Disability Studies; developed first undergraduate and postgraduate courses in Autism Spectrum Disorders (ASD) in Australia. Her research focus on ASD includes social cognition, development of friendships, bullying and strategies for coping with stress and anxiety. verity.bottroff@flinders.edu.au

BRIGHI, Antonella, PhD. Senior Lecturer of Developmental Psychology and Education at Bologna University, Italy. Professional history includes: Professor of Developmental Psychology; coordinator of European and national projects on bullying and cyberbullying; International Research Fellow at Flinders University, Australia. Her research focuses on risk factors, incidences and programs for the prevention of bullying and cyberbullying and for promoting mental health, and social and emotional development from infancy to adolescence. antonella.brighi @unibo.it

CAPP, Gordon, MSW, LCSW. PhD student in the School of Social Work, University of Southern California. Professional experience includes teaching public school (elementary and middle) in Colorado, and several years of clinical practice in California as a child and family therapist in community mental health. His research interests include the influence of school environments on mental health outcomes, school climate and youth resiliency and wellbeing. capp@usc.edu

CHEN, Junwen, PhD. Lecturer in the School of Psychology, Flinders University. She held several academic positions at universities in Japan and also worked as a clinical psychologist before joining Flinders. Her research focuses on investigating underlying mechanisms of, and developing and evaluating treatments for, anxiety and depression in adults and adolescents. She has over 60 peer-reviewed publications in Japanese and English. junwen.chen@flinders.edu.au

CROSS, Donna, BEd, Ed D. Winthrop Professor with the Faculty of Medicine, Dentistry and Health Sciences at the University of Western Australia and Telethon Kids Institute; Adjunct Professor, Edith Cowan University. Her research focuses on the development and implementation of school-based interventions to prevent bullying and associated mental health harms among young people. donna.cross @telethonkids.org.au

ESSAU, Cecilia A., BA (Hons.), MA, PhD. Professor of Developmental Psycho-pathology and Director of Centre for Applied Research and Assessment in Child and Adolescent Wellbeing, University of Roehampton, UK. She obtained her undergraduate and Masters degrees from Lakehead University, her PhD from the University of Konstanz and her post-doctoral degree (Qualification for tenure-track professorships in Germany) from the University of Bremen. She has authored 180 articles and authored/edited 17 books on youth mental health. c.essau@roehampton.ac.uk

GLADSTONE, Emilie J., BA, MPH. School of Population and Public Health, University of British Columbia, Canada; researcher with the pharmaceutical policy team at the Centre for Health Services and Policy Research. Her research addresses sex and gender disparities in patterns of prescription opioid use and related harms. She has expertise in managing and analysing large population health databases and has worked with Bonnie Leadbeater on the WITS programs. emilie.gladstone @ubc.ca

GRAETZ, Brian, MPsych (Clin), PhD. Until 2015, General Manager at *beyondblue,* a major national Australian mental health organisation, and Adjunct Senior Clinical Lecturer in the Department of Paediatrics at the University of Adelaide. Professional history includes school teaching, clinical psychology, research and project delivery managing national research projects (e.g., Australian National Child and Adolescent Mental Health Survey) and school-based initiatives in primary schools (*KidsMatter*) and secondary schools (*MindMatters*). brian.graetz@healthstrategy.com.au

GREENBERG, Mark, PhD. Bennett Endowed Chair in Prevention Research in Penn State's College of Health and Human Development. Founding Director of the Prevention Research Center for the Promotion of Human Development; co-author of the PATHS Curriculum (*Promoting Alternative Thinking Strategies*). His research focuses on developmental psychopathology, wellbeing and the effects of prevention efforts on children and families. One current interest is how to help nurture awareness and compassion in our society. mxg47@psu.edu

GUARINI, Annalisa, PhD. Associate Professor of Developmental Psychology at Bologna University, Italy. Professional history includes: Professor of Developmental Psychology and Psychology of Education; coordinator of European and national projects on bullying and cyberbullying; Director of Clinical Service (SERES) for children and adolescents. Her research focuses on risk factors, incidences and programs for the prevention of bullying and cyberbullying, and cognitive and linguistic skills in children with typical and atypical development. annalisa.guarini @unibo.it

HUGHES, Jennifer, LLB, BA (Hons), MSc, PhD. Chartered Health Psychologist and Assistant Clinical Psychologist at the Child and Adolescent Health Service, Royal Edinburgh Hospital, Scotland. Professional history includes: Head of Clinical Effectiveness; Research Fellow in Cancer Care; provision of child and adolescent psychological interventions. Research areas include: experiences of cancer care, migrant health and access to health services. jennifer.hughes@nhslothian.scot.nhs.uk

HUMPHREY, Neil, BA (Hons), PG Cert, PhD, CSci, CPsychol, FBPsS. Professor of Psychology of Education and Research Director for Education at the University of Manchester, UK. Neil's research focuses on social and emotional learning, mental health and special educational needs (particularly autism). He recently completed *Social and Emotional Learning: A Critical Appraisal* (Sage). neil.humphrey@manchester.ac.uk

ISHIKAWA, Shin-ichi, PhD. Associate professor in the Faculty of Psychology, Doshisha University, Kyoto, Japan. He obtained his undergraduate and MA degrees from Waseda University and his PhD from Health Sciences University of Hokkaido. He also attended Swarthmore College, Pennsylvania as a Fulbright scholar. His research has focused on clinical psychology for children and adolescents, especially treatment, prevention and psychopathology. ishinn@mail.doshisha.ac.jp

JARVIS, Jane M., BA, PGDipEdStudies (Psych), M Ed Psych, PhD. Senior Lecturer, School of Education, Flinders University, Australia. Professional history includes: school counsellor, teacher, learning specialist (special education), behaviour intervention specialist and educational consultant in gifted education, special education and disability services in Australia and the United States. She currently works with schools in Australia and overseas on differentiating curriculum and instruction to meet the needs of diverse learners. jane.jarvis@flinders.edu.au

KHAMMASH, Umaiyeh, is a Palestinian medical doctor and senior public health specialist with over 30 years of experience in running various local and international health programs. Currently he serves as the Chief of Health Programs for the United Nations Relief and Works Agency (UNRWA) in the West Bank. He integrated mental health into primary health care and established the family & child protection model in the UNRWA Health system. ukhammash@juzoor.org

LEADBEATER, Bonnie J., PhD. Professor in Psychology at the University of Victoria, Canada. She holds degrees in Nursing and Educational Psychology from the University of Ottawa and in Developmental Psychology from Columbia University, New York. She has made internationally recognised contributions to research on adolescent parenting, emerging adulthood, adolescent depression, resilience in high-risk youth and the prevention of peer victimisation in elementary school children. bleadbea@uvic.ca

LENDRUM, Ann, BSc (Hons), PhD. Lecturer and program director of the Psychology of Education Master's programme at the Manchester Institute of Education, University of Manchester, UK. Her research focuses on the implementation of school-based social and emotional learning interventions. Recent work includes an evaluation of the Promoting Alternative Thinking Strategies (PATHS) program in English primary schools. She is currently leading a feasibility study of Second Step in the UK. http://www.manchester.ac.uk/research/ann.lendrum/

MARTIN, Jon, BA (Hons - Psych), Grad Dip Psych Prac, Grad Cert HRM, MAICD, Registered Psychologist (Non-Practising), CEO Community Support Incorporated. Jon has 17 years of service with Autism SA (South Australia), being CEO from 2003 to 2014. He has been involved in various national projects including autism training for the education sector and hosting the third Asia Pacific Autism Conference in August 2013, attracting 1,300 delegates from 20 countries. jonmartin@csisa.org.au

MASSAD, Salwa George, MCPH, PhD. Research manager at the World Health Organization Palestinian National Institute of Public Health and Adjunct Associate Research Scientist at the Institute of Human Nutrition, Columbia University/US. She has worked as assistant professor at BirZeit University, research officer at UNRWA and at Juzoor for Health and Social Development. Research interests: mental health, quality of life, nutrition, non-communicable diseases, mortality statistics, HIV research and monitoring and evaluation. salwamassad@gmail.com

McMILLAN, Julie M., BTeach, MEd, PhD. Senior Lecturer, School of Education, Flinders University. Previously at University of Illinois and teacher of students with disabilities. Her research interests include teacher professional learning and the effect of service provision and practice on student outcomes, specifically in the areas of augmentative and alternative communication, assistive technologies and instruction of students with complex support needs. julie.mcmillan@flinders.edu.au

MOORE, Hadass, MSW, PhD student, School of Social Work, University of Southern California. Professional experience includes: counsellor and teacher of high-school individuals who immigrated to Israel; therapist and case manager in a mental-health transition home in Israel; social worker with refugees and victims of torture. Her research interests include: conflict zones with the emphasis on gender; cultural diversity among adolescents and children in the education system; military social work. hadassmo@usc.edu

MURRAY-HARVEY, Rosalind, BEd, MEd, PhD. Adjunct Professor in the School of Education at Flinders University, Adelaide, Australia. Research and teaching interests are in educational and developmental psychology. Peer-reviewed journal article and book chapter publications and reports that draw on research involvement in national mental health promotion evaluations have focused on teacher professional learning and innovative research methodologies. www.flinders.edu.au/people/rosalind.murray-harvey

NICOLETTI, Sandra Maria Elena, Psychologist – Psychotherapist, Research Assistant in Developmental Psychology at Department of Educational Sciences – University of Bologna. Professional history includes: Adjunct Professor of developmental and educational psychology at the University of Bologna; teacher of clinical psychology at the School for Specialisation in Psychotherapy. Expert in traumatic stress and conflict management. Her research focuses on characteristics and diffusion of bullying and cyberbullying and implementation of support programs for children at risk of violence. sandra.nicoletti2@unibo.it

PEARCE, Natasha, BAppSc, PGDip Health Promotion, PhD. Honorary Research Fellow at the Telethon Kids Institute, University of Western Australia. Her research interests are child and adolescent wellbeing, school-based health promotion and using knowledge translation and implementation science to achieve real-world impact from evidence-based interventions. She is part of the Global Implementation Society Development Committee within the Global Implementation Initiative and part of the Australian Implementation Network. natasha.pearce@telethonkids.org.au

RICHARDS, Cathy, BSc (Hons), MSc. Lead Clinician and Head of Psychology, Child and Adolescent Mental Health Service, NHS Lothian Scotland. Professional history includes: chair of the Scottish CAMHS Lead Clinicians network, external advisor for *Preventing Depression and Improving Awareness through Networking in the EU* intervention program. Her interests include developing low-intensity resources such as healthy reading for public libraries and websites for young people (www.edinburgh.gov.uk/healthyreading; www.depressioninteenagers.com; www.stressandanxietyinteenagers.com). cathy.richards@nhslothian.scot.nhs.uk

SASAGAWA, Satoko, PhD from Waseda University, Japan (2007). She has published many articles in the area of clinical psychology, developmental psychopathology and cross-cultural research. Areas of interest include treatment and prevention/early intervention for mental disorders, as well as cultural diversity in the presentation of psychological symptoms. She also has a strong background in psychological statistics. She is currently a full-time lecturer at Mejiro University, and devotes significant time to treating patients clinically. sasagawa@mejiro.ac.jp

SHUTE, Rosalyn H., BSc (Hons), PhD. Adjunct Professor of Psychology at Flinders University and Federation University, Australia. Professional history includes: university Head of Psychology; teacher of developmental and clinical child psychology; coordinator of clinical and educational psychology postgraduate programs; paediatric psychologist. She researches peer victimisation and psychosocial aspects of child health. She and Phillip Slee recently completed *Child Development: Theories and Critical Perspectives* (Routledge). ros.shute@flinders.edu.au

SLEE, Phillip T., BEd, PhD. Professor of Human Development, School of Education, Flinders University. Trained teacher and registered psychologist. Director of the Student Wellbeing and Prevention of Violence (SWAPv) Research Centre at Flinders. He has published extensively on child development, mental health and wellbeing, bullying, school violence and stress, and produced educational resources (videos and resource packages). He is currently undertaking several international research projects on school violence. phillip.slee@flinders.edu.au

SPEARS, Barbara, DipT, BEd, MEd, PhD. Senior Lecturer, School of Education, University of South Australia. Research areas include cyberbullying; covert bullying; bullying behaviours; girls' friendships and peer relationships, conflict management, negotiation and wellbeing. Recent publications include Costabile, A., & Spears, B. A., (Eds.) (2012), *The Impact of Technology on Relationships in Educational Settings* (Routledge). barbara.spears@unisa.edu.au

THOMAS, Laura, BSc, MPH, PhD. Senior Lecturer, Edith Cowan University. Professional history includes: Deputy Head, Child Health Promotion Research Centre, Edith Cowan University; tutor of research methods and project units; youth health promotion coordinator. Her research focuses on youth engagement and mental health and wellbeing promotion. l.thomas@ecu.edu.au

WOTHERSPOON, Alison, BA, Dip Ed, PhD. Head of Screen and Media and Senior Lecturer, Flinders University, South Australia. She has worked in film and television at the BBC, Film Australia, ABC and SBS, studied Producing at AFTRS and worked as an independent producer in Sydney. She is currently in production for a series of documentaries on bullying research in India. Her most recent work is the series *Asperger's and Bullying.* Her educational resource *Come into My World,* about Alzheimer's, was nominated for an ATOM award in 2009. alison.wotherspoon @flinders.edu.au

FOREWORD

The coincidence of homophones is of special relevance in the case of the foreword to this book because the focus of the book is expressed in its subtitle: What is the way *forward* in the promotion of mental health and wellbeing in schools?

Schools have probably been seen as sites for the promotion of student mental health and wellbeing from the time of the establishment of the first school, though our sense of what mental health and wellbeing constitute has changed. Medical doctors were given a role in schools in the United Kingdom right at the end of the nineteenth century and Constance Davey was appointed as a school psychologist in this state of South Australia in 1924. So the importance of the school as a site for promotion of mental health and wellbeing is not a new realisation.

What has become clear in recent decades is the significance of the school as a site for the promotion of mental health and wellbeing in a broad sense. As has happened in the conceptualisation of 'health', it has become clear that mental health and wellbeing is not just about negatives – the illness, problems and difficulties likely to be prevalent in special populations. Rather, it is now recognised that the health, including mental health, and wellbeing of students should also be seen as encompassing positive, proactive elements that build the strength and wellbeing of all students to assist them to deal with any illness and difficulties that may arise. For the promotion of mental health and wellbeing in this broad sense, the school is a now recognised as a key site for action.

In Australia and in many other countries major resources have recently been applied to the generation and systematic evaluation of school-based mental health and wellbeing programs. In general, the efficacy of these trial programs has been established. Several of the key people involved in the generation and evaluation of these programs have contributed to this book. Their insights provide important foundations for the consideration of where the future efforts of governments, school systems, teachers and parents need to be focused.

Looking to the future of the current mental health and wellbeing programs in schools in Australia and in other countries is critical. Once the success of trial programs has been demonstrated, the programs have been spread to much larger school populations. As is discussed here, this use of the programs with larger numbers of students provides important challenges. So we can ask, for example, how do we ensure that the integrity of a proven program is maintained outside the controlled conditions of a trial? How do we ensure that the benefits of the programs can be sustained and developed across time? Such challenges for future promotion of mental health and wellbeing are the very timely focus of this book. Its editors and contributors are to be congratulated. The book includes the contributions of key researchers and practitioners from different countries that will provoke consideration of possible and effective programs for the future promotion of mental health and wellbeing in schools.

Mike Lawson
Emeritus Professor
School of Education, Flinders University

PREFACE

Children have the right to live a full life (Article 6, United Nations Convention on the Rights of the Child). Governments should ensure that children survive and develop healthily. Furthermore, Article 28 of the Convention states that children have a right to education. Against this backdrop of two of the fundamental rights of the child, this edited work presents chapters by prominent researchers and writers from around the globe on the subject of promoting mental health and wellbeing through schools.

How far, though, is a right to *mental* health encompassed by a right to health? Gable and Gostin (2009) observe that the "affirmative right to mental health has evolved comparatively slowly and gradually within international human rights law" (p. 253). It is a salutary fact that an Internet search provides precious little in the way of research or writing relating to the idea of mental health as a basic human right. Only 60 per cent of countries report having a dedicated mental health policy, 71 per cent a mental health plan and 59 per cent dedicated mental health legislation (World Health Organization Mental Health Atlas, 2011).

Gable and Gostin (2009) further note that, "The goal of achieving good mental health remains an important global concern, although one that is often overlooked and undermined by policymakers and politicians" (p. 249). Politically powerless groups such as children and young people are particularly disadvantaged and vulnerable in relation to the provision of mental health services. This is despite the fact that, as Margaret Chan, Director General of the World Health Organization observed in 2010, "Positive mental health is linked to a range of development outcomes, including better health status, higher educational achievement, enhanced productivity and earnings, improved interpersonal relationships, better parenting, closer social connections and improved quality of life" (2010, p. 1). Improving mental health and wellbeing through schools is therefore an important part of efforts directed towards creating a better quality of life for today's children and tomorrow's adults around the world.

The term 'mental health' is often taken to signify that an individual does not have a diagnosable mental illness. We did not impose any definitions on the contributors to this book, but the general approach they have taken is much broader, in accord with both a public health perspective and the understandings of many communities around the world. For example, Australia's Aboriginal and Torres Strait Islander peoples have no term for 'health' as a separable entity, so intimately is individuals' wellbeing tied to that of the community and their traditional lands (O'Neill, 2011, cited in Slee, Skrzypiec, Dix, Murray-Harvey, & Askell-Williams, 2012). Although recent influential perspectives continue to reflect a Western focus on the individual, their scope has widened considerably:

> [M]ental health . . . is conceptualized as a state of well-being in which the individual realizes his or her own abilities, can cope with the normal stresses of life, can work productively and fruitfully, and is able to make a contribution to his or her community. With respect to children, an emphasis is placed on the developmental aspects, for instance, having a positive sense of identity, the ability to manage thoughts [and] emotions, and to build social relationships, as well as the aptitude to learn and acquire an education, ultimately enabling their full active participation in society.
>
> (Sixty-sixth World Health Assembly, 2013, p. 3)

This approach, together with recognition of the foundational importance of the early years, has strongly influenced the development of school-based programs to promote young people's wellbeing, to prevent mental health difficulties and to intervene early when they do occur. It is now understood that mental health and educational attainment go hand in hand, and that schools and other sites of education offer significant advantages for addressing mental health. Several decades of experience have been accumulated and the field is rapidly developing further but, in many respects, aspirations and practice are outstripping knowledge. In this age of evidence-based practice, this book brings together international experts from a range of disciplines to identify and address a range of current challenges in addressing the delivery of mental health programs in schools.

The production of this book was prompted by two initiatives by *Student Wellbeing and Prevention of Violence* (*SWAPv*), a research centre at Flinders University, South Australia. The first initiative was a previous edited book (Shute, Slee, Murray-Harvey, & Dix, 2011) that brought together the expertise of *SWAPv*'s members with that of other Australian and international experts to address issues surrounding mental health and wellbeing from educational perspectives. The second initiative was a research forum in December 2012, where keynote speaker Dr Brian Graetz gave an inspiring presentation about the next round of challenges facing the implementation of mental health programs in schools. As General Manager of

Research for Child and Youth at *beyondblue*, a major Australian mental health NGO, Dr Graetz had gained deep insights into these issues; in particular, he had oversight of *KidsMatter*, the national mental health initiative in Australian preschools and primary schools, which was evaluated by members of *SWAPv*. The demonstrated success of the latest versions of the program places Australia at the forefront of developing, implementing and evaluating such initiatives. We wanted to share Australian experience and learn from other initiatives around the world. It had become clear that the time was ripe for a second book, building upon some of the themes of the first, as well as addressing new issues.

We are most grateful to Joanne Forshaw and her colleagues at Routledge Mental Health for taking up the idea, and for their invaluable assistance with publication. Dr Graetz kindly agreed to contribute the opening chapter, and the remainder of the book addresses many of the challenges he raises. They fall into four broad but related categories: challenges for organisations and leaders; challenges for teachers; new technologies; and targeted interventions. We specifically asked our contributors to focus on solutions, with the intention of producing a helpful and practical resource. Children and adolescents are referred to as pupils, students or young people, depending on country of origin, and authors use the spelling conventions of their own countries.

We hope the book will be of value to those involved in researching, developing, evaluating and implementing mental health initiatives in schools, including academics, educators and educational and mental health policy makers, as well as postgraduate students in relevant disciplines, such as education, social policy, psychology, mental health nursing and public health. We have sought out expertise from various parts of the world, and our authors come from Australia, Canada, England, Italy, Israel, Japan, Palestine, Scotland and the United States. The chapters encompass a wide (though by no means comprehensive) range of national contexts and stages of development of school-based mental health initiatives.

The professional backgrounds of our contributors are varied, and include the broad areas of education, psychology, public health and social work; many are experienced practitioners or policy-makers, as well as researchers, in their fields. We are most grateful to all of them for their scholarly input and unfailing gracious-ness throughout the process of collating and editing the chapters. We are delighted that Professor Ron Avi Astor and his colleagues agreed to read and reflect on the chapters and, in the light of that, to contribute a chapter of their own. As editors, we round off the book with our own reflections and suggestions.

Our hope is that the book will make a valuable contribution towards the international efforts now being made to promote, through schools, the mental health and wellbeing of children around the world.

Rosalyn H. Shute and Phillip T. Slee
Flinders University, Adelaide
April 2015

References

Chan, M. (2010). Mental health and development: Targeting people with mental health conditions as a vulnerable group. *World Health Organization*. Accessed 25.02.2015 at www.who.int/mental_health/policy/mhtargeting/en

Gable, L., & Gostin, L. O. (2009). Mental health as a human right. In A. Clapham, M. Robinson, and S. Jerbi (Eds.), *Realising the right to health. Swiss Human Rights Book. V. III*. Detroit: Ruffer & Rub, pp. 249–261.

Shute, R. H., (Ed.), with Slee, P. T., Murray-Harvey, R., & Dix, K. (2011). *Mental health and wellbeing: Educational perspectives*. Adelaide: Shannon Research Press.

Sixty-sixth World Health Assembly (2013). *Comprehensive mental health action plan 2013–2020*. Accessed 13.02.2015 at http://apps.who.int/gb/ebwha/pdf_files/WHA66/A66_R8-en. pdf?ua=1

Slee, P. T., Skrzypiec, G., Dix, K., Murray-Harvey, R., & Askell-Williams, H. (2012). *KidsMatter early childhood evaluation in services with high proportions of Aboriginal and Torres Strait Islander children*. Adelaide: Research Centre for Student Wellbeing and Prevention of Violence, Flinders University.

United Nations Office of the High Commissioner for Human Rights. *Convention on the Rights of the Child*. Accessed 25.02.2015 at www.ohchr.org/en/professionalinterest/pages/crc.aspx

World Health Organization Mental Health Atlas (2011). Accessed 25.02.2015 at www.who.int/mental_health/publications/mental_health_atlas_2011/en/

SECTION 1
Overview of challenges

1

STUDENT MENTAL HEALTH PROGRAMS

Current challenges and future opportunities

Brian Graetz

This introductory chapter draws upon the research literature and experience in developing, implementing and evaluating Australia's national government-funded secondary and primary school mental health initiatives. It raises various challenges in four areas: for leaders and organisations; for teachers; new technologies; and the need for targeted interventions. It therefore acts as a springboard for the chapters that follow, which take up aspects of these various themes.

Schools have long been viewed as a natural setting in which to deliver student mental health initiatives and programs (Ross, 1980). This view has largely been born from the twin observations that youth mental health represents a major public health issue and that schools provide the optimal ready-made vehicle for reaching large numbers of young people (as well as the key adults critical to their development). Advocacy for student mental health programs in schools is routinely observed in research, policy and mainstream news. For example, epidemiological studies typically find youth mental health difficulties to be relatively common (the figure of around one in five young people being often identified), and they invariably conclude with a recommendation for the broad scale roll-out of school-based programs – particularly those that can prevent mental health difficulties so as to reduce the impact on individuals and demand on limited services. Stories about mental health or social issues affecting youth (such as suicide, self-harm, and drug and alcohol misuse) are commonly reported in the media, with accompanying commentary regarding the need for schools to run programs that 'teach' students how to manage various challenges such as bullying, stress, anxiety and depression.

Over the past 30 years there have been numerous youth mental health and wellbeing programs developed for delivery in primary and secondary schools (Catalano, Bergland, Ryan, Lonczak, & Hawkins, 2002; Greenberg, Domitrovich, & Bumbarger 2001; Weare & Nind, 2011). Programs have varied enormously in their goals, theoretical underpinnings, intervention targets and delivery models – reflecting the diversity of funding sources and academic disciplines involved. While not always readily classifiable, some of the common 'program' types include: social and emotional learning programs; problem prevention or early intervention programs for specific mental health difficulties; resilience programs; mental health education ('literacy') programs; and programs focused on strengthening connections to the 'school community'. Individual programs may or may not be delivered as part of a whole school approach or broader framework seeking to generate collective action and encompassing multiple elements and targets (e.g., the Health Promoting Schools Framework, World Health Organization, 2000).

Today, there is a relatively large number of evidence-based student mental health and wellbeing programs available for schools. The Collaborative for Academic, Social and Emotional Learning (CASEL) in the United States identifies around 20 evidence-based social and emotional learning programs for primary schools. In Australia, *KidsMatter* – the national primary schools mental health initiative – identifies nearly 100 programs spanning the mental health promotion through to early intervention spectrum (Graetz *et al.*, 2008). There is also now a compelling body of research showing that student mental health and wellbeing have a significant impact on the core business of schools. Numerous studies have shown student mental health difficulties to be strongly associated with poorer classroom behaviour, academic performance, school attendance and retention (Masten *et al.*, 2005; Mihalas, Morse, Allsopp, & McHatton, 2009). Conversely, developmental science has shown that cognitive development goes hand in hand with social and emotional development and that enhancing children's social and emotional competencies has significant academic payoffs (Dix, Slee, Lawson, & Keeves, 2011; Durlak, Weissberg, Dymnicki, Taylor, & Schellinger, 2011; Heckman, 2008).

However, despite the availability of programs and the strong evidence for their benefits to students and the broader school community, large-scale roll-out and the sustainment of programs in schools remain the exception rather than the norm. The more common picture observed over the years is one of student mental health and wellbeing programs being delivered in the 'margins' of school life, sustained by a few dedicated staff members with minimal – and often precarious – short-term funding (Adelman & Taylor, 2000).

Researchers examining why dissemination has been so challenging often bemoan the lack of resourcing and inadequate policy frameworks, particularly curriculum (Weist, 2004). The general view is that these have been at insufficient levels for schools to effectively plan, integrate and sustain student mental health and wellbeing programs into 'normal' school practices (Adelman & Taylor, 2000; Han & Weiss, 2005). Difficulty in securing ongoing funding has been a constant theme over the years and, while frustrating, reflects the ongoing reality of funders managing competing and evolving budget priorities. In particular, programs developed and initially funded by organisations external to education jurisdictions understandably struggle when they seek to obtain jurisdiction 'buy-in' in terms of funding or staffing resources to secure a program's longer-term future.

A related issue, which probably receives less critical attention, is the quality of individual programs and the implementation demands they place on school communities (Han & Weiss, 2005). The extent to which individual programs understand the 'real world' needs and limitations of schools is a critical question. Programs developed and trialled under optimum conditions with significant funding and staffing resources often struggle when they are rolled out in the real world of reduced funding, tightly controlled curriculum, leadership turnover, and time-poor and stressed staff with limited opportunities for professional learning during school hours (Ringeisen, Henderson, & Hoagwood, 2003). There are also obvious tensions with respect to what is known about successful program implementation and school realities. As a general rule the more ambitious the program goals in terms of student mental health impacts, the greater the implementation and resourcing requirements. For example, evidence indicates that mental health problem prevention and social and emotional competency programs are effective when they are delivered over the longer term with sufficient intensity and a reasonable level of fidelity (National Research Council and Institute of Medicine, 2009; Nation *et al.*, 2003; Weare & Nind, 2011). Many schools understandably struggle to meet such program demands even with reasonable resourcing.

Ultimately, the extent to which student mental health and wellbeing programs can be incorporated into mainstream school practice with appropriate funding and resourcing may well depend on whether greater clarity and agreement can be achieved at senior government levels (and the broader community) on the central questions of: 'What is the appropriate role and function of schools with respect to student mental health and wellbeing?' and 'How does the role of schools relate to that of other sectors whose remit specifically covers youth and family mental health?'

Historically, schools have been provided with limited guidance on these crucial questions. While education policy frameworks identify student wellbeing as important, they tend to provide little detail beyond the need for schools to attend to students' social and emotional development as well as their cognitive and academic development (although the recent inclusion of social and emotional competencies into the new national curriculum in Australia reflects a notable exception). In particular, there has been relatively little guidance given to schools as to how they should respond to those complex student mental health or social issues, such as suicide and self-harm, that negatively impact on individuals and the broader school community. Even amongst the experts there is ongoing debate about the types of program that would produce the greatest benefits: for example, whether schools should focus more on universal mental health promotion or problem prevention efforts or early intervention programs targeting students with elevated risk or exhibiting difficulties – as well as whether screening for risk or difficulties should occur (Craig, 2009; Spence & Shortt, 2007). These debates at times reflect the differing views (and occasional positioning) of the various experts involved and are often played out with program funders, policy makers and school leaders, resulting in even greater confusion. It is not surprising that schools report being unsure of their role and, as a consequence, tend to remain reactive in this space (Hopkins, 2014).

Disappointingly, there has been only limited research on the views of school leaders, staff, parents and students with respect to youth mental health programs being delivered in schools and the types of program preferred. Recent research in the United Kingdom and Australia with students and school staff indicates a high level of awareness of youth mental health issues and the need for practical education and 'upskilling' such as how to support a student who is distressed (Graham, Phelps, Maddison, & Fitzgerald, 2011; Kidger, Donovan, Biddle, Campbell, & Gunnell, 2009). Notably, staff identified a clear link between the mental health of students and their own mental wellbeing. The findings from the 2009 Intercamhs (International Alliance for Child and Adolescent Mental Health and Schools) survey of 1,200 principals across 27 countries indicates that school leaders appreciate the significance of student wellbeing with over 80 per cent identifying student emotional/mental health as being 'very important' for academic achievement. When asked to rank the main student mental health and wellbeing issues confronting schools, principals identified the following three in order of priority: (1) bullying and harassment; (2) impulse control; and (3) anger management. With respect to training, education materials and resourcing supports the following four were given highest priority: (1) student and family supports for those with serious problems; (2) programs/strategies to teach students social and emotional competencies; (3) knowledge of effective promotion/prevention strategies and implementation; and (4) how to identify mental health problems early.

Taken together, these findings indicate that school leadership, staff and students believe student mental health and wellbeing to be an important issue for school communities and, moreover, that they are seeking practical support to deal with a range of issues. Working to identify and address the needs of school communities may well provide the foundation for more effective advocacy with respect to funding and improve program uptake and sustainability. For example, if school staff view a clear link between student mental health and their own wellbeing, then greater buy-in for student programs may be achieved if they also encompass self-care strategies for staff (Graham, Phelps, Maddison, & Fitzgerald, 2011; Kidger et al., 2009).

A second – and perhaps more telling – point that can be drawn from the above research is that school leaders are seeking effective responses to 'pointy end' or complex issues which often cause the greatest distress and impact on students, staff and the broader school community. Today, schools are grappling with a host of challenging issues such as suicide, self-harm, drug use, depression, anxiety, bullying and school violence, which – on anecdotal evidence at least – are becoming more prominent (Eckersley, 2011). Although these problems are not new, they are not static either and their immediate drivers and manifestations (e.g., cyberbullying) are continually evolving, as are their likely 'remedies'. Increasingly, many of the key youth mental health issues are being viewed as 'wicked problems' – not in the sense of being evil but because they are not readily solvable within any one sector of the community (Sanson, Havinghurst, & Zubrick, 2011) – see Chapter 2. Schools, with their need to focus on student learning and academic outcomes, understandably tend to look for 'quick fixes' that require minimal resourcing or the need for time-consuming community engagement and collaboration. Unfortunately, few ready-made solutions exist for many of the significant youth mental health issues, and schools will probably continue to struggle to identify effective responses until models are in place that can drive better coordination and integration between schooling, mental health, family and community services (Greenberg, 2004; Sanson *et al.*, 2011). Not that this means schools have the luxury of opting out: being on the 'front line' means that schools and staff have little choice but to manage as best they can.

The above discussion is not to suggest that schools cannot have a significant impact on students' mental health and wellbeing. It is, however, meant to highlight the need for school leadership to be well educated about programs and approaches that seek to impact across whole student groups or year levels, and to give careful consideration to their choices. This includes having a good appreciation of school community priorities and a realistic understanding of what can be achieved with the available resources, time and commitments, and knowing that a school can only do so much by itself and that support from the broader service (and parent) community is likely required to make any serious headway. Ideally, schools should be able to make conscious decisions regarding such things as the relative priority they give to universal mental health promotion or problem prevention efforts versus more-targeted strategies for those students at risk or already experiencing difficulties.

The need for schools (and jurisdictions) to become more discerning about their choices is becoming increasingly apparent as more student mental health programs or resources are becoming available. Advancements in web-based technologies are rapidly expanding the possibilities for schools in this space, not only in terms of student mental health programs and services, but also in areas such as staff professional learning and online tools for monitoring or evaluating the mental health and wellbeing of students and the broader school community.

Historically, student mental health programs have been predominantly delivered 'face-to-face' to students by either mental health professionals or school staff, often after completing some level of training. The level of funding required for face-to-face delivery has been one of the main limiting factors for broadscale program roll-out in schools as the costs quickly become prohibitive. Many youth mental health programs are now being developed or converted for online delivery, which enables program content to be directly delivered to students in a standardised manner (Christensen & Hickie, 2010). Online programs have been found to be particularly promising for problem prevention or for treatment programs for high-prevalence mental health disorders such as depression and anxiety, where studies have found similar mental health outcomes for online as for face-to-face delivery (Cuijpers, van Straten, Warmerdam, & Anderssan, 2008). Similarly, online technologies are expanding counselling or support options for youth (e.g., webchat) – an age group that has been traditionally poor at accessing help, often because of concerns over privacy (Gulliver, Griffiths, & Christensen, 2010). The introduction of smartphones has further expanded the frontiers with the explosion of mental health apps, ranging from the basic (e.g., apps that provide mental health information) to the sophisticated such as those which seek to monitor a young person's mental health and provide a tailored response via the automatic collection of data on such things as physical activity, social media use, and even music preferences (Donker *et al.*, 2013; Proudfoot, 2013).

Online mental health programs, apps and services are still in their infancy and the extent to which these will provide schools with effective vehicles to support student mental health and wellbeing is unknown. While they potentially provide options across the mental health promotion, prevention and early intervention spectrum, there remain some significant challenges. Many of the emerging programs have limited evaluations (evaluations for apps are virtually non-existent) and low completion rates for online programs are noted (Christensen, Reynolds, & Griffiths, 2011). Questions also exist regarding the school and staff roles: will schools make curriculum space available and will staff support young people to complete online programs, or will schools limit themselves to general promotion? Furthermore, to what extent will online programs or services facilitate the necessary links and integration between schools and mental health, family and community services?

Similar questions exist with respect to staff professional learning. Although web-based technologies provide for the direct delivery of programs and services to students, ongoing demand for staff professional learning with respect to individual programs and their broader role in supporting student mental health is likely. Online professional learning for school staff is rapidly emerging, providing a reach that was previously unattainable. Staff professional development is often seen as a cornerstone of successful mental health program delivery (Han & Weiss, 2005), but the extent to which school staff will engage with online learning is unknown, particularly where professional learning is not linked to registration or continuing professional development requirements. There is a need to identify the most-effective online professional learning models for staff engagement and learning, including whether online learning models can achieve the type of collaborative learning that has historically been successful in this field (Mellin & Weist, 2011).

Even with the above uncertainties, the use of web-based technologies to deliver mental health programs, services and professional learning in schools will continue to be keenly pursued by funders as vehicles to increase program reach and to minimise the difficulties (and political risks) attached to recurrent funding. While this will provide schools with greater opportunities, it also presents some obvious challenges. Schools are increasingly being viewed as a 'market' for developers of youth mental health programs, staff professional learning packages and student assessment tools, and anecdotally school principals are reporting a steady stream of digital and print solicitations. There is an obvious need for models that will help schools make sense of the student mental health and wellbeing 'market'; for example, the type of programs available, where they fit on the intervention spectrum, their resourcing requirements and their evidence base. Useful also would be research that provides for a better understanding of the factors that influence the program selections of schools and jurisdictions. Data collected on the *KidsMatter* national pilot involving over 100 primary schools in Australia suggests that research evidence of effectiveness is not the overriding consideration, with the vast majority of schools selecting one of two social and emotional learning programs which had not been formally evaluated (Slee *et al.*, 2009). This issue has been identified in a number of other countries and further discussed by Shute (2012).

A related issue is the need for broader 'public-health' models that help schools to recognise that such things as depression, anxiety, behavioural problems, bullying, self-harm and suicide, obesity, body-image issues, and drug and alcohol misuse are not unrelated issues and that their underlying risk and protective factors at a population level are likely to have more similarities than differences (Scott, Varghese, & McGrath, 2010). Often, schools are presented with separate programs or initiatives to tackle these issues which may well represent a duplication of effort as well as increasing the risk that school staff will feel overwhelmed and resentful of being asked to do too much. Unfortunately, funding bodies and program developers are often 'issue' based and as such produce programs specific to their issue without thinking about the other public health agendas being pushed onto schools.

Ultimately, it is unrealistic to view schools as the vehicles to achieve significant improvements in the major social and mental health issues impacting on the broader community and the public purse without major changes to their current role, function and resourcing. Without high-level government intervention, schools have limited capacity to alter their existing parameters and to achieve the level of integration and coordination required with other key service sectors to achieve impact. Nevertheless, schools are increasingly aware of the importance of student (and teacher) mental health and wellbeing for their core business and are seeing the need for practical support. Supporting schools to achieve greater clarity around their role and function in supporting student mental health and wellbeing, and a realistic and pragmatic approach to what can be achieved within individual school communities with the level of resourcing and commitment available, is suggested as a necessary starting point for progress.

References

Adelman, H. S., & Taylor, L. (2000). *Moving prevention from the fringes into the fabric of school improvement. Journal of Educational and Psychological Consultation, 11*, 7–36.

Catalano, R. F., Bergland, L., Ryan, J. A. M., Lonczak, H. S., & Hawkins, J. D. (2002). Positive youth development in the United States: Research findings on evaluations of positive youth development programs. *Prevention and Treatment, 5, Article 15*, 1–111.

Christensen, H., & Hickie, I. B. (2010). E-mental health: A new era in delivery of mental health services. *Medical Journal of Australia, 192*, S2–S3.

Christensen, H., Reynolds, J., & Griffiths, K. M. (2011). The use of e-health applications for anxiety and depression in young people: Challenges and solutions. *Early Intervention in Psychiatry, 5* (Suppl. 1), 58–62.

Craig, C. (2009). *Wellbeing in schools: The curious case of the tail wagging the dog.* Scotland: Centre for Confidence and Wellbeing. Accessed 22.01.2016 at www.centrefor confidence.co.uk

Cuijpers, P., van Straten, A., Warmerdam, L., & Anderssan, G. (2008). Psychological treatment of depression: A meta-analytic database of randomized studies. *BMC Psychiatry*, 8, 36.

Dix, K. L., Slee, P. T., Lawson, M. J., & Keeves, J. P. (2011). Implementation quality of whole-school mental health promotion and students' academic performance. *Child and Adolescent Mental Health*, 17, 45–51.

Donker, T., Petrie, K., Proudfoot, J., Clarke, J., Birch, M., & Christensen, H. (2013). Smartphones for smarter delivery of mental health programs: A systematic review. *Journal of Medical Internet Research*, 15, e247.

Durlak, J. A., Weissberg, R. P., Dymnicki, A. B., Taylor, R. D., & Schellinger, K. B. (2011). The impact of enhancing students' social and emotional learning: A meta-analysis of school-based universal interventions. *Child Development*, 82, 405–432.

Eckersley, R. (2011). Troubled youth: An island of misery in an ocean of happiness, or the tip of an iceberg of suffering? *Early Intervention in Psychiatry*, 5 (Suppl. 1): 6–11.

Graetz, B., Littlefield, L., Trinder, M., Dobia, B., Souter, M., Champion, C., Boucher, S., Killick-Moran, C., & Cummins, R. (2008). KidsMatter: A population health model to support student mental health and wellbeing in primary schools. *International Journal of Mental Health Promotion*, 10, 13–20.

Graham, A., Phelps, R., Maddison, C., & Fitzgerald, R. (2011). Supporting children's mental health in schools: Teachers' views. *Teachers and Teaching: Theory and Practice*, 17, 479–496.

Greenberg, M. T. (2004). Current and future challenges in school-based prevention: The researcher perspective. *Prevention Science*, 5, 5–13.

Greenberg, M. T., Domitrovich, C., & Bumbarger, B. (2001). The prevention of mental disorders in school-aged children: Current state of the field. *Prevention and Treatment*, 4, 1–59.

Gulliver, A., Griffiths, K. M., & Christensen, H. (2010). Perceived barriers and facilitators to mental health help-seeking in young people: A systematic review. *BMC Psychiatry*, 10, 113.

Han, S. S., & Weiss, B. (2005). Sustainability of teacher implementation of school-based mental health programs. *Journal of Abnormal Psychology*, 33, 665–679.

Heckman, J. J. (2008). Schools, skills and synapses. *Economic Inquiry*, 46, 289–324.

Hopkins, L. (2014). Schools and adolescent mental health: Education providers or health care providers? *Journal of Public Mental Health*, 13, 20–24.

Kidger, J., Donovan, J. L., Biddle, L., Campbell, R., & Gunnell, D. (2009). Supporting adolescent emotional health in schools: A mixed methods study of student and staff views in England. *BMC Public Health*, 9, 403.

Intercamhs (2009). *International survey of principals concerning emotional and mental health and well-being.* Accessed 1.08.2014 at www.intercamhs.org/html/principals_survey.html

Masten, A. S., Roisman, G. I., Long, J. D., Burt, K. B., Obradovic, J., Riley, J. R., Boelcke-Stennes, K., & Tellegen, A. (2005). Developmental cascades: Linking academic achievement and externalizing and internalizing symptoms over 20 years. *Developmental Psychology*, 41, 733–746.

Mellin, E. A., & Weist, M. D. (2011). Exploring school mental health collaboration in an urban community: A social capital perspective. *School Mental Health*, 3, 81–92.

Mihalas, S., Morse, W., Allsopp, D., & McHatton, P. (2009). Cultivating caring relationships between teachers and secondary students with emotional and behavioural disorders: Implications for research and practice. *Remedial and Special Education*, 30, 108–125.

Nation, M., Crusto, C., Wandersman, A., Kumpfer, K. L., Seybolt, D., Morrisey-Kane, E., & Davino, K. (2003). What works in prevention: Principles of effective prevention programs. *American Psychologist, 58*, 449–456.

National Research Council and Institute of Medicine (2009). *Preventing mental, emotional and behavioral disorders among young people: Progress and possibilities.* Washington, DC: National Academies Press.

Proudfoot, J. (2013). The future is in our hands. The role of mobile phones in the prevention and management of mental disorders. *Australian and New Zealand Journal of Psychiatry, 47*, 111.

Ringeisen, H., Henderson, K., & Hoagwood, K. (2003). Context Matters: Schools and the 'research to practice gap' in children's mental health. *School Psychology Review, 32*, 153–168.

Ross, C. P. (1980). Mobilizing schools for suicide prevention. *Suicide and Life-Threatening Behavior, 11*, 239–243.

Sanson, A. V., Havinghurst, S. S., & Zubrick, S. R. (2011). The science of prevention for children and youth. *Australian Review of Public Affairs, 10*, 79–93.

Scott, J., Varghese, D., & McGrath, J. (2010). As the twig is bent, the tree inclines: Adult mental health consequences of childhood adversity. *Archives of General Psychiatry, 67*, 11–112.

Shute, R. H. (2012). Promoting mental health through schools: Is this field of development an evidence-based practice? *The Psychologist, 25*(10), 752–755.

Slee, P. T., Lawson, M. J., Russell, A., Askell-Williams, H., Dix, K. L., Owens, L., Skrzypiec, G., & Spears, B. (2009). *KidsMatter Primary Evaluation Final Report.* Centre for Analysis of Educational Futures, Flinders University of South Australia.

Spence, S. H., & Shortt, A. L. (2007). Can we justify the widespread dissemination of universal, school-based interventions for the prevention of depression among children and adolescents? *Journal of Child Psychology and Psychiatry, 48*, 526–542.

Weare, K., & Nind, M. (2011). Mental health promotion and problem prevention in schools: What does the evidence say? *Health Promotion International, 26*, S1.

Weist, M. D. (2004). Fulfilling the promise of school-based mental health: Moving toward a public mental health promotion approach. *Journal of Abnormal Child Psychology, 33*, 735–741.

World Health Organization (2000). Local Action: Creating health promoting schools. *Information Series on School Health.* Geneva: Author.

SECTION 2

Challenges for organisations and leaders

2

LEADERSHIP FOR 'WICKED' SCHOOL MENTAL HEALTH PROBLEMS

Richard H. Beinecke

This chapter introduces the concept of 'wicked problems': problems that are technically and socially complex, ill-defined and with no clear end-point. Those attempting to address mental health difficulties within the school setting often face problems of this type. This is illustrated by considering the multiple and complex challenges facing school counselors and social workers in the United States. Adaptive leadership is needed in order to address the mental health challenges that the rapidly changing world is bringing to our schools.

The challenges

We are in a period of complexity, with unprecedented change, interconnectivity, innovations and structures. Staff in school mental health programs must provide services and lead and manage many complex, multi-dimensional, and interconnected issues. Among these are diverse child psychological and academic problems, family disruption, and societal issues such as violence and child abuse, drug dependency and (especially in the United States) guns. Staff must assist students who are not doing well academically or who may have difficulty finding jobs, consult with teachers and administrators, develop education and prevention programs, and be advocates for more programs and greater service funding. Doing more of the same will not work. Increasing demand, greater complexity, and rising expectations mean that we need to be school leaders, collaborating closely and engaging many stakeholders to provide high quality services to children, their families, and other caregivers. School mental health issues can be seen as 'wicked problems' – a concept that is helpful in understanding their complexity and the challenges we face in addressing them.

Background

Wicked problems

'Wicked problems' is a term first used by Rittel and Webber (1973). They are wicked,

> [n]ot because these problems are ethically deplorable. We use the term 'wicked' in a meaning akin to that of 'malignant' (in contrast to 'benign') or 'vicious' (like a circle) or tricky (like a leprechaun) or 'aggressive' (like a lion, in contrast to the docility of a lamb).
>
> (Rittel & Webber, 1973, p. 160)

They contrast wicked problems with 'tame problems', which are not necessarily simple (they can be technically complex), but are those that can be tightly defined and a solution readily identified or worked through.

> Wicked problems often crop up when organizations have to face constant change or unprecedented challenges. They occur in a social context; the greater the disagreement among stakeholders, the more wicked the problem. In fact, it is the social complexity of wicked problems as much as their technical difficulties that make them tough to manage.
>
> (Camillus, 2008, p. 100)

Wicked problems fall within Types II and III of Heifetz's (1994) categorization of three problem types. In Type I problems, the challenge is technical, the problem definition is clear, and the solution can be solved with technical knowledge and abilities. Type II problems are both technical and adaptive. While the problem is clearly defined, the solution is unclear and may be achieved in different ways. Type III problems are adaptive, the focus of much of Heifetz's writing. There are many ways of defining the unclear problem. The solution (or solutions) is also unclear. Thus, they are very complex.

Wicked problems often have no definite formulation and are difficult to diagnose. Each problem is essentially unique, and often has not been faced before. Stakeholders may have different points of view and different ways of understanding the problem. People may disagree on what the real problem is, or there may be multiple issues and it is a challenge to determine what to address and when and where to do it. Wicked problems are resistant to solutions and frequently entwined with other problems. They may have many interdependencies, are often multi-causal and can be considered a symptom of other problems. They have no stopping rule or clear end-point but are frequently not stable, and evolve (Beinecke, 2009).

Wicked problems are therefore difficult to resolve. Solutions are often unclear or need to be non-linear, and attempts to address them often lead to unforeseen circumstances. Solutions are not true or false or good or bad but are judgment calls and often difficult to measure. The solution depends on how the problem is framed (and vice versa). Solutions that may have worked in one setting may not work in another, and evidence to guide change is open to challenge. The search for solutions never stops, and involves changing behavior (Australian Public Service Commission, 2014; Conklin, 2006; Rittel & Webber, 1973).

The problems are socially complex and thus need coordination and networking by a variety of stakeholders since they seldom ever sit within the responsibility of one organization. The constraints to which the problem is subject, and the resources to solve it, change over time. While wicked problems are challenging, they can become opportunities for creativity and change, and new paradigms and ways of viewing the world and ourselves.

Wicked mental health problems

Mental health is a particularly untamed and wicked field of practice (Hannigan & Coffey, 2011). Complex divisions of work have evolved, with services provided by many types of caregivers in a wide variety of settings often simultaneously, making networking especially critical. Many clients present with multiple diagnoses and sometimes multiple disabilities. Roles and responsibilities among service organizations are often unclear or disputed. Professional knowledge remains open to contest, and differing views can be found (even in single teams) on the interventions which practitioners might use, and between workers and those being helped (Mental Health Commission, Eire, 2006). The emergence of new physical and psychosocial therapies has helped shape the system as a whole. Families and children are becoming more involved in what services should be delivered, and values and interests often collide. New rules about record keeping make it a challenge to share information while protecting confidentiality.

> These system features mean that a potentially endless array of problems present themselves as a focus for action. The problems of modern mental health systems can, therefore, be explained in a multitude of often competing ways: too little understanding of disease, lack of suitable and/or available treatments, poorly trained and/or too few workers, too few and/or the wrong types of teams or facilities, poverty, unemployment, poor housing, poor mental hygiene, too much or too little surveillance, mental health laws which are either too liberal or too coercive, and so forth. Each of these positions (or combinations of positions) reflects certain standpoints and interpretations of the available evidence. Each offers a direction of travel. No rules exist, however, to guide progress in the 'correct' way, and problem formulations and their attempted solutions are differentially assessed in ways which reflect stakeholders' values, their appraisals of 'the evidence' and their location within the system. Even where a dominant view might be detected, there still remain vocal minorities and a range of alternative positions held by combinations of professionals, service users, carers and others.
>
> (Hannigan & Coffey, 2011, p. 223)

Wicked problems in school mental health programs

Many children in schools have psychosocial problems. In the United States, for example, 12–20 percent of all youngsters under age 18 need services for mental, emotional, or behavioral problems. Twenty percent of children and adolescents experience the signs and symptoms of a *DSM-IV* disorder during a year, with 11 percent experiencing significant impairment and about 5 percent experiencing "extreme functional impairment", 40 percent in "bad educational shape" and therefore not fulfilling their potential, while over 50 percent in many large urban schools "manifest significant behaviors, learning, and emotional problems" (Adelman & Taylor, 2010, pp. 7–8). Schools can be important venues for meeting the mental health needs of children and their families, and doing so is critical to school performance.

In the United States and globally, we are in a period of rapid social change. Children face many forms of family structures such as divorce, remarriage, cohabitation, dual careers, blended families, homelessness, and same-sex unions (e.g., Organization for Economic Cooperation and Development, 2011). Serious societal issues such as changing population demographics, poverty, shifting educational profiles, chemical dependency, and the spread of guns affect them. There is violence by students to others, an epidemic of suicide, and violence by parents and other adults. Adverse child experiences include physical and emotional abuse by a parent, sexual abuse, family, alcohol or drug abuse, domestic violence, incarceration of a household member, living with a family member experiencing mental illness, loss of a parent, and/or emotional or physical neglect. Immigrant children, children of incarcerated parents, children of soldiers and veterans and those with physical and intellectual disabilities have unique needs. Technology, especially the Internet and social media, has many positive effects but can also lead to loneliness, fewer opportunities for social interaction, and cyberbullying (e.g., Byrne, Katz, Lee, Linz, & McIlrath, 2014; Livingstone, 2008).

Thompson (1992) observed that, "[a]s the stabilizing and socializing influence of home and church has waned, our reliance on the school has grown" (p. 8), and such social issues form a backdrop for school-based mental health initiatives and referral to school counselors. Workers such as Auger (2011), Jarolman (2014), Sink (2011) and Thompson (1992) and the author's own experience as a child and adolescent therapist indicate the nature of problems encountered in schools. Some of the most common are autism, severe behavioral and conduct problems, depression and mood disorders, self-injury and suicidal behavior, hyperactivity and attention deficit disorder, post-traumatic stress, anxiety disorders, eating disorders, and substance abuse. Others are failing school subjects, delinquency and dropouts, short-term crises such as loss of loved ones and parents getting divorced, bullying, and abuse and neglect of many kinds. More children with learning disabilities and developmental disabilities are staying in schools, and many services in the United States are now mandated through IEPs (Individual Education Plans). Violence and, especially in the United States, weapons in schools present special challenges.

High student unemployment and teenage pregnancy and sexual behavior also affect student performance.

Solutions

Leadership for wicked problems

The concept of wicked problems provides a framework for developing solutions to these problems. School mental health staff need to be adaptive leaders. Adaptive leadership (Heifetz, 1994; Heifetz, Grashow, & Linksy, 2009) is the practice of mobilizing and orchestrating multiple stakeholders to tackle tough problems and enable change. It is present when responses within the current repertoire are inadequate, difficult learning is required, new stakeholders across boundaries need to be engaged, a longer time frame is necessary, and/or disequilibrium is experienced as a sense of crisis is starting to be felt.

Successful adaptive change builds on the past. Experimentation is important, and adaptation relies on valuing diverse views, and having diverse processes and solutions. It may significantly displace, reregulate, and rearrange some 'old DNA': it takes time. Mobilizing people to meet their immediate adaptive challenges lies at the heart of leadership in the short term. Over time, such mobilization and other culture-shaping efforts build an organization's adaptive capacity, fostering processes that will generate new norms that will enable the organization to meet the ongoing stream of adaptive challenges and opportunities (Beinecke, 2009; Heifetz *et al.*, 2009).

Adaptive work requires figuring out what to save from past practices, inventing new ways to build from the best of the past, and avoiding our tendency to treat problems as technical when they are not. One needs to listen to the song beneath the words – look beyond what people are saying. People try to avoid adaptive challenges or fail to adapt when there is a gap between espoused values and behavior, when there are competing and conflicting commitments, when the nature of the problem is misperceived, when the problem is perceived but the challenge seems to exceed the culture's adaptive capability, and/or when the distress provoked by the problem and the changes it demands are felt to be too high. In an adaptive organization, issues including the 'elephants in the room' are discussed. Members share responsibility for the organization's future, independent judgment is respected and valued, leadership capacity is developed, and reflection and continuous learning are institutionalized (Heifetz *et al.*, 2009).

Tasks

To be adaptive leaders, school counselors and social workers provide a wide range of services:

> When I was asked what I did for a living at a cocktail party once by a business professional, I said "I'm a school social worker. I help teachers and administrators ensure the academic, emotional, and professional success of

the students I serve." I then added, "I conduct individual and group counseling for high school students, handle crisis interventions and incidents – including child abuse, suicidal ideation, and bullying – and lead professional development and training for teachers." School social workers provide direct counseling services to students in need and support teachers in working with difficult students and serve in an administrative or leadership role and implement school programs.

(Varianides, 2013, pp. 3–4)

Historically, school counselors had two roles. One was therapeutic, drawing on the facilitating relationship of counselor and student, to enhance the personal and psychiatric competencies of students. The second was more administrative: the guidance administrator, planning programs, and helping students with college placement and job placement (Thompson, 1992). School mental health professionals now have many more complex and broader tasks, including the areas of prevention and mental health promotion, youth and family engagement and empowerment, and intervention for specific problems (Weist, Lever, Bradshaw, & Owens, 2014).

The American School Counselor Association (ASCA) sets standards that are the basis for the evaluation of school counseling programs in the United States. Overall, "Effective school counseling programs are a collaborative effort between the school counselor, parents, and other educators to create an environment that promotes student achievement" (ASCA, 2012, p. xii). This includes both prevention and intervention activities. The work areas include educational development, career development, and personal and social development. Essential services are counseling, consulting, coordinating data, referrals and follow-up, and school-wide events, educational planning and career development, and student and environmental appraisal (Schmidt, 2003).

School counselors and social workers have varied responsibilities (Thompson, 1992; Varianides, 2013). They:

1. Counsel students individually and in groups regarding academic readiness, discipline, and emotional development, substance abuse, conflict mediation, graduation requirements, and make appropriate referrals to outside agencies.
2. Provide crisis intervention and mediation between students, dealing with loss, grief counseling, and post-traumatic stress.
3. Communicate with in-service teachers and administrators on effective behavioral management practices in the classroom as well as other professional development areas of need.
4. Act as consultants and collaborative problem solvers with people in the school, home, and community.
5. Offer educational and occupational guidance, advice on college decision making, and occupational help for those not college-bound.
6. Maintain regular and open communication with parents, including assistance in creating regular forums for parents and guardians to explore issues important to the community.

7. Work closely with the Special Education Department to ensure the coordination of services for students with special needs.
8. Promote a positive school climate.
9. Carry out program development and evaluation of services.
10. Coordinate and participate in the School Code of Conduct Committee and offer clinical expertise in regards to disciplinary interventions to teachers and administrators.
11. Follow guidelines for reporting incidents of child abuse.
12. Abide by all school regulations and requirements regarding confidentiality and education laws.
13. Maintain student files including progress notes, treatment plans, assessments, behavior contracts, and so on.
14. Attend and participate in staff and administrator meetings and trainings.
15. Support effective school public relations.

Paisley and McMahon (2001) discussed the ambiguous role definition of school counselors and the challenge of priority setting. The list of their many roles was:

1. Provide individual and small group counseling sessions.
2. Conduct classroom guidance interventions.
3. Consult with parents, teachers, administrators, and community agency representatives.
4. Advocate for all students to enhance educational experiences and outcomes.
5. Build partnerships and teams within and outside the school.
6. Be a member of school leadership and policy-making groups.
7. Provide individualized, focused, and intensive interventions for at-risk students.
8. Be the developmental specialist in the school setting.
9. Be the mental health specialist in the school setting.
10. Provide family counseling interventions.
11. Coordinate school-wide programs including peer helping, peer mediation, conflict resolution, violence prevention, character education, and teacher advisory programs.
12. Prevent suicides, pregnancies, dropouts, drug use, and general moral decay.
13. Maintain the necessary expertise in all of the above areas to ensure quality in all interventions and programs.

In addition, counselors must address increasingly diverse populations and be culturally competent and responsive, deal with the increasing reliance on technology and changes in it, be more accountable, and measure the effectiveness of their work.

Advocacy is an especially important role. It includes student empowerment (self-advocacy), advocacy for students, school and community collaboration, systems advocacy, public information, and social and political advocacy (ASCA, 2012). Martin (2002) believes that school counselors should undertake the following:

1. Focus on improving student achievement.
2. Help children learn, help their teachers motivate them, and help parents successfully navigate the school bureaucracy so that they, too, can advocate for their children.
3. Understand and use social advocacy skills to challenge the status quo in schools and systems where inequities impede students' access to quality academic preparation.
4. Use data to effect change and advocate for those students who need help in navigating school bureaucracies to get access to rigorous courses and quality teaching.
5. Understand organizational change and how to intervene to make change happen for children.
6. Become competent users of technology to monitor individual students' progress, and help students and their families gather information needed for critical decisions about their children's future options and plans.
7. Use their group and problem-solving skills with other educational professionals for the purpose of systemic problem solving.
8. Understand and be able to operate competently in a diverse and multicultural school setting and community.

Workshop development and leadership now is a core role. Topics noted by Varianides (2013) include anti-bullying, dropout prevention, substance abuse, suicide prevention, test anxiety, peer mediation, and racism/prejudice.

School health systems are very complex and fragmented. In addition to mental health and counseling services, school related health programs may include formal health services and health education, for example: HIV/AIDS prevention; nutrition education and school lunch programs; after school and physical education programs; special education; psychological testing; violence and crime prevention; a wide variety of social services and child protective services; juvenile court services; and drug and alcohol programs (Adelman & Taylor, 2010). Many of these services are addressed by groups outside of the school setting and need comprehensive approaches. Thus, counselors are more and more moving beyond the classroom to making referrals and linking students with community agencies, communicating with parents and other professionals, and expanding comprehensive school improvement plans to include community involvement (Waller, 2006). Adelman and Taylor (2010) reflected on this expanding role as follows:

> Mental health in schools will move away from an orientation that mainly plans and implements services for a relatively few students. What will emerge is a broad approach that encompasses health promotion, problem prevention, and early-after-onset interventions as well as special assistance for those with chronic and severe problems.
>
> (p. 71)

These authors also point out the need for a wide continuum of interconnected school-community systems for promoting healthy development and preventing problems, for early intervention, and for systemic collaboration to address the needs of all children.

Competencies for mental health leadership

Multiple competencies are needed to address these challenges. According to the ASCA (2012), school counselors should spend 80 percent of their time on effective service delivery. Leadership is also critical, and a number of ways of looking at this have been developed.

ASCA suggests that four situations or contexts are needed: structural (building of viable organizations), human resources (empowerment and inspiration of followers), political (use of personal and organizational power), and symbolic (interpretation and re-interpretation of change) (ASCA, 2012; based on Bolman & Deal, 2008). Slaten and Baskin (2014) build further on the ASCA guidelines as well as those of the Council of Counseling Psychology Training Programs (CCPTP) training clusters to say that school counselors need to be competent in the areas of confiding relationships, systems (healing settings), science (rationale), application (procedural), and professionalism.

The US Substance Abuse and Mental Health Services Administration (SAMHSA) (2005) lists six areas of transformational leadership competence:

- individual leader attributes (e.g., being visionary);
- knowledge and information management (e.g., applying research findings);
- future trends in mental health (e.g., family-relevant outcomes);
- transformation management (e.g., strategic alliances);
- process 'toolkit' (e.g., negotiation skills);
- business acumen (e.g., human resource development).

Based on a study of leadership models in eight countries, Beinecke and Spencer (2007) identified five priority leadership competencies (Figure 2.1). Personal skills include competencies such as emotional intelligence (self-awareness, personal style), leaders' values and beliefs, ethics, flexibility and creativity, critical thinking, intelligence, and customer orientation. Important interpersonal skills are effective written and verbal communication, teamwork and group skills, enabling others, negotiating and resolving conflict, networking, and working with people of different cultures. Burns (1978) and many others have described transactional (management) and transformative skills. Among the transactional skills are quality management, data use, evaluation, evidence-based practices, human resource management, finance and budgeting, organizational design, information systems and technology and service systems design and management. Transformational skills are also needed: visioning and strategic thinking, managing and leading change and innovation, goal and direction setting, mobilizing support and inspiring others,

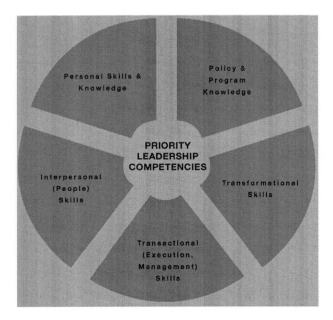

FIGURE 2.1 The leadership and management skill set (Beinecke & Spencer, 2007)

networking and working across complex organizational systems, and political astuteness. Policy and program knowledge is the knowledge about particular areas such as clinical and service areas, political knowledge and history, organization, funding, policies, and legislation. All are needed to some degree by every clinician, manager, and leader. Not everyone needs to be highly skilled in all, but members of a team should share these competencies.

Conclusion: a way forward

This book covers many areas that are needed for improving mental health services in schools. Health promotion, use of new technologies, targeted interventions for youth with disabilities and other challenging situations are among the areas that are addressed. As we look at particular types of interventions, we must not forget the broader context that school mental health staff face. The numbers and variety of wicked problems are increasing in industrial and postindustrial societies and are even greater in the Majority World (formerly referred to as 'developing' countries). In industrial and postindustrial countries, schools are becoming centers for helping to address a wide variety of social issues, moving far beyond just academic studies. In the Majority World, education, especially for girls and young women, is the key to economic and political development (and sadly, in some countries, a tool for repression).

To address wicked problems and achieve sustained behavioral change, one needs innovative, adaptive, and flexible approaches. Holistic rather than linear and narrow thinking is important. One should both work on the dance floor where much of the action takes place as well as regularly move to the balcony to step back and get a view of the whole (Heifetz, 1994).

Collaborative strategies and work across organizational and agency boundaries are critical. Stakeholders need to be effectively engaged and citizens to have a shared understanding of the problems and solutions (Australian Public Service Commission, 2014; Heifetz *et al.*, 2009). School mental health workers need to move beyond their narrow but important role as counselors to seeing themselves as leaders and change agents. It is not enough to see one's role as simply addressing Type I problems. Transformative as well as transactional leadership is needed. Managerial, networking, and leadership skills as well as clinical competencies need to be developed. This broader framework can help to create a culture whereby the multiple needs of diverse students can be met, future leaders are nurtured, and schools can play a growing role in addressing society's issues in this millennium.

References

Adelman, H. S., & Taylor, L. (2010). *Mental health in schools: Engaging learners, preventing problems, and improving schools*. Thousand Oaks, CA: Corwin.

American School Counselor Association (2012). *ASCA National Model: A framework for school counseling programs* (3rd edn). Alexandria, VA: ASCA.

Auger, R. (2011). *The school counselor's mental health sourcebook: Strategies to help students succeed*. Thousand Oaks, CA: Corwin.

Australian Public Service Commission (2014). ARCHIVE: Tackling wicked problems: A public policy perspective. Accessed 10.04.2014 at www.apsc.gov.au/publications-and-media/archive/publications

Beinecke, R. H. (2009). Introduction: Leadership for wicked problems. *The Innovation Journal*, *14*(1), 1–17.

Beinecke, R. H., & Spencer, J. (2007). *Leadership training programs and competencies for mental health, substance use, health, and public administration in eight countries*. International Initiative for Mental Health Leadership. Accessed 22.08.2014 at www.iimhl.com

Bolman, L. G., & Deal, T. E. (2008). *Reframing organizations: Artistry, choice and leadership*. San Francisco: John Wiley & Sons.

Burns, J. (1978). *Leadership*. New York: Harper and Row.

Byrne, S., Katz, S. J., Lee, T., Linz, D., & McIlrath, M. (2014). Peers, predators, and porn: Predicting parental underestimation of children's risky online experiences. *Journal of Computer-Mediated Communication*, *19*, 215–231.

Camillus, J. (2008). Strategy as a wicked problem. *Harvard Business Review*, *86*(5), 98–106.

Conklin, J. (2006). *Dialogue mapping: Building shared understanding of wicked problems*. Chichester, West Sussex: John Wiley & Sons.

Hannigan, H., & Coffey, M. (2011). Where the wicked problems are: The case of mental health. *Health Policy*, *101*(3), 220–227.

Heifetz, R. (1994). *Leadership without easy answers*. Cambridge, MA: The Belknap Press of Harvard University.

Heifetz, R., Grashow, A., & Linksy, M. (2009). The practice of adaptive leadership. Cambridge, MA: Cambridge Leadership Associates.

Jarolman, J. (2014). *School social work: A direct practice guide.* Thousand Oaks, CA: Sage Publications Inc.

Livingstone, S. (2008). Taking risky opportunities in youthful content creation: Teenagers' use of social networking sites for intimacy, privacy and self-expression. *New Media & Society, 10*(3), 393–411.

Martin, P. J. (2002). Transforming school counseling: A national perspective. *Theory Into Practice, 41*(3), 148–153.

Mental Health Commission (Eire) (2006). *Multidisciplinary team working.* Discussion paper. Accessed 15.08.2014 at www.mhcirl.ie/file/discusspapmultiteam.pdf

Organization for Economic Cooperation and Development (2011). *Doing better for families.* Accessed 22.01.2016 at : www.oecd.org/social/soc/doingbetterfor families.htm

Paisley, P. O., & McMahon, H. G. (2001). School counseling in the 21st century: Challenges and opportunities. *Professional School Counseling, 5*(2), 106–116.

Rittel, H., & Webber, M. L. (1973). Dilemmas in a general theory of planning. *Policy Sciences, 4,* 155–169.

SAMHSA (May/June 2005). Leadership is everyone's business in mental health. *Transformation Trends: A Periodic Briefing, 1*(2), p. 2, cited in Beinecke, R. H. and Spencer, J. (2007). Leadership training programs and competencies for mental health, substance use, health, and public administration in eight countries. *International Initiative for Mental Health Leadership.* Accessed 22.08.2014 at www.iimhl.com

Schmidt, J. J. (2003). *Counseling in schools: Essential services and comprehensive programs* (4th Edn.). Boston, MA: Allyn & Bacon.

Sink, C. (2011). *Mental health interventions for school counselors.* Belmont, CA: Brooks/Cole.

Slaten, C. D., & Baskin, T. W. (2014). Contextual school counseling: A framework for training with implications for curriculum, supervision, practice, and future research. *The Counseling Psychologist, 42*(1), 97–123.

Thompson, R. (1992). *School counseling renewal strategies for the twenty-first century. Accelerated Development.* Indiana: Muncie.

Varianides, A. (2013). *The School Social Work Toolkit.* Washington, DC: NASW Press.

Waller, R. J. (2006). *Fostering child and adolescent mental health in the classroom.* Thousand Oaks, CA: Sage Publications Inc.

Weist, M. D, Lever, N. A., Bradshaw, C. P., & Owens, J. S. (Eds.). (2014). *Handbook of school mental health research, practice, and policy* (2nd edn.). New York: Springer.

3

SUPPORTING SCHOOLS FOR THE WIDESPREAD IMPLEMENTATION OF EVIDENCE-BASED MENTAL HEALTH PROMOTION PROGRAMS

What is needed?

Bonnie J. Leadbeater and Emilie J. Gladstone

The implementation of evidence-based mental health promotion and prevention programs in schools has many advantages but also faces numerous obstacles, such as the complexity and diversity of school contexts, fragmented infrastructure support, funding limitations and competing attractive programs lacking an evidence base. This chapter offers a framework for conceptualizing the challenges and opportunities for program implementation. The framework is applied to experience in the adoption, implementation and sustaining of the WITS Programs, which are designed to create responsive communities that promote social responsibility, prosocial leadership and positive school climates, and to reduce peer victimization and bullying among children in grades one to six.

The challenge

Evidence-based mental health promotion and risk prevention efforts frequently target school-age children and youth, and schools are often seen as ideal contexts for reaching many children simultaneously. However, the capacity of schools and educators to fulfil this expanded role is not well understood or well supported. Already burdened with growing curriculum demands, increasing class sizes, and more special needs children, it is not clear whether or how schools will be able to respond. While it is assumed that schools are 'ready targets' for the implementation of prevention programs addressing a variety of social problems, the reality of their capacity to undertake these initiatives may be quite different.

This chapter outlines the challenges and opportunities for schools as implementers of evidence-based programs. It suggests a framework for engaging schools that identifies what is needed to support this emerging role, and offers as an exemplar the successful implementation in elementary schools (particularly in rural and remote areas of Canada) of online open access evidence-based bullying prevention programs: the *WITS Programs* (Leadbeater & Sukhawathanakul, 2011; Leadbeater, Thompson, & Sukhawathanakul, 2014). We argue that there is a clear need for national, provincial and local policy and practices that support the utilization of evidence-based programs in schools (Moore, Bumbarger, & Cooper, 2013; Tibbits, Bumbarger, Kyler, & Perkins, 2010).

There are many advantages to the implementation of mental health promotion programs in schools: they can overcome barriers to access by reaching many children at once; schools engage many highly trained professional staff who can undertake and support program implementation; schools are governed by mandated educational policies; and children attend school across childhood and adolescence, allowing for sustained efforts across developmental phases. Social science researchers, working in community-based partnership with educators, government organizations, not-for-profit groups, or youth-serving agencies, parents or youth, have produced a wealth of evidence-based prevention programs and resources that are effective in improving children's mental health (Durlak, Mahoney, Bohnert, & Parente, 2010).

However, the adoption and high-quality implementation of evidence-based prevention programs in school settings not involved in the original research alliances remain extremely limited. Indeed, proven programs are rarely distributed at a scale that could influence population levels of children's mental health and behaviours, and serious gaps exist between the extensive research base and resources, and their widespread use. This severely hampers the impact that we can have on critical social problems (Rhoades, Bumbarger, & Moore, 2012). The barriers to large-scale program dissemination, adoption, implementation and sustainability are beginning to be identified, but the organizational structures and iterative processes required to improve implementation have only begun to be documented (Metz & Albers, 2014; Rhoades *et al.*, 2012).

Background

Mobilizing evidence-based programs in school settings

Early research in this area addressed efforts to disseminate innovations in treatments and technology that showed clear health or economic benefits. However, even within these interacting systems there are many influences on, and challenges to, the spread of tested solutions and innovations. For example, although penicillin was discovered in 1928, the drug was not used to treat infections in humans until 15 years later (Brownson, Colditz, & Proctor, 2012). Its widespread adoption in the mid-1940s is often attributed to the increased demand for antibiotics during the Second World War and the subsequent innovation of methods for mass production that facilitated wide-scale military use. This example illustrates that features of the innovation itself (e.g., the efficacy of penicillin) are not the sole factors determining the adoption of a solution. Settings and climates are intrinsically linked to the success or failure of an innovation, and developers can design and package innovations to meet the demands of target settings to increase the speed and likelihood of adoption (Oldenburg & Glanz, 2008).

Models that address the challenges of implementing public health interventions in school and community settings are emerging (e.g., Fixsen, Naoom, Blase, Friedman, & Wallace, 2005; Schell, Luke, & Schooley, 2013; Wandersman, Duffy, Flaspohler, *et al.*, 2008). School settings pose unique challenges related to, for example, defining roles and responsibilities of multiple stakeholders, wide variation in capacities and needs across sites (e.g., urban or rural schools), and less hierarchically organized structures of authority within schools and regulators of schools (Saunders, Pate, Dowda, *et al.*, 2012). Without a better understanding of this complexity and how to support schools in the use of evidence-based programs, schools' participation in efforts to reduce serious social problems is unlikely to improve.

What are the obstacles to implementation of evidence-based programs in schools?

The characteristics of schools that enable or hinder the widespread implementation of evidence-based programs are under-studied (Leadbeater, 2010; Lee & Gortmaker, 2012; Sandler *et al.*, 2005). Barriers that have been identified include the following.

1. Schools are complex organizations with numerous stakeholders (communities, children, parents, teachers and counselors) who cannot be reached through a single marketing strategy (Sandler *et al.*, 2005).
2. The university–community partnerships that often form alliances to develop and evaluate programs typically lack the capacity or funding and expertise to support their large-scale dissemination (Spoth, Guyll, Lillehoj, Redmond, & Greenberg, 2007). There is a growing need for intermediaries with expertise in both understanding school and community needs and in implementing evidence-based programs under real-world conditions (Tibbits, Bumbarger, Kyler, & Perkins, 2010).
3. Provincial and school-wide politics in the education system can hinder or enable dissemination. Changing policies relating to bullying may favour broad approaches and locally supported strategies over evidence-based programs, with power dynamics and conflict between administrators and teachers fueling resistance to new programs.
4. Implementing programs in diverse settings such as rural and remote regions and bilingual populations presents additional challenges, and program adaptations are needed to meet such specific needs. Funding for adaptation is not always available for programs or in schools (Leadbeater, Gladstone, Yeung Thompson, Sukhawathanakul, & Desjardins, 2012).

5.   National, provincial and local infrastructures that support informed choices and foster the use of evidence-based programs are fragmented and rarely connected to schools (Leadbeater, 2010).
6.   There is extensive competition in the resources marketed to schools, including celebrity-endorsed or widely used programs that are not evidence-based. Educators can therefore be burdened by an array of 'flavour-of-the-day' innovations that demand learning new skills without the potential to sustain training across staff turnovers or resist the next 'new discovery'.
7.   Web-based approaches with self-paced training modules and access to live coaching or consultants have increased clinician training for evidence-based mental health interventions (Kolko, Hoagwood, & Springgate, 2010). Education resources for the implementation of prevention programs in schools are also proliferating; however, the usefulness, acceptability, uptake, fidelity and impact of these online, open-access resources and programs are not well understood, even at local levels.

Solutions

A framework for the implementation of evidence-based programs in schools

Fixsen and colleagues (2005) outlined a framework for implementation *at the community level* that draws attention to the multi-level, transacting influences of: i) core evidence-based program characteristics; ii) core features of the implementation approaches used; iii) core components of the targeted organization; and iv) contextual factors that can influence implementation and outcomes. This framework is used here to organize the challenges and opportunities that need to be considered at the local, state/province and national level for the implementation of evidence-based programs in schools.

What are the core characteristics of evidence-based prevention programs for schools?

Knowing the core components of programs can help schools to integrate their ongoing strategies with adopted evidence-based approaches and avoid the pressures of trying to implement multiple programs with separate goals. Studies of the components of successful prevention programs (Bohanon & Wu, 2011; Domitrovich & Greenberg, 2000; Jones & Bouffard, 2012) demonstrate the need for programs that: a) are integrated into children's daily activities; b) address risk and protective factors; c) engage and address key ecologies that surround children and youth; and d) are sustained across multiple years. Implementation of programs may also be more likely if they pose low demands for additional highly qualified staff, can be integrated into the usual roles of school members, have high accessibility and low demands for training and retraining (to accommodate staff turnover), can be delivered at low cost, and allow for flexibility, local adaptations and choice. Programs also benefit from effective administrative leadership and program champions, ongoing coaching from program developers, and opportunities to assess their local impact.

What are the core features of implementation approaches?

Key characteristics of schools and their communities also influence their ability to adopt, implement and sustain evidence-based programs (Lee & Gortmaker, 2012). Core processes can be identified that support implementation strategies, and these take time to unfold. Based on a synthesis of past research, Durlak and DuPre (2008) identified four phases of program diffusion that include: *dissemination* – how well information about the program's existence and value is supplied to potential users; *adoption* – whether the user decides to try the program; *implementation* – how well the program is conducted; and *sustainability* – how well it is maintained over time. Situating program implementation efforts within a long-term perspective that recognizes these component processes provides a more accurate picture of the complexity of what is involved. Beyond initial training, program implementers need ongoing support from developers to support the:

1. integration of the program into the users' routine activities, website, and codes of conduct;
2. deepening of the program's infusion into an organization's daily practice;
3. costs of maintaining the programs across school years and staff turnover;
4. sustainability of program funding; and
5. evaluation, feedback, revisions and renewal.

What are the core features of schools as complex organizations embedded in local community contexts?

The ability of professionally trained educators is central among the many advantages of the choice of schools for the delivery of evidence-based programs to promote the mental health and wellbeing of children. It is also important to recognize that schools are complex social organizations with heterogeneous characteristics (Sandler *et al.*, 2005). This complexity encompasses:

1. differences in characteristics of students (e.g., beliefs in the value of using aggression);
2. organizational relationships between administrators and teachers (in some Canadian provinces administrators and teachers are in different unions, in others they are not);
3. levels of staff experience (new teachers may be assigned to inner-city schools, whereas teachers with more seniority may have greater choice regarding school placement);

4. connectedness to parents and community leaders (many schools have established interactions with school-based police liaisons, but many do not);
5. school climate (quality of relations among people in the school, safety, access to resources); and
6. demographic settings (rural vs. urban settings can influence resource bases for prevention programs).

The influence of such distinctive features of schools and communities in enabling or hindering implementation approaches is rarely addressed in implementation efforts (Leadbeater *et al.*, 2012).

What are the core features of enabling social, economic and political influences on schools?

The social and political context can have an important and direct role in creating enabling contexts for implementation (Rhoades *et al.*, 2012). Moreover, the social, economic and political contexts in which evidence-based programs or resources are disseminated influence each phase of the program adoption, implementation and evaluation processes. Local legislation and policies can compete with funding and support for evidence-based mental health promotion programs. However, they can also mandate that choices come from the pool of tested resources. Many US states and Canadian provinces have responded to high-profile youth suicide incidents by mandating that schools develop plans for bullying prevention. Some such initiatives encourage school boards to utilize evidence-based programs and also provide funding for program costs and support for implementation.

Challenges and opportunities for school-based action: Adoption, implementation and sustaining of the WITS Programs

The WITS Programs

In the next section, we use our experience with the development of these programs over the past 16 years to provide a case study of emerging success in widespread program implementation. The *WITS Programs* have been extensively evaluated (e.g., Leadbeater, Thompson, & Sukhawathanakul, 2014; Leadbeater & Sukhawathanakul 2011). We are now documenting the challenges and opportunities that are apparent as *WITS* 'goes to scale' across Canada with the support of the Public Health Agency of Canada's Innovation Strategy entitled *Taking Action to Reduce Health Inequalities in Canada*.

Our findings are based on a longitudinal qualitative approach that examined factors affecting the adoption, implementation and sustainability processes of the *WITS Programs* in remote and rural communities in British Columbia, Canada (Leadbeater *et al.*, 2012). Semi-structured interviews were conducted with more than 30 self-identified program 'champions' – school staff or community members who are leaders in adopting, implementing and sustaining the program. Interviews were conducted individually by researchers at the University of Victoria four times between 2011 and 2013, in seven elementary schools across three school districts. We also report on some of what we have learned in observing and carefully monitoring the implementation of the *WITS Programs* in 15 schools involved in a Cluster Randomized Trial of the program.

What are the core characteristics of the WITS Programs that enhance and support implementation?

The programs were designed to create responsive communities that promote social responsibility, prosocial leadership and positive school climates to reduce peer victimization and bullying among children in grades one to six. Resources for school staff, parents, community leaders and children are accessible online at www.wits progams.ca (or, in French, at www.leprogrammeDIRE.ca). The programs are launched each year in a 'Swearing-in Ceremony' led by a notable 'Community Leader' − often a member of the local RCMP, city police or other first responder. Children and school staff members pledge to use their **WITS** to **W**alk Away, **I**gnore, **T**alk it Out and **S**eek Help to deal with teasing and bullying and to help other children use their WITS. The programs uniquely work to create a common language to enable communities to talk proactively about 'using your WITS' to solve peer conflicts and increase social responsibility. Principals also can use the language to inquire about and respond to disciplinary problems. Each month, teachers can choose from many book-based lesson plans that facilitate conversations about WITS messages. These lesson plans are integrated with academic learning objectives to reduce time demands on teachers. Support also comes from community leaders who re-visit the school throughout the school year to ask children about their successes in using their WITS and to deliver take-home gifts (pencils, rulers, etc.). Parents are also encouraged to use the WITS language at home and are reminded about WITS activities and online resources for parents through school newsletters and school-wide posters and contests. Older children in grades four to six are taught prosocial leadership skills that enable them to be more effective bystanders using the **LEAD**er**S** lesson plans to **L**ook and Listen, **E**xplore Points of View, **A**ct, ask **D**id it Work and to **S**eek Help in order to feel competent and empowered to help younger children in the playground and neighbourhood.

What are the core features of WITS implementation processes?

Most of the resources for the *WITS Programs* are online, needing little or no support from the research team. Online training modules allow individuals or groups of educators to use the program and a separate module is available for community leaders. However, in many instances face-to-face training was requested by schools and police groups (acting as community leaders) − at least at the initial start-up phase. These face-to-face meetings were highly valued by the school and *WITS*

Programs staff and quickly expanded knowledge about the program and uptake in communities. Trained staff used the online modules to deal with staff turnover and train new members. Strong collaborative relationships among stakeholders within schools (and often between schools and their communities) are needed to implement and sustain multi-systemic programs. Schools are embedded in, and connected to, communities that can support programs. *WITS* has partnered with the Canadian Red Cross and RCMP, who already have direct roles in supporting bullying prevention programs in schools through highly trained program implementers or school–police liaisons (Leadbeater, 2008). Renewed commitment to the *WITS Programs* was also made possible each year through the initiative of community leaders who contacted schools to conduct the annual *WITS* Swearing-in Ceremonies.

Many popular and publicly available children's books are needed to implement the program. Schools and communities were creative in covering costs of these books (often amounting to $1,000 per school) through available library funds, community fund-raising events, local support from philanthropies, or applications to the Rock Solid Foundation (www.rockfoundation.bc.ca) – a not-for-profit group that raises funds specifically for the implementation of the *WITS Programs*.

What are the characteristic of schools that facilitate uptake and implementation and sustain the WITS Programs?

In our interviews, school staff called attention to the importance of the fit of the program with their ongoing activities and values, and the need for the integration of program materials with current curriculum demands, as well as the potential for program flexibility, adaptability and sustainability. Self-selected program champions reviewed and personally piloted the programs for a substantial amount of time with children they taught or supervised prior to sharing it with others. They articulated personalized motivations for using the programs and drew connections between the programs and their existing beliefs and teaching strategies and with their schools' existing programs and codes of conduct. They then used their own knowledge and experience with the programs to influence others to use the programs, occasionally recruiting endorsements from other school staff who knew about the programs from other settings. In most schools, staff members were highly responsive to the champions' advocacy for starting the programs, but in a few schools champions faced resistance to their efforts to engage others in program activities.

What are the enabling school contexts that promote and sustain the WITS Programs' implementation?

Schools that successfully sustained the *WITS Programs* across two years identify the programs as durable because they became part of their school culture and every-day programming. The *WITS Programs* fit with other programs in the schools and in some instances provide a core language and approach for linking other social skills and values-oriented programs together. Continuity in leadership support was important to keeping the program 'fresh' and present. Principal and staff-member turnover presented challenges for continuity and sustainability. These threats were reduced in schools where several teachers and users had significant buy-in to the programs or where children continued to use the language and introduced it to new staff members. Sustaining program use in these schools required ongoing communication about the program among staff members and planning for the program at the beginning of each school year. Setting goals for the program annually also allowed the staff to prioritize and re-commit to the program. Some schools had difficulty recruiting a community leader to do the annual Swearing-in Ceremony and follow-up visits due to staff turnover, lack of support for the program from local commanding officers, and demands for police to implement other programs (e.g., bicycle or drug safety). Despite difficulties, community leaders were active each year in all but one school. Some participants suggest that the program development staff played an important role in sustaining the program by continuously updating (and providing) new program materials (e.g., books and lesson plans) and by continuing regular communication with the school. The danger of falling into a kind of automatic 'cruising zone' was cited as a threat to sustainability.

What are the core features of enabling social, economic and political influences on schools?

In the process of implementing the *WITS Programs*, we have also learned a great deal about enabling legislation, policies and economic conditions. The formation of national partnerships among the *WITS Program* team, the RCMP, Red Cross and PREVNet (a national network that works for the promotion of healthy relationships and the prevention of relationship violence) has also greatly facilitated national dissemination and implementation. In Canada, responsibility for education is under provincial jurisdiction, with no national ministry. The implementation of evidence-based programs can be affected in many ways by provincial policies and legislation that recommend, mandate, prioritize, or fund these programs. For example, in Ontario, passage of Bill 13 (June 2012) mandated school action against bullying and mandated, and partially funded, the use of evidence-based programs. School boards began searching for, and became open to implementing, new programs. A coordinated approach to prevention of mental health concerns was also facilitated through the School Mental Health-ASSIST office that is "designed to help Ontario school boards to build capacity to support student mental health and well-being, through effective implementation of research-based programs and strategies" (see www.smh-assist.ca). In Ontario, uptake of the *WITS Programs* increased 121 percent from 71 schools in the 2012–2013 academic year to 154 in the 2013–2014 academic year. In contrast, British Columbia adopted the *Erase Bullying Strategy*, which focused on training all educators in 'threat assessment' and appointed staff in school districts to follow up online reports of bullying. This policy for action competed with implementation of prevention strategies. In this political environment, uptake of the *WITS Programs* (while recommended) declined 36 percent in the 120 schools in the 2012–2013 academic year to 76 in 2013–2014. Labor disputes in BC also reduced communication between teachers and administrators and may have reduced enthusiasm for the start-up of new programs in some schools. Indeed, while there are many possible explanations for these differences in uptake (e.g., differences in school level priorities, difference in decision making for program uptake, and accessibility of competing prevention programs), it is possible that these policy influences also contributed.

Conclusions and recommendations

Despite the availability of many evidence-based prevention programs, we are not yet leveraging their full value for the children's benefit. This may, in part, explain why Canada and many other countries have shown little progress on the world stage in reducing bullying and victimization among children and youth (Pickett *et al.*, 2011). Widespread social problems that threaten their mental health may require the widespread adoption of evidence-based solutions. Overcoming barriers to adoption, implementation and sustainability of evidence-based mental health promotion programs in schools may be essential to improving our capacity for effective action.

For educators, the way forward can, and likely should, be built on increasing the utilization of evidence-based resources, many of which are already available. Rather than adding to workloads, when programs are selected by local program champions to fit with existing approaches to advancing children's social emotional development and social competence, they may in fact reduce teacher burden (for example in class management and disciplinary actions) and mesh with existing curriculum. Several Internet portals now exist that can guide smart choices among evidence-based mental health promotion programs for schools and also locate resources and support for their implementation (e.g., Canadian Best Practice Portal (http://cbpp-pcpe.phac-aspc.gc.ca/interventions) and in the United States SAMHSA's National Registry of evidence-based programs and practices (www.nrepp.samhsa.gov). School districts would benefit from having knowledgeable champions who are able to search for evidence-based resources and support schools not only with what is needed to start up programs but also what is needed to advance the capacity to sustain them over many years (see *School Mental Health ASSIST*; http://smh-assist.ca/). Innovation and change, while sometimes appealing, can exhaust resources, limit full implementation, and undermine positive and sustainable change. Early planning for sustaining programs, often across changes in leadership and staff, may be needed to realize the impact of mental health promotion programs. Support for local implementation facilitators and program champions' efforts to assess the integration and synergies among new and existing programs within a school may also help to reduce pressures to implement multiple distinct programs (Bohanon & Wu, 2011). It may also be that pressures on schools could be relieved if program developers begin to reach out to other organizations that routinely engage children, including after-school programs, sports teams, religious and community service groups, Scouting or 4-H groups, or Big Brothers and Sisters (Durlak *et al.*, 2010; Hirsch, Deutsch, & DuBois, 2011).

Continued research is needed to contribute to an understanding of successful processes that can enhance how evidence-based programs and resources are discovered, adopted and implemented by new users across varied contexts in ways that improve their impact on bullying, victimization and cyber-bullying. These findings will be important to program developers, educators, parents and politicians seeking feedback about the influence of their bullying prevention initiatives on Canadian children and youth. While this chapter centers on bullying-related concerns, it is likely that these findings will be generalizable to other areas of public health, including the prevention of other serious social problems with onset in childhood and adolescence, such as obesity, head injuries and anxiety.

References

Bohanon, H., & Wu, M. (2011). Can prevention programs work together? An example of school-based mental health with prevention initiatives. *Advances in School Mental Health Promotion, 4,* 35–46.

Brownson, R. C., Colditz, G. A., & Proctor, E. K. (Eds.) (2012). *Dissemination and implementation research in health: Translating science to practice.* New York: Oxford University Press.

Domitrovich, C. E., & Greenberg, M. T. (2000). The study of implementation: Current findings from effective programs that prevent mental disorders in school-age children. *Journal of Educational and Psychological Consultation, 11*(2), 193–221.

Durlak, J. A., & DuPre, E. P. (2008). Implementation matters: A review of research on the influence of implementation on program outcomes and the factors affecting implementation. *American Journal of Community Psychology, 41*(3–4), 327–350.

Durlak, J. A., Mahoney, J. L., Bohnert, A. M., & Parente, M. E. (2010). Developing and improving after-school programs to enhance youth's personal growth and adjustment: A special issue of AJCP. *American Journal of Community Psychology, 45*(3–4), 285–293.

Fixsen, D. L., Naoom, S. F., Blase, K. A., Friedman, R. M., & Wallace, F. (2005). *Implementation research: A synthesis of the literature.* Tampa, FL: University of South Florida, Louis de la Parte Florida Mental Health Institute, The National Implementation Research Network (FMHI Publication #231).

Hirsch, B. J., Deutsch, N. M. L., & DuBois, D. L. (2011) *After-school centers and youth development: Case studies of success and failure,* New York: Cambridge University Press.

Jones, S. M., & Bouffard, S. M. (2012) Social and emotional learning in schools: From programs to strategies. *Social Policy Report, 24*(4), 1–30.

Kolko, D. J., Hoagwood, K., & Springgate, B. (2010). Treatment research for children and youth exposed to traumatic events: Moving beyond efficacy to ramp up public health impact. *General Hospital Psychiatry, 32,* 465–476.

Leadbeater, B. (2008). Engaging community champions in the prevention of bullying. In: D. Pepler, & W. Craig (Eds.), *Understanding and addressing bullying: An international perspective, Volume 1.* PREVNet Series. Bloomington (IN): AuthorHouse, 166–183.

Leadbeater, B. (2010). The fickle fates of push and pull in the dissemination of mental health programs for children. *Canadian Psychology/Psychologie Canadienne, 51*(4), 221–230.

Leadbeater, B., & Sukhawathanakul, P. (2011). Multicomponent programs for reducing peer victimization in early elementary school: A longitudinal evaluation of the WITS Primary Program. *Journal of Community Psychology*, *39*(5), 606–620.

Leadbeater, B., Gladstone, E., Yeung Thompson, R., Sukhawathanakul, P., & Desjardins, T. (2012). Getting started: Assimilatory processes of uptake of mental health promotion and primary prevention programs in elementary schools. *Advances in School Mental Health Promotion*, *5*(4), 1–19.

Leadbeater, B. J., Thompson, R., & Sukhawathanakul, P. (2014). Enhancing protective processes to prevent bullying and peer victimization: A randomized control trial of the WITS Programs. Manuscript submitted for publication.

Lee, R., & Gortmaker, S. (2012). Health dissemination and implementation within schools. In R. C. Brownson, G. A. Colditz, & E. K. Proctor, (Eds.), *Dissemination and implementation research in health: Translating science to practice*. New York: OUP.

Metz, A., & Albers, B. (2014). What does it take? How federal initiatives can support the implementation of evidence-based programs to improve outcomes for adolescents. *Journal of Adolescent Health*, *54*(3, Suppl.l), S92–S96.

Moore, J. E., Bumbarger, B. K., & Cooper, B. (2013). Examining adaptations of evidence-based programs in natural contexts. *The Journal of Primary Prevention*, *34*(3), 147–161.

Oldenburg, B., & Glanz, K. (2008). Diffusion of innovations. In K. Glanz, B. Rimer, and K. Viswanath, (Eds.), *Health behavior and health education: Theory research and practice*, *4th edn*. San Francisco: Jossey-Bass.

Pickett, W. T., King, M., Freeman, J., Craig, W., Elgar, F., Janssen, I., & Klinger, D. (2011). *The health of Canada's young people: A mental health focus (HBSC) study: International report from the 2011/2012 survey, World Health Organization*. Accessed 15.04.2015 at Public Health Agency of Canada website: www.phac-aspc.gc.ca/hp-ps/dca-dea/publications/hbsc-mental-mentale/assets/pdf/hbsc-mental-mentale-eng.pdf.

Rhoades, B. L., Bumbarger, B. K., & Moore, J. E. (2012). The role of a state-level prevention support system in promoting high-quality implementation and sustainability of evidence-based programs. *American Journal of Community Psychology*, *50*(3–4), 386–401.

Sandler, I., Ostrom, A., Bitner, M. J., Ayers. T., Wolchik, S., & Daniels, V. S. (2005). Developing effective prevention services for the real world: A prevention service development model. *American Journal of Community Psychology*, *35*, 127–142.

Saunders, R. P., Pate, R. R., Dowda, M., *et al.* (2012). Assessing sustainability of Lifestyle Education for Activity Program (LEAP). *Health Education Research*, *27*(2), 319–330.

Schell, S. F., Luke, D. A., & Schooley, M. W. (2013). Public health program capacity for sustainability: A new framework. *Implementation Science*, *8*, 15–30.

Spoth, R., Guyll, M., Lillehoj, C. L., Redmond, C., & Greenberg, M. (2007). Prosper study of evidence-based intervention implementation quality by community-university partnerships. *Journal of Community Psychology*, *35*, 981–999.

Tibbits, M. K., Bumbarger, B. K., Kyler, S. J., & Perkins, D. F. (2010). Sustaining evidence-based interventions under real-world conditions: Results from a large-scale diffusion project. *Prevention Science*, *11*(3), 252–262.

Wandersman, A., Duffy, J., Flaspohler, P., *et al.* (2008). Bridging the gap between prevention research and practice: The Interactive Systems Framework for Dissemination and Implementation. *American Journal of Community Psychology*, *41*, 171–181.

4

MENTAL HEALTH AND WELLBEING THROUGH SCHOOLS IN SITUATIONS OF POLITICAL CONFLICT AND ADVERSITY

The Palestinian case

Salwa George Massad and Umaiyeh Khammash

Governments must do everything they can to protect and care for children affected by war.

(The Convention on the Rights of the Child)

Conflict-affected parts of the world are challenging contexts for addressing children's mental health and wellbeing. Not only are war-torn situations a threat to mental health, but difficulties in service provision are significant. This chapter illustrates some of the complex issues involved in the case of Palestine. Bearing in mind a broad range of possible psychological responses to adversity, schools are identified as places where children can receive services and develop resilience. However, early intervention is hampered by a lack of preschools.

The challenge

Most current mental health programs in Palestine reflect the adoption of western cultural trends towards the medicalization of trauma and distress and are mostly psychological therapies (Giacaman, Rabaia, Nguyen-Gillham, Batniji, Punamaki, & Summerfield, 2010). This focus on trauma alone has resulted in inadequate attention to factors associated with resilient mental health outcomes. There is a shortage of trained mental health professionals, and mental health services and programs are fragmented and lack the required material and financial resources to scale them up (Save the Children, 2012). In addition, there are no mental health programs at the preschool level for early intervention.

Background

Children living in conflict-affected areas

Approximately 1 billion children live in conflict-affected areas – 300 million of whom are under the age of five. Apart from the direct physical impact, armed conflict has broad-ranging consequences for the mental health and wellbeing of children and adolescents (Lokuge *et al.*, 2013). Evidence-based interventions are vital to adequately address the needs of populations affected by disasters and mass violence. Inadequate responsiveness increases the risk of mental health problems in war-affected children and families (Betancourt, Meyers-Ohki, Charrow, & Tol, 2013). Five intervention principles are considered as 'essential elements' of immediate and midterm mass trauma interventions: (i) a sense of safety; (ii) calming; (iii) a sense of self- and community efficacy; (iv) connectedness; and (v) hope (Betancourt *et al.*, 2013).

In this chapter some background is provided to enable a consideration of the specific case of Palestine. The chapter is written from a particular Palestinian perspective where the underlying political situation is complex. Palestine is located in the Middle East and divided into the West Bank, which borders Jordan, and the Gaza Strip, which borders Egypt and the Mediterranean Sea. The total population (end-2013) was about 4.5 million: 2.8 million in the West Bank and 1.7 million in the Gaza Strip (Palestinian Central Bureau of Statistics, 2014a). In 2013, 47 percent of the Palestinian population was under 18 (Palestinian Central Bureau of Statistics, 2014b).

In 1948, around 700,000 Palestinians were displaced by the emerging Israeli State. Today there are around 5.3 million registered refugees, about one-third living in camps in Jordan, Lebanon, Syria, the West Bank and the Gaza Strip (UNRWA, n.d.). About 41 percent of the population in Palestine comprises refugees; a Palestinian child has fewer chances of having a parent who is not traumatized than the average child in the world. Some consider camps as sites of poverty, marginalization and terror, but also of remarkable creativity (Peteet, 2009).

The first uprising (intifada), which occurred from 1987 to 1993, represented the zenith of Palestinian popular resistance against the Israeli military occupation. In the course of the first intifada, over 1,500 civilians were killed (25 percent were children), with many thousands injured (Giacaman *et al.*, 2010). The violent Israeli response to the second Palestinian intifada in 2000 led to even more difficult, dangerous and insecure living conditions for Palestinians. More than 4,800 people, including over 950 children, were killed by Israeli military action between 29 September 2000 and 12 June 2008 (B'Tselem, n.d). In the few weeks since this chapter was first drafted in mid-2014, there has been a further escalation of violence in Gaza, with thousands of civilians killed and severely injured, more than 290,000 displaced, homes, schools, clinics and hospitals destroyed or damaged and concerns expressed around the world about the bombing of United Nations facilities (World Health Organization [WHO], 2014).

Even before this, direct and indirect exposure to violence was common among children in Palestine, especially in Gaza (Palestinian Central Bureau of Statistics, 2005). The Israeli attack on the Gaza Strip 27 December 2008–18 January 2009 killed about 1,400 and injured 5,380 Gazans, including many civilians (Abu-Rmeileh et al., 2011). In 2002, in a study of a representative sample of 1,266 children living in the West Bank and Gaza Strip, 93 percent of children reported not feeling safe and feeling exposed to attack, 48 percent had personally experienced violence or witnessed violence against an immediate family member, and 21 percent had to move out of their homes, temporarily or permanently, for conflict-related reasons (Arafat, 2003). In another study of the mental health of preschoolers in the Gaza Strip in 2007, 94 percent had heard sounds of jetfighters, 93 percent saw mutilated or injured bodies on television, 84 percent had heard shelling by artillery, and 50 percent witnessed signs of shelling on the ground (Massad et al., 2009). Child witnesses of violence display an increased incidence of internalizing behaviors, such as depression, and externalizing behaviors, such as aggressiveness and noncompliance (Lieberman, van Horn, & Ozer, 2005).

Such reactions intensify with increasing levels of violence (Thabet, Karim, & Vostanis, 2006). In 2003, Thabet looked at the behavioral and emotional problems of 309 Palestinian preschoolers and found that direct and indirect exposure to war trauma increased the risk of poor mental health (Thabet et al., 2006). In 2007, the quality of life of preschoolers in the Gaza Strip was very low and comparable to US children with severe cardiac diseases, end-stage renal disease, and to children receiving chemotherapy and radiation treatment for newly diagnosed cancer (Massad et al., 2011). Qouta, Punamaki, and El Sarraj (2005) assessed the mental health problems of 121 Palestinian children aged 6–16 and found that 54 percent suffered from severe levels of post-traumatic stress disorders. In addition, suicide attempts were increasing (Save the Children, 2012). However, children participating in active resistance against Israeli soldiers during the first intifada were having fewer PTSD symptoms than those not engaged in active resistance (e.g., demonstrations, throwing of stones, burning tires, etc.), although both groups were exposed to similar violent events from the Israeli soldiers. This could be attributed to better coping strategies among children who felt that they could actively resist the occupation, as opposed to those who felt helpless and stayed home (Srour, 2003). In fact, the Atfal Al-Hijara – children of the stones – were the most visible symbol of the first uprising: the frontline of a war of liberation that cut across class, religion, and political affiliation.

The challenge of responding to mental health needs of school children

Exposure to violent events is not the only stressor affecting the mental health of Palestinian children, as their wellbeing is also threatened by poverty, poor living conditions and overcrowding in camps. Moreover, these camps are turning into slums with high levels of violence, food insecurity, forced relocation, mothers' poor mental health (Massad *et al.*, 2009), and patriarchal social structures that dispro-portionately affect the most-vulnerable population groups – women and children.

Until the 1980s, the mental health of war-affected Palestinians had received little attention from health practitioners and humanitarian aid providers (Giacaman *et al.*, 2010). However, since the first Palestinian uprising in the late 1980s and the accompanying media attention to Israeli military violence, the emphasis on psychological 'trauma' has increased and subsequently become a major concern of international mental health initiatives. In fact, international organizations have contributed to the increased attention to mental health by putting it on their agenda and providing funding. In the first years following the uprising, there was significant funding for psychosocial interventions under emergency funding for different activities that were not integrated into the health or school system. In fact, there was overfunding at one point without programs being integrated into the health system or system development to ensure sustainability. Furthermore, this funding came with minimal to no monitoring or evaluation, bearing in mind the nature of the considerable long-standing conflict. At that time, international organizations imported a variety of intervention methods designed to mitigate post-traumatic stress disorder, providing local staff with short training programs and limited follow-up (Nguyen-Gillham, Giacaman, Naser, & Boyce, 2008). Many local organizations that worked with youth and children carried out psychosocial interventions that were mostly debriefing activities, such as school trips and face-painting. The imposed psychosocial programming model reflected the adoption of western cultural trends towards the medicalization of trauma and distress and the rise of psychological therapies (Giacaman *et al.*, 2010). However, the second intifada was a turning point for mental health, with developing anti-stigma campaigns and improving mental health, with less focus on individual counseling.

In Palestine, international and local Non-Governmental Organizations (NGOs) played a big role in introducing mental health services. Most services are offered in schools through the Ministry of Education and United Nations Relief and Works Agency (UNRWA), through which school counselors serve as the first contact for students needing additional support or guidance regarding preventative services (Ciftci & Shawahin, 2013). However, governmental organizations and NGOs often provide overlapping services to the same populations, and many of the NGOs' services and interventions are driven mostly by the agenda of funders, rather than by the needs of the community, with the availability and continuity of services and training heavily dependent on intermittent western sources of funding (Ciftci & Shawahin, 2013).

Before the Ministry of Health officially adopted the Mental Health policy in 2004, public services ran vertical programs driven by donors, without having enough resources for rehabilitation, reintegration into society, and promotion of wellbeing. Despite the progress in recent years, stigma is still associated with mental illness, and health services are far from being optimal (WHO, 2012) and the system continues to suffer from funding deficits. There is no specifically defined budget for mental health services costs. In 2006, for example, an estimated 2.5 percent of the Palestinian Authority health care expenditures were used for mental health, the bulk of which went to the two psychiatric hospitals (Giacaman *et al.*, 2010). There is also a shortage of trained mental health professionals, with 0.87 psychiatrists, 3.43 psychiatric nurses, 0.98 psychologists and 0.21 occupational therapists per 100,000 people in Palestine (Giacaman *et al.*, 2010). Intervention is primarily focused on the provision of medicines, rather than prevention and early detection in at-risk children. Mental health services are still fragmented between and within sectors. Public mental health services are offered by both the education and health systems, with suboptimal coordination. There is no operational policy, no guidelines for referral, and there are different health information systems. Although there is currently a mental health policy set to establish community mental health centers, hospital-based care is still predominant. So far, there are no mental health departments in general hospitals.

Access to mental health services is another critical issue; lack of complete Palestinian control puts areas such as Area C, that includes all 125 Israeli settlements in the West Bank (B'Tselem, 2014) and seam zone areas (areas of the West Bank between the Green Line and the separation wall), Gaza Strip, and East Jerusalem at risk of marginalization and creates discrepancies in services received by children in these areas compared to those in areas under the control of the Palestinian Authority (Save the Children, 2012).

The emphasis of most current mental health programs is on the victimization of children, which takes the focus away from their sense of empowerment (Giacaman *et al.*, 2010). Such a treatment modality assumes that the pathological effects of war can be cured through individual treatment, as if the individual were recovering from an illness rather than suffering from the long-protracted consequences of a historical and ongoing political injustice (Giacaman *et al.*, 2010). As a result, the majority of the research on the mental health of war-affected children has focused on risk factors and subsequent psychopathology (Betancourt & Khan, 2008). However, the focus on trauma alone has resulted in inadequate attention to factors associated with resilient mental health outcomes. Exposure to adversity or trauma does not necessarily lead to impairment and the development of psychopathology in all exposed children. Some are resilient in the face of stressful life events and appear to develop healthy psychosocial functioning (Massad *et al.*, 2009). In a study of Palestinian children aged 5–17 years in 2002, 70 percent believed that they could improve their own lives by developing academically first and foremost, but also personally and socially (Arafat, 2003).

Opportunities for responding to mental health needs of school children

An alternative to the vulnerability and medical symptoms approach is linking mental health to indicators of social wellbeing and quality of life. This approach places social suffering within an ease–disease continuum ranging from mental wellbeing to mental disease, where Palestinians, who live in severe distress as they endure the suffering and trauma of chronic and acute warlike conditions, are seen as oscillating in the grey areas between ease and disease (Giacaman *et al.*, 2010).

An important paradigm shift is currently underway as scientific work is moving its focus from the factors and mechanisms that determine vulnerability to mental ill health, to the factors and mechanisms that stimulate resilience to enable individuals to remain healthy or to recover quickly when facing severe adversities over the course of their lives (Rutten *et al.*, 2013). Resilience is not only an individual quality of certain children; rather, it is more useful to focus on 'resilient outcomes' in children faced with adversity (Betancourt & Khan, 2008). The focus on resilience is based on the theory that the mechanisms operating to produce resilience and vulnerability are different. In addition to the home setting, the quality of relations in schools and neighborhoods are also implicated in the mental health and coping of war-affected children (Betancourt & Khan, 2008).

Addressing the challenge and opportunities

Early interventions at preschool level

Research indicates it is more effective and economical to intervene early to promote optimal development, as opposed to intervening after problems become established (Miller-Lewis, Searle, Sawyer, Baghurst, & Hedley, 2013). Early childhood is considered an opportune time for implementing early intervention strategies aimed at altering the trajectory of pathways that lead to the emergence of mental health difficulties. Children with behavior problems as preschoolers are at an increased risk of psychiatric disorders as adolescents (Loeber, 1982). The identification of factors that may either protect children from adverse effects of violence and deprivation or exacerbate these effects is crucial for both the theoretical understanding of child development and for the design of effective intervention strategies (Lieberman *et al.*, 2005).

Although early intervention is crucial for wellbeing (Miller-Lewis *et al.*, 2013), it was dropped by the Palestinian health system in an effort to focus on older children who are more cooperative and less challenging. In Palestine, there are no public preschools, and as a result no interventions or psychosocial activities at that level. Most private preschools in Palestine are weak and not affordable by poor families. There are no integrated psychosocial interventions in most preschool programs other than debriefing activities. As a result, children enter schools with their mental health issues untouched by the education system.

Mental health and wellbeing through schools

During crisis events and in the longer term, schools, and child and youth clubs, become important sources of stability and care, and may contribute to the resilience outcome (Miller-Lewis *et al.*, 2013). Within the school setting, interventions can be aimed at preventing mental health problems and promoting wellbeing in all children in the school, or targeting specific at-risk groups (Betancourt et al., 2013). It has been shown that secure attachment can prevent negative outcomes in children otherwise at risk of developing less optimal outcomes (Rutten et al., 2013).

In discussing ecological approaches to interventions for children affected by war, Elbedour, ten Bensel, and Bastien (1993) emphasized the importance of schools in mitigating trauma's effects. In a review, Betancourt and colleagues identified three preventive school-based interventions that focused on developing resiliency as a mechanism for addressing mental health (Betancourt et al., 2013). The first (ERASE-Stress) uses psycho-education and skill training with meditative and narrative practices to re-process traumatic experiences and boost self-esteem and access to social supports. The second is a primary prevention intervention that focuses on strengthening social support, self-efficacy, and meaning attribution. The third is a school-based psychosocial intervention that focuses on positive aspects of wellbeing, such as good family and community relationships, trust, problem solving, and hope.

Mental health programs in Palestinian Schools

During the first intifada, all Palestinian schools were closed for periods ranging from several months to two years at a time, where a number were taken over as detention centers. In the first four years of the intifada, approximately one-third of school days were lost. The mobility restrictions in these areas caused by the Israeli military curfews, closures and home confinement necessitated the creation of a substitute alternative schooling system or 'popular education' as a means of resistance. Many children were home-schooled, or gathered in makeshift classrooms such as mosques, basements, and alleyways to learn. The Israeli authorities considered the popular education initiatives illegal; students caught participating were subject to harassment and arrest, and were liable to be jailed for a period of up to ten years and fined up to USD 5,000; however, these Israeli measures somewhat backfired, as they effectively encouraged further youth involvement in the intifada (Nicolai, 2007). Furthermore, the emergency popular education provided children and youth with a sense of security and predictability amidst the chaos of displacement, traumatic events, and loss. Such tangible and practical activities restored order and stability and fostered resilience (Nguyen-Gillham et al., 2008). In a study among Palestinian children following the second intifada, while parents and teachers were alarmed about decreases in students' attention spans and rising absenteeism, children continued to value their education. Almost all (96 percent) viewed education as one of their main means of peaceful resistance, and considered it their main means to improve their situation, both presently and in the future (Arafat, 2003).

Almost 91 percent of Palestinian children are in UNRWA and public schools. The Ministry of Health (MoH) and UNRWA are currently emphasizing mental health as a priority, given the historic lack of appropriate services combined with the present socio-political crisis. This combination further reduces the health services' capacity to cope with mental health problems and increases the needs of the population in terms of mental health care. The Ministry of Education (MoE) runs a school counseling program in most public schools, working in synergy with the school health program and dealing with students in need of professional counseling, addressing anxiety, fears, problems related to stress, family support, and referrals. The program is specifically sensitive to targeting children at risk of school dropout and those with low attainment and performance at school, offering guidance to students on the advantages of staying in school and avoiding early marriage and dropout. The program also identifies those who may have been exposed to violence, abuse and/or exploitation and is part of the national child protection network; it refers children in need of more intensive treatment, or for certain treatments by more specialist professionals at the MoH or in the NGO sector (Save the Children, 2012).

UNRWA has been running a mixture of mental health and counseling services within the health and school system in the West Bank and Gaza Strip with programs fluctuating in response to the availability of funding (Giacaman *et al.*, 2010). UNRWA schools implement different psychosocial interventions through various activities, such as creative arts, theatre, summer camps, dabka (a folkloric dance), animation films, puppets, and introduction of capoeira (a Brazilian martial art that is used as a tool to provide debriefing), rehabilitation and therapy, as well as psychological support for vulnerable children through storytelling, movement and exercise, song and instruments, dance, social talks, and community spirit. As part of a holistic approach in tackling mental health issues of school children, UNRWA produced a booklet on positive parenting to work with parents on their parenting skills in an effort to provide a relaxing home environment, bringing psychological relief to children.

Current policy initiatives

Among Palestinian MoH policy priorities in 2012 was the inclusion of community mental health as a first line of defense to protect children's mental health, and equip them with protective mechanisms to increase their ability to deal with life's pressures through schools, primary health care clinics, the family and community. Community mental health is intended to provide psychological support, life skills and defense mechanisms to enhance children's immunity against adverse influences and life pressures through school, primary health care clinics, the family unit, and the community (Save the Children, 2012).

The UNRWA's *Community Mental Health Program* (*CMHP*) was established in 2002 to assist Palestinian refugees who had lost their ability to cope with the deteriorating conditions characterized by high levels of violence and economic decline. With a particular focus on children and youth, CMHP helps to mitigate the psychological impact resulting from the prevailing violence and economic hardship (Massad *et al.*, 2009). Mental health counselors are based in schools to provide children with basic life skills, such as appropriate forms of communication, stress coping mechanisms, and self-confidence-building exercises. These structured exercises and drawing activities attempt to provide students with the necessary tools to live a normal life in challenging conditions (UNRWA, 2013).

In response to a growing awareness of cases of violence, abuse, and neglect among Palestinian refugee families, in 2009, UNRWA established the *Family and Child Protection Program* as part of the *CMHP*. This program was intended to work with UNRWA *Health, Education, and the Relief and Social Services Program* in partnership with the refugee communities to prevent and respond to cases of abuse, neglect, and violence in homes, schools, and communities. The program has a public health approach as well: tackling the causes of abuse and violence to promote wellbeing. It developed three modules on sexual reproductive and health rights, early marriage, and sexual abuse and sexually transmitted diseases that are going to be incorporated into the UNRWA school curriculum. The program's work with children focuses on child participation. Children who participated in training, awareness sessions, and peer groups engaged their families and started to attract other peers (e.g., siblings, friends, neighbors' children) to attend the sessions. The training provided for children made them feel comfortable to facilitate other groups themselves (UNRWA, 2012).

Conclusions

Poor mental health and PTSD are only one aspect of a complete set of responses to adversity or trauma. Children can defy chaos and overcome severe risk factors by establishing routine and normality within their daily lives. For Palestinian children, a key to active coping is the completion of everyday tasks at home and at school. Social capital, in the form of a tight network of family support, peers, friends, caring adults, clubs, and schools, can nurture and sustain their sense of optimism and hope (Giacaman *et al.*, 2010).

In light of the ongoing exposure to violence, shortage of skilled mental health professionals, inability to equitably reach all areas and groups, limited financial resources, and discontinuity of interventions and services, kindergartens and schools are the best place to target a large segment of children. This provides a window of opportunity to combat adversity and promote resilience. There is also a need to invest in preschool-level health education and development for psychosocial interventions, in order to promote wellbeing and early detection to allow timely intervention (Save the Children, 2012). The school has grown in importance as a social forum and source of support for Palestinian children. Both governmental and nongovernmental service providers and educational programs need to work together to develop appropriate operational policies and avoid duplication and wasting of resources. Such cooperation will lead to policy development that is more organized and consistently serves the needs of the community, especially children (Ciftci & Shawahin, 2013).

School-based mental health programs need to build on the UNRWA's *Family and Child Protection Program* model that is based on partnership with communities; it focuses on child participation and empowerment using the Child-to-Child approach, and peer groups to combat adversity and promote resilience among schoolchildren. That said, schools should be assisted in broadening their extra-curricular facilities, turning them into 'multi-functional centers' where children can study, play, and socialize throughout the day, with a view to bolstering their 'sense of normality'. This will require improvements in physical infrastructure designed to make schools more child-friendly, the training of psychosocial facilitators who can support children in the context of both in- and out-of-school activities, and programs that train teachers – not only school counselors – to deploy proper psychosocial methods in dealing with children (Arafat, 2003). There is also a need for rehabilitation programs within the education system to support the re-integration of victims of conflict-related violence into schools and society. However, there is a need for more counselors, especially in high-risk areas: Jerusalem suburbs, East Jerusalem, Hebron, Jordan Valley, areas adjacent to the Wall, or areas close to settlements and military camps, among others, as well as a need to invest in preschool-level health education (Save the Children, 2012).

References

Abu-Rmeileh, N., Hammoudeh W., Husseini, A., Khawaja, M., Shannon, H. S., Hogan, D., . . . Giacaman, R. (2011). Health-related quality of life of Gaza Palestinians in the aftermath of the winter 2008–2009 Israeli attack on the Strip. *The European Journal of Public Health, 22*(5), 732–737.

Arafat, C. (2003). Psychosocial assessment of Palestinian children. Save the Children. Accessed 15.04.2015 at http://resourcecentre.savethechildren.se/library/psychosocial-assessment-palestinian-children

Betancourt, T. S., Meyers-Ohki, S. E., Charrow, A. P., & Tol, W. A. (2013). Interventions for children affected by war: An ecological perspective on psychosocial support and mental health care. *Harvard Review of Psychiatry, 21*(2), 70–91.

Betancourt, T. S., & Khan, K. T. (2008). The mental health of children affected by armed conflict: Protective processes and pathways to resilience. *International Review of Psychiatry, 20*(3), 317–28.

B'Tselem (2014). Area C. Accessed 12.11.2015 at www.btselem.org/area_c/what_is_area_c

B'Tselem (n.d). The Israeli Information Center for Human Rights in the Occupied Territories. Statistics. Accessed 20.01.2014 at www.btselem.org/statistics/fatalities/before-cast-lead/by-date-of-event

Ciftci, A., & Shawahin, L. (2013). Counseling and mental health care in Palestine. *Journal of Counseling and Development, 90*, 378–382.

Elbedour, S., ten Bensel, R., & Bastien, D. T. (1993). Ecological integrated model of children of war: Individual and social psychology. *Child Abuse and Neglect, 17*(6), 805–819.

Giacaman, R., Rabaia, Y., Nguyen-Gillham, V., Batniji, R., Punamaki, R. L., & Summerfield, D. (2010). Mental health, social distress and political oppression: The case of the occupied Palestinian territory. *Global Public Health, 6*(5), 1–13.

Lieberman, A. F., Van Horn, P., & Ozer, E. J. (2005). Preschooler witnesses of marital violence: Predictors and mediators of child behavior problems. *Developmental Psychopathology, 17*(2), 385–396.

Loeber, R. (1982). The stability of antisocial and delinquent child behavior: A review. *Child Development, 53*(6), 1431–1446.

Lokuge, K., Shah, T., Pintaldi, G., Thurber, K., Martinez-Viciana, C., Cristobal, M., . . . Banks, E. (2013). Mental health services for children exposed to armed conflict: Medecins

Sans Frontières' experience in the Democratic Republic of Congo, Iraq and the occupied Palestinian territory. *Paediatrica and International Child Health, 33*(4), 259–272.

Massad, S., Nieto, F. J., Palta, M., Smith, M., Clark, R., & Thabet, A. A. (2009). Mental health of Palestinian children in kindergartens: Resilience and vulnerability. *Child and Adolescent Mental Health, 14,* 89–96.

Massad, S., Nieto, F. J., Palta, M., Smith, M., Clark, R., & Thabet, A. A. (2011). Health-related quality of life of Palestinian preschoolers in the Gaza Strip: A cross-sectional study. *BMC Public Health, 11*(253).

Miller-Lewis, L. R., Searle, A. K., Sawyer, M. G., Baghurst, P. A., & Hedley, D. (2013). Resource factors for mental health resilience in early childhood: An analysis with multiple methodologies. *Child and Adolescent Psychiatry and Mental Health, 7*(6). Accessed 15.04.2015 at www.capmh.com/content/7/1/6

Nguyen-Gillham, V., Giacaman, R., Naser, G., & Boyce, W. (2008). Normalising the abnormal: Palestinian youth and the contradictions of resilience in protracted conflict. *Health & Social Care in the Community, 16*(3), 291–298.

Nicolai, S. (2007). Fragmented foundations: Education and chronic crisis in the Occupied Palestinian Territory. UNESCO International Institute for Educational Planning, Save the Children UK. Accessed 15.04.2015 at http://unesdoc.unesco.org/images/0015/001502/150260e.pdf

Palestinian Central Bureau of Statistics (2005). *Impact of Israeli measures on the well-being of the Palestinian children, women, and household - Press Release.* Child Statistics 2005. Accessed 15.04.2015 at www.pcbs.gov.ps/Portals/_pcbs/PressRelease/chld_00/texte.pdf

Palestinian Central Bureau of Statistics (2014a). *Special Statistical Bulletin on the 66th Anniversary of the Palestinian Nakba. Press Release 2014.* Accessed 15.04.2015 at www.pcbs.gov.ps/site/512/default.aspx?tabID=512&lang=en&ItemID=1111&mid=3171&wversion=Staging

Palestinian Central Bureau of Statistics (2014b). *The Palestinian Child's Day. Press Release.* Accessed 15.04.2015 at www.pcbs.gov.ps/portals/_pcbs/PressRelease/Press_En_ChilDay2014E.pdf

Peteet, J. P. (2009). *Landscape of Hope and Despair: Palestinian Refugee Camps.* Philadelphia: University of Pennsylvania Press.

Qouta, S., Punamaki, R. L., & El Sarraj, E. (2005). Mother–child expression of psychological distress in war trauma. *Clinical Child Psychology and Psychiatry, 10*(2), 135–156.

Rutten, B. P., Hammels, C., Geschwind, N., Menne-Lothmann, C., Pishva, E., Schruers, K., . . . Wichers, M. (2013). Resilience in mental health: Linking psychological and neurobiological perspectives. *Acta Psychiatr Scand. 128*(1), 3–20.

Save the Children (2012). *Ministry of Health – Palestinian Child Public Health Policy: Palestinian child health priorities based on the child's rights to health.*

Srour, R. (2003). *Palestinian children in war zone: Coping strategies and their long term effects.* Palestinian Counseling Center. Accessed 15.04.2015 at www.pcc-jer.org/english/article7_en.php

Thabet, A. A., Karim, K., & Vostanis, P. (2006). Trauma exposure in pre-school children in a war zone. *British Journal of Psychiatry, 188,* 154–158.

United Nations Relief and Works Agency (UNRWA) (2013). *UNRWA Community Mental Health Programme.* Retrieved 27.11.15 from www.unrwa.org/sites/default/files/20100118151854.pdf

United Nations Relief and Works Agency (UNRWA) (2012). *The Annual report of the Department of Health 2011.* Accessed 15.04.2015 at http://unispal.un.org/pdfs/UNRWA_HealthDept2011Rpt.pdf

United Nations Relief and Works Agency (UNRWA) (n.d). *Palestine Refugees*. Accessed 15.04.2015 at www.unrwa.org/palestine-refugees

World Health Organization (WHO) (2012). *Transforming mental health services and attitudes: Phase 2 of EU-funded mental health initiative in the West Bank and Gaza Strip, 10 October 2012*. Accessed 20.01.2014 at www.emro.who.int/ar/palestine-press-releases/2012/transforming-mental-health-services-and-attitudes-palestinian-moh-and-who-launch-phase-2-of-eu-funded-mental-health-initiative-in-west-bank-and-gaza.html

World Health Organization (WHO) (2014). Occupied Palestinian Territory - Conflict escalation in Gaza - complex emergency Situation Report #7 6-August 2014. Accessed 13.08.2014 at www.emro.who.int/images/stories/palestine/documents/WHO_Sitrep_on_Gaza_-__7_-_Aug_6.pdf?ua=1

SECTION 3
Challenges for teachers

5

IMPLEMENTING FOR SUCCESS IN SCHOOL-BASED MENTAL HEALTH PROMOTION

The role of quality in resolving the tension between fidelity and adaptation

Ann Lendrum, Neil Humphrey and Mark Greenberg

Research in implementation science has shown that interventions are rarely implemented as designed, and that variability in implementation is associated with variability in outcomes. Lack of programme fidelity has been seen as the prime cause of poor outcomes, though it has also been suggested that this must be balanced against adaptation. In this chapter, we argue that what is required is a focus on quality, of both fidelity and adaptation. This reframing has implications for programme development processes, research and evaluation, and the training and support of practitioners in the field.

The challenge

The challenge addressed in this chapter is the long-standing tension between programme developers' requirement for fidelity and practitioners' need for adaptability in the implementation of school-based interventions. Drawing upon recent theory and research in implementation and prevention science, we propose an increased focus on the *quality* of both fidelity and adaptation as a means to resolve this tension.

Background

Mental health difficulties are changes in thought, feelings and/or behaviour that are maladaptive and impair functioning. Around one in five students experience such difficulties, and up to half of adult mental health problems originate in childhood and adolescence (Belfer, 2008). Schools are increasingly expected to play a central role in addressing these problems and promoting wellbeing, with good reason. They play a central role in the lives of children and their families, and their reach is unparalleled (Greenberg, 2010). Drawing on the inoculation metaphor that 'an ounce of prevention is worth a pound of cure', a universal approach to intervention has become a defining characteristic of education policy and practice in this area. Social and emotional learning (SEL) programmes, which seek to help all children understand their emotions, manage their behaviour and work well with others, offer particular promise. SEL theory suggests that developing such competencies in the context of a caring, participatory classroom environment engenders resilience to the onset of mental health difficulties because it fosters greater attachment to school, enables more effective coping in adverse circumstances, and reduces risky behaviours (CASEL, 2007).

Two recent meta-analyses have demonstrated that SEL interventions can make meaningful improvements to a range of outcomes for children, including their mental health (Durlak *et al.*, 2011; Sklad, Diekstra, De Ritter, Ben, & Gravesteijn, 2012). Drawing on these and other analyses, a range of online databases is currently available that enables practitioners to identify those interventions for which there is a robust evidence base (e.g., see www.kidsmatter.edu.au). However, the adoption of evidence-based SEL programmes is only the first step, and does not guarantee that intended outcomes will be achieved. The 'bridge' to these outcomes is implementation, that is, the process by which an intervention is put into practice (Lendrum & Humphrey, 2012). Decades of research in the field of implementation science has shown that interventions are rarely implemented as designed, and that variability in implementation is associated with variability in outcomes – put simply, implementation matters (Durlak & DuPre, 2008). In studying this process, we may refer to:

- *fidelity* – was the intervention delivered as intended by its developers?
- *dosage* – how much of the intervention was delivered?
- *adaptation* – what changes/modifications were made and why?
- *quality* – how well was the intervention delivered?
- *participant responsiveness* – did recipients engage with the intervention?
- *reach* – was the intervention delivered to all intended recipients?
- *programme differentiation* – was the intervention distinct from usual practice?

Of these aspects, fidelity has inarguably predominated. So, for example, in Durlak and DuPre's (2008) seminal review, 63 per cent of studies focused on fidelity as the primary indicator of implementation effectiveness, compared with only 10 per cent focusing on quality. This is based on an implicit assumption that for the outcomes of a 'proven' programme to be replicated, the exact delivery regime under which it was validated must also be replicated. This is the 'zero-sum-game' view of fidelity and adaptation: higher fidelity results in better outcomes, and any deviation from the intended intervention model must therefore be detrimental (e.g., Elliott & Mihalic, 2004).

Evidence supporting the fidelity–outcome relationship is indeed robust (see Durlak & DuPre, 2008, for a review), and programme developers therefore strongly advocate this aspect in their dissemination/promotion work, particularly for manualised interventions. However, this evidence is typically gathered in the absence of concurrent consideration of other aspects of implementation such as adaptations and quality (Berkel, Mauricio, Schoenfelder, & Sandler, 2011). This has led to a kind of self-fulfilling prophecy in which fidelity is routinely identified as the most important aspect of implementation because it is the one most often studied. Furthermore, the zero-sum-game view arguably promotes a model of educational practice that is anathema to the autonomy and professional identity of teachers. Dixon (2012) summarises this objection well in his satirical ponderings about how a modern-day Gradgrind (a character in Charles Dickens' *Hard Times* who embodies a purely rationalist approach to human experience) would approach SEL:

> He would seek, from any programme of emotional education, a package of activities that could be mechanically, identically, practiced in every classroom in the land, regardless of the fanciful foibles of individual teachers or the cultural inheritance of individual children . . . he would thus impose a single pedagogical scheme and a universal emotional language.
>
> (p.12)

At this point it might be important to differentiate between SEL interventions that are short term and discrete (for example, an eight- or twelve-lesson programme on life skills) and more comprehensive models intended to teach skills as well as change the culture of the classroom and be infused throughout the day. In the first case, it is quite reasonable to assess fidelity by asking whether each activity was completed. In the second case, where the goal is for the teacher to integrate the lessons and larger conceptual model of action into the fabric of the classroom, there are broader questions to be addressed regarding the teacher's ability to nurture and generalise the skills, attitudes and behaviours learned in the lessons throughout the remainder of the school day.

In the real-world implementation of school-based interventions, adaptations are inevitable (Durlak & DuPre, 2008; Ringwalt & Ennett, 2003). Practitioners are likely to modify or change an intervention to improve its fit to the local context and their students' needs, both of which may be different from the circumstances under which it was originally validated (Chambers, Glasgow, & Stange, 2013; Hansen *et al.*, 2013). When interventions are first tested, the focus is on optimising internal validity. This inevitably means less focus on external validity and how the programme will work in a wider range of contexts, perhaps based on an assumption that 'one size fits all'. Of course, this isn't the case – multiple contextual factors can influence implementation, including preplanning and foundations, the implementation support system, the implementation environment, implementer factors, and programme characteristics (Humphrey, 2013). School contexts are also dynamic. Changing student populations, and indeed cultural contexts (Ferrer-Wreder, Sundell, & Mansoory, 2011), may mean that different adaptations will be needed for each group receiving a given intervention. Moreover, practitioners in naturalistic settings may not have access to the same resources and expertise present when the programme was first tested or validated (e.g., number of hours, curriculum time, staffing support), meaning that adaptation is unavoidable. Finally, they may also adapt interventions to incorporate their own experience or to suit their pedagogical approach.

With a predominant focus on fidelity in implementation science and programme dissemination, adaptations may be unhelpfully dismissed as 'implementation failure'. However, while certain types of adaptation may be detrimental, some can be beneficial or even crucial to the success of an intervention, increasing local ownership and sustainability (US Department of Health and Human Services, 2002). Furthermore, adapting to the needs of students may improve their engagement with an intervention and thus enhance programme effectiveness (Botvin, 2004). Teachers who adapt interventions should not, therefore, be dismissed as failing. Indeed, they may be more motivated, creative and effective implementers than those who slavishly 'stick to the script' (Dusenbury, Brannigan, Falco, & Hansen, 2003).

Backer and others have advocated a balanced approach to the fidelity–adaptation debate that contrasts sharply with the zero-sum-game view (US Department of Health and Human Services, 2002). In this model, there is a dual acknowledgement that while fidelity to core intervention components is critical for success, some level of adaptation may also be necessary due to variations in context. A major review by Durlak and DuPre (2008) would seem to support this; very few studies report greater than 80 per cent implementation fidelity and positive outcomes have been achieved with only 60 per cent, suggesting that some form of adaptation is acceptable. What can be adapted and what must be implemented with fidelity is, however, likely to be programme-specific and require increased dialogue between implementers and programme developers. For the latter, identifying and operationalising critical components is therefore crucial (Blase & Fixsen, 2013). For the former, understanding how and why interventions work will prove beneficial.

Quality matters?

One approach to resolving the tension between programme developers' requirement for fidelity and practitioners' need for adaptability is to increase the focus on the *quality* of these aspects of implementation. We begin with fidelity, "the degree to which teachers and other programme providers implement programs as intended by the programme developers" (Dusenbury *et al.*, 2003, p. 240). Recall that the push for full fidelity is to achieve replication of a validated delivery regime, and thus achieve the same results. However, researchers and practitioners often have different views about this. Practitioners aim to achieve improved outcomes for their students in whatever way they feel is best, and may be less interested in validity and evidence of effectiveness than researchers and programme developers. Rigid fidelity requirements may therefore influence the 'science to practice gap', which has seen schools more likely to rely on home-grown approaches than those with a strong evidence base (see, for example, Vostanis, Humphrey, Fitzgerald, Wolpert, & Deighton, 2013). Furthermore, at an intuitive level, myopic adherence to an intervention model alone is surely insufficient to trigger lasting change (Harn, Parisi, & Stoolmiller, 2013). The engagement of students is crucial for effective learning; without this, internalisation of lesson content and the development of competencies are unlikely to occur. For programmes that have both a skills and environmental/ climate focus, this rigid model is not considered appropriate.

Thus, a reconceptualisation of fidelity as more than just replication, unthinkingly repeating scripts, messages and activities, is warranted. It is important not just that practitioners 'do it right', but that they also 'do it well'. Quality is therefore central, and there is emerging evidence that its importance is at least equal to that of fidelity in the achievement of expected outcomes. A recent example of this can be seen in our implementation and process evaluation of the Promoting Alternative Thinking Strategies (PATHS) curriculum, in which quality (operationalised as teacher preparedness, enthusiasm, and engagement with and responsiveness to students) was routinely more strongly associated with improved outcomes than fidelity when both were assessed concurrently in a comprehensive analysis of all of the aspects of implementation noted above (Humphrey, Lendrum, & Wigelsworth, 2014).

'Quality' can, however, be a somewhat elusive term. It is subjective and more challenging to assess or quantify and measure than other aspects of implementation.[1] As a term, it is also bound up confusingly in the existing discourse of implementation, such that it is often used interchangeably with 'fidelity' (Humphrey, 2013). This in itself is an example of the zero-sum-game view outlined earlier – such is the dominance of the fidelity discourse, it has come to be viewed as *synonymous with quality*, implying, perhaps, that any adaptation may thus be seen as a threat to quality.

So what do we mean by quality of implementation? Domitrovich *et al.* (2008) define it as practitioners' affective engagement, sensitivity, and responsiveness in their delivery of intervention content. Odom *et al.* (2010) assessed quality as relating to teachers' preparedness, the skill with which they delivered lessons, their integration of concepts into activities across the day and their response to children. More recently, Vo, Sutherland and Conroy (2012) defined quality as competence, that is an implementer's level of skill and responsiveness in delivering an intervention. The emphasis in all of these definitions is not just on what is taught, but how well. How might this distinction be reconciled in a modified conceptualisation of fidelity? Both Odom *et al.* (2010) and O'Donnell (2008) draw a useful line between assessing *structure* and *process* in fidelity, with the former reflecting the 'what' and the latter revealing the 'how well'. A similar dichotomy is drawn by Century, Rudnick, and Freeman (2010) in their discussion of *structural* and *instructional* components of fidelity. In this paradigm, fidelity to critical intervention components and the quality of their delivery are equally important aspects of implementation, and it is their *interaction* that triggers change. This proposal is offered credence by Odom *et al.*'s (2010) finding that both dimensions were differentially related to a range of intervention outcomes in the Children's School Success project.

Turning now to adaptation, it is evident that despite having received less attention than fidelity when considering effective implementation, more is perhaps known about the role played by quality. An adaptation is essentially, "any addition, subtraction or modification to the original program model, quality of delivery or participant responsiveness" (Moore, Bumbarger, & Cooper, 2013, p. 148). Adaptations may be beneficial or detrimental, intentional or accidental, reactive or proactive, and superficial or structural. They may be made to improve goodness of fit to context (Hansen *et al.*, 2013; US Department of Health and Human Services, 2002), align with a practitioner's preferred teaching style (Miller-Day, Pettigrew, & Hecht, 2013), improve sustainability (Chambers *et al.*, 2013; Harn *et al.*, 2013), remove resistance and/or improve acceptability (US Department of Health and Human Services, 2002). Adaptations also facilitate a sense of ownership, as practitioners 'reinvent' interventions by infusing their personal experiences and altering content to make it more relevant to their student population (Harn *et al.*, 2013; Miller-Day *et al.*, 2013; Rogers, 2003). This may be particularly important where there is significant cultural diversity in the classroom (Castro, Barrera, & Martinez, 2004). More specifically, for SEL programmes that teach skills and seek to improve climate, it is usually the case that they are also intended to be adapted to align with other academic curriculum areas (e.g., reading, social studies). In addition, to increase the interest in implementing SEL programmes, often there is a desire to align with other educational initiatives or mandates that are required (for example, other aspects of school inspections or national curriculum requirements) (Domitrovich, Moore, & Greenberg, 2012; Domitrovich *et al.*, 2010).

Drawing on the above body of work, Moore *et al.* (2013) suggest that to truly understand this phenomenon, we need to determine, "when adaptations are being made, why they are being made, what they consist of, and how they align with the program's goals and theory" (p. 150). They propose three dimensions of adaptation: *fit, timing* and *valence*. In terms of fit, Moore *et al.* (2013) suggest that we can distinguish between adaptations that are made for *logistical* reasons and those that are made for *philosophical* reasons. The former are those that are made to accommodate pragmatic constraints (e.g., delivering an abbreviated version of a lesson in order to fit a pre-set timetable), with the latter reflecting differences in underlying conceptualisation (e.g., changing intervention content where it is considered inappropriate for a given audience). Timing may be *pro-active* or *reactive*. Pro-active adaptations are those that occur when problems of fit to local context/need are anticipated and changes made in advance. Reactive adaptations, by contrast, are made in response to issues that arise during the course of implementation. Finally, the valence of adaptations may be *positive* (in keeping with the goals and theory of the intervention), *neutral* (neither aligned with nor deviating from goals and theory) or *negative* (deviating from goals and theory). Empirical study of this taxonomy is still emergent and tentative, but that which has been published provides us with powerful insights. Moore *et al.*'s (2013) study of the implementation of a variety of evidence-based prevention curricula in natural contexts demonstrated that most adaptations made by teachers were logistical rather than philosophical, reactive rather than proactive, and negative rather than neutral or positive. The most frequently cited adaptations were those made to intervention procedures, dosage and content, and were primarily attributed to a lack of time, limited resources, recruitment of participants and implementer resistance. Taken in sum, these findings suggest that many evidence-based intervention models may fail to adequately account for the demands and challenges of implementation in naturalistic contexts, in which busy teachers struggle to accommodate delivery requirements and thus make spontaneous changes that may ultimately be detrimental to outcomes.

What role, then, for an increased focus on quality? Arguing that "whatever the type and frequency with which adaptations are made, it is essential to assess quality", Hansen *et al.* (2013, p. 360) equate quality with *positive valence*. In their study of the implementation of a middle school drug prevention programme ('*All Stars*'), observers coded the valence of adaptations relating to method (e.g., a change in structure or instructions, adding steps, questions, examples or stories) and message (e.g., introducing a new concept, adding a normative message). Positively valenced changes in method were associated with better student outcomes. This suggests very clearly that it is not the act of adaptation itself that is critical (as is implied in the zero-sum-game viewpoint) but its nature and quality that determine the ultimate effect on outcomes.

Given the above, we might begin to tentatively explore what high-quality adaptation looks like. Hansen *et al.*'s (2013) study offers further useful insights in this regard. First, they suggest that adaptation should be used sparingly, with fewer but positively valenced adaptations being considered the optimal model. This of course has concurrent implications for fidelity – implying the need to avoid 'throwing the baby out with the bathwater'. Second, quality adaptations must demonstrably serve the goals and objectives of the intervention (e.g., where a teacher simplifies language/instructions to make an activity or concept clearer for his or her students). A natural corollary of this proposition is that proactive adaptations are more likely to be high quality as these are anticipated, reasoned actions. However, an underlying knowledge and understanding of the intervention itself is critical. So, for example, a teacher may pro-actively 'streamline' a programme by omitting what s/he considers to be the least important elements due to time constraints. In order for this adaptation to be high quality, s/he needs to know and understand *what* is important, *why* different aspects of content have been included, and *how* they interact/relate to one another. Harn *et al.* (2013) concur, arguing that if teachers are experienced, understand an intervention and how/why it works, and know their students well, they are more than able to make reasoned adaptations that support the achievement of outcomes.

A way forward

Thus far we have argued that variability in the implementation of school-based mental health programmes is likely to influence variability in the achievement of intended outcomes. We have focused our discussion of implementation around two contrasting viewpoints of the relationship between fidelity and adaptation (the zero-sum-game and balanced viewpoints, respectively) and the tension therein. As a means to resolve this tension, we have proposed an alternative viewpoint defined by an increased focus on quality in both of these aspects of implementation. On the basis of this thesis, we make three related recommendations for the advancement of research and practice in this area.

In terms of assessment, we argue that implementation and process evaluations of school-based mental health and related interventions need to move beyond simplistic notions of fidelity and routinely examine the full range of aspects of implementation outlined at the beginning of this chapter. This will lead to a better understanding of how these aspects interact and provide a more balanced science of implementation. If we *only* assess fidelity, it is tempting to conclude that low fidelity is causal if there are poor outcomes. In fact, these poor outcomes may be more accurately attributed to an aspect that has not been measured. Similarly, if not all aspects of implementation are considered, and fidelity is measured as high, poor outcomes may be incorrectly seen as programme or theory failure (e.g., a 'Type III error') (Humphrey, 2013).

In terms of programme design and validation, we argue that developers need to more fully and explicitly specify the proposed critical components, that is, 'active ingredients' of their interventions, such that the 'must dos' can be separated from the 'may dos' (Greenberg, Domotrovich, Graczyk, & Zins, 2005). Empirical validation is necessary as part of this, but it may be a challenging endeavour, as it would require sophisticated component analysis and be highly resource intensive. This may be why developers tend to validate their programmes as a single unit (Elliot & Mihalic, 2004). It is perhaps unsurprising, then, that there are "few adequately defined programs in the research literature that clearly detail the core components with recommendations on the dosage, strength and adherence required to produce positive outcomes" (Blase & Fixsen, 2013, p. 5). However, where such work has been undertaken, it has proven extremely useful. For example, documentation of the natural variation in implementation of different constituent components of the Achievement for All programme in England (a wide-ranging, multi-level intervention designed to improve a range of outcomes for students with special needs, including their behaviour and relationships with others) allowed our research team to identify several 'kernels' that were associated with positive outcomes (e.g., the school's programme lead being part of the senior leadership team), which were subsequently included in guidance to schools when the programme was brought to scale (Humphrey & Squires, 2011).

Once critical components have been identified and validated, this information needs to be communicated to practitioners as part of a broader training and support package that offers increased emphasis on the different aspects of implementation and a given intervention's theory of change/logic model. With an improved understanding of *how* and *why* a given programme is theorised to work, teachers are arguably better equipped to be more effective implementers. For example, they will be more likely to make pro-active, positively valenced adaptations that serve to enhance programme outcomes while also increasing goodness-of-fit to local context.

Conclusion

Implementation processes are undoubtedly critical to the achievement of expected outcomes in school-based mental health interventions. However, the field of implementation science has long been dominated by a debate on the relative merits of fidelity and adaptation that has arguably stifled progress and impacted upon practice in schools. We argue that for this challenge to be overcome, the debate needs to be reframed in such a way as to focus on the *quality* of both of these aspects of implementation. This reframing has implications for programme development processes, research and evaluation, and the training and support of practitioners in the field. Some of these bring new challenges in themselves, requiring an approach that may go against the grain (e.g., empirical determination of critical intervention components requires developers to suppress their natural urge to minimise implementation variability – Blase & Fixsen, 2013). However, we propose that these are challenges worth facing, as they will be to the benefit of all concerned: programme developers, researchers, practitioners, and, ultimately, the children and young people who are in receipt of the interventions.

Note

This may, of course, offer additional insight regarding the predominance of fidelity in implementation research. In contrast with quality, fidelity is reasonably straightforward to assess.

References

Belfer, M. L. (2008). Child and adolescent mental disorders: The magnitude of the problem across the globe. *Journal of Child Psychology and Psychiatry, and Allied Disciplines, 49*, 226–236.

Berkel, C., Mauricio, A. M., Schoenfelder, E., & Sandler, I. N. (2011). Putting the pieces together: An integrated model of program implementation. *Prevention Science, 12*, 23–33.

Blase, K., & Fixsen, D. (2013). Core intervention components: Identifying and operationalizing what makes programs work. *ASPE Research Brief, February 2*, 1–21.

Botvin, G. J. (2004). Advancing prevention science and practice: Challenges, critical issues, and future directions. *Prevention Science, 5*, 69–72.

CASEL. (2007). *How evidence-based SEL programs work to produce greater student success in school and life*. Chicago: CASEL.

Castro, F. G., Barrera, M., & Martinez, C. R. (2004). The cultural adaptation of prevention interventions: Resolving tensions between fidelity and fit. *Prevention Science, 5*, 41–45.

Century, J., Rudnick, M., & Freeman, C. (2010). A framework for measuring fidelity of implementation: A foundation for shared language and accumulation of knowledge. *American Journal of Evaluation, 31*, 199–218.

Chambers, D. A, Glasgow, R. E., & Stange, K. C. (2013). The dynamic sustainability framework: Addressing the paradox of sustainment amid ongoing change. *Implementation Science, 8*, 117–128.

Dixon, T. (2012). Educating the emotions from Gradgrind to Goleman. *Research Papers in Education, 27*, 481–495.

Domitrovich, C. E., Bradhsaw, C. P., Poduska, J. M., Hoagwood, K., Buckley, J. A., Olin, S., . . . Ialongo, N. S. (2008). Maximising the implementation quality of evidence-based preventive interventions in schools: A conceptual framework. *Advances in School Mental Health Promotion, 1*, 6–28.

Domitrovich, C. E., Bradshaw, C. P., Greenberg, M. T., Embry, D., Poduska, J. M., & Ialongo, N. S. (2010). Integrated models of school-based prevention: Logic and theory. *Psychology in the Schools, 47*, 71–88.

Domitrovich, C., Moore, J. E., & Greenberg, M. T. (2012). Maximising the effectiveness of social-emotional interventions for young children through high-quality implementation of evidence-based interventions. In B. Kelly & D. F. Perkins (Eds.), *Handbook of implementation science for psychology in education* (pp. 207–229). Cambridge: Cambridge University Press.

Durlak, J. A., & DuPre, E. P. (2008). Implementation matters: A review of research on the influence of implementation on program outcomes and the factors affecting implementation. *American Journal of Community Psychology, 41*, 327–350.

Durlak, J. A., Weissberg, R. P., Dymnicki, A. B., Taylor, R. D., & Schellinger, K. B. (2011). The impact of enhancing students' social and emotional learning: A meta-analysis of school-based universal interventions. *Child Development, 82*, 405–432.

Dusenbury, L., Brannigan, R., Falco, M., & Hansen, W. B. (2003). A review of research on fidelity of implementation: Implications for drug abuse prevention in school settings. *Health Education Research, 18*, 237–256.

Elliott, D., & Mihalic, S. (2004). Issues in disseminating and replicating effective prevention programs. *Prevention Science, 5*, 47–53.

Ferrer-Wreder, L., Sundell, K., & Mansoory, S. (2011). Tinkering with perfection: Theory development in the intervention cultural adaptation field. *Child & Youth Care Forum, 41*, 149–171.

Greenberg, M., Domotrovich, C., Graczyk, P., & Zins, J. (2005). *The study of implementation in school-based preventive interventions: Theory, research and practice.* Washington: USDHHS.

Greenberg, M. T. (2010). School-based prevention: Current status and future challenges. *Effective Education, 2*, 27–52.

Hansen, W. B., Pankrantz, M. M., Dusenbury, L., Giles, S. M., Bishop, D., Albritton, J., . . . Strack, J. (2013). Styles of adapation: The impact of frequency and valence of adaptation on preventing substance abuse. *Health Education, 113*, 345–363.

Harn, B., Parisi, D., & Stoolmiller, M. (2013). Balancing fidelity with flexibility and fit: What do we really know about fidelity of implementation in schools? *Exceptional Children, 79*, 181–193.

Humphrey, N. (2013). *Social and emotional learning: A critical appraisal.* London: Sage Publications.

Humphrey, N., Lendrum, A., & Wigelsworth, M. (2014). PATHS to Success: Interim findings from a cluster-randomised trial of a universal social-emotional learning intervention. *Paper presented at the Society for Prevention Research Annual Meeting*, Washington, DC.

Humphrey, N., & Squires, G. (2011). *Achievement for All national evaluation: Final report.* London: DFE.

Lendrum, A., & Humphrey, N. (2012). The importance of studying the implementation of school-based interventions. *Oxford Review of Education, 38*, 635–652.

Miller-Day, M., Pettigrew, J., & Hecht, M. (2013). How prevention curricula are taught under real-world conditions: Types of and reasons for curriculum adapations. *Health Education, 113*, 324–344.

Moore, J. E., Bumbarger, B. K., & Cooper, B. R. (2013). Examining adaptations of evidence-based programs in natural contexts. *The Journal of Primary Prevention, 34*, 147–161.

Odom, S. L., Fleming, K., Diamond, K., Lieber, J., Hanson, M., Butera, G., . . . Marquis, J. (2010). Examining different forms of implementation in early childhood curriculum research. *Early Childhood Research Quarterly, 25*, 314–328.

O'Donnell, C. L. (2008). Defining, conceptualizing, and measuring fidelity of implementation and its relationship to outcomes in K-12 curriculum intervention research. *Review of Educational Research, 78*, 33–84.

Ringwalt, C., & Ennett, S. (2003). Factors associated with fidelity to substance use prevention curriculum guides in the nation's middle schools. *Health Education & Behaviour, 30*, 375–391.

Rogers, E. M. (2003). *Diffusion of innovations*. New York, NY: Free Press.

Sklad, M., Diekstra, R., De Ritter, M., Ben, J., & Gravesteijn, C. (2012). Effectiveness of school-based universal social, emotional, and behavioral programs: Do they enhance students' development in the area of skills, behavior and adjustment? *Psychology in the Schools, 49*, 892–909.

US Department of Health and Human Services. (2002). *Finding the balance: Program fidelity and adaptation in substance abuse prevention*. Washington: USDHHS.

Vo, A. K., Sutherland, K. S. & Conroy, M. (2012). Best in Class: A classroom-based model for ameliorating problem behaviour in early childhood settings. *Psychology in the Schools, 49*(5), n.p. Accessed 13.11.2015 at http://onlinelibrary.wiley.com/doi/10.1002/pits.21609/pdf

Vostanis, P., Humphrey, N., Fitzgerald, N., Wolpert, M., & Deighton, J. (2013). How do schools promote emotional wellbeing among their pupils? Findings from a national scoping survey of mental health provision in English schools. *Child and Adolescent Mental Health, 18*, 151–157.

6

"PROMOTION WITH PARENTS IS CHALLENGING"

The role of teacher communication skills and parent–teacher partnerships in school-based mental health initiatives

Rosalyn H. Shute

Governments and education authorities often promote the development of partnerships between schools and parents or other carers. There is some evidence that such partnerships benefit children academically, emotionally and behaviourally. Teachers' skills in communicating with parents are central to such partnerships, but little addressed in pre-service and in-service teacher education. This chapter outlines some promising ways forward.

The challenge

Schools and governments in many countries seek to promote parent–teacher partnerships in order to support not just children's education but their mental health and wellbeing. However, the research base in this area is not extensive. In seeking to assist in guiding such partnership endeavours, this chapter reviews the evidence from teaching and other professions. Teacher communication skills are the main focus, but the broader context is also considered.

Background

The ultimate purpose of school–parent collaborations is to benefit children, and ideally we would like to see evidence of positive results. However, there is a dearth of research, especially regarding mental health outcomes. Despite the limited number of studies and their methodological weaknesses, they suggest that improvements in academic progress and school behaviour can be achieved, especially when programs treat parents as equals and incorporate a two-way flow of information (Cox, 2005). The strongest evidence comes from a well-designed US study, in which a parent-teacher action research intervention for children at risk of emotional and behavioural problems produced substantial improvements (McConaughy, Kay, & Fitzgerald, 1999).

Although further evidence about efficacy is needed, since the 1970s government and school policies in many countries have supported the building of effective relationships between schools and parents (or other caregivers). This is in accord with ecological models that consider the various social systems within which children develop, and their interactions (Bronfenbrenner & Morris, 1998). One-way parental 'involvement' in schools is yielding to 'dialogue', 'collaboration' and 'partnership' – terms denoting more dynamic and equitable relationships (e.g., Cox, 2005). School-based mental health policy documents now often refer to the importance of strong family–school communication, examples being the Joint Consortium for School Health in British Columbia, Canada (JCSH, 2010) and *KidsMatter*, Australia's primary school mental health initiative (Slee *et al.*, 2009). The latter includes a specific component aimed at engaging parents in schools' efforts to promote children's wellbeing, but this was the least successful aspect of an otherwise efficacious initiative. While up to two-thirds of teachers agreed strongly that parents felt able to discuss their children's social or behavioural difficulties with school staff, fewer than half of parents did so. As one school principal said, "Promotion with parents is challenging" (p. 50). Furthermore, teachers themselves often feel ill-equipped to deal with mental health issues, as 'out of their area' and surrounded by stigma and uncertainty (Askell-Williams & Lawson, 2011). More research is clearly needed on the best ways and the value of promoting parent–teacher collaboration in school-based mental health initiatives, but it is without question that communication is fundamental to any such partnership.

Teaching is inherently relational (Giles, 2010), and communication both forms and serves our relationships. As Graham-Clay (2005) observed, "[E]very positive interchange [between teachers and parents] will serve to increase trust and build stronger relationships" (p. 124). Conversely, every negative encounter will undermine them. For instance, a mother who considered her child's pre-school as unsupportive gave as an example the time she was upset because the family pet had died; the workers' failure to pause or make eye contact, when she told them, sent an uncaring message (Rolfe & Armstrong, 2010). Parents have reported serious communication problems when reporting bullying to teachers (Brown, Aalsma, & Ott, 2013), and teachers report that their most difficult school-related relationships are with other adults, including parents (Burrows, 2011). Some schools and teachers send out messages that parents are not welcome and yet blame parents (especially from disadvantaged backgrounds) for not engaging with the school (Symeou, Roussounidou, & Michaelides, 2012). Enhancing teacher communication skills, while not a complete solution, has the potential to smooth parent–teacher interactions and pave the way for more effective home–school collaboration. We can note here the distinction between 'training' (in specific skills), and the broader concept of teacher 'education' or 'development' (concerned with personal and professional growth; Bayrakcı, 2009).

Employers often take it for granted that job applicants will have the specific skills of their field, and use oral communication ability as their primary selection criterion (Ihmeide, Al-Omari, & Al-Dababneh, 2010). However, a lack of such skills in the workforce has been identified and it is uncommon for communication skills training to be incorporated into professional courses (Ihmeide *et al.*, 2010). There may be explicit or implicit government or accreditation requirements for teachers to have good communication skills. For example, graduates of Australian teacher education courses are required to "understand strategies for working effectively, sensitively and confidentially with parents/carers" (Australian Institute for Teaching and School Leadership (AITSL), 2011); however, there is no explicit requirement for communication skills to be developed. Indeed, interpersonal skills are not generally a criterion for entering the profession in Australia, though in some other countries this is the case (Masters, 2012) (n.b., the Australian standards are under review at a time of great volatility and public scrutiny regarding teacher education).

In terms of the pre-service development of communication skills, there is a lack of attention to preparing teachers for interactions with parents (Dotger, Dotger, & Maher, 2010), and the addressing of parent–teacher partnerships has been described as "haphazard" (Epstein, 2013, p. 115). For in-service teachers, educational opportunities to address their own workplace-related social-emotional issues are rare (Burrows, 2011). Those working in early childhood settings may be unwilling to speak to parents or feel unsure how to communicate with them (Rolfe & Armstrong, 2010). Dotger, Harris, Maher and Hansel (2011) maintain that deliberate preparation for communicating with parents is vital for teacher education, with opportunities for practice required, not just the odd reading or lecture. As Symeou *et al.* (2012) have said, "It will take more than good intentions and empathy on the part of teachers to provide meaningful support for parents" (p. 81). It seems that there is a need to provide more pre-service and in-service opportunities for the development of teachers' communication skills. By contrast, such training has long been integral to professional education in psychology and medicine. Drawing upon models from these fields, some very promising programs for pre-service teachers have recently been developed.

Solutions

Microskills training

Several methods for teaching counselling skills have been extensively developed and evaluated within the discipline of psychology. While most teachers probably do not see themselves as counsellors (unless they have undertaken specific training as school counsellors), training in counselling begins with basic oral communication skills that are applicable in a broad range of contexts. Of a variety of methods that have been developed and evaluated, the microskills method (e.g., Ivey, 1988) is effective and widely used (Baker, Daniels, & Greely, 1990; Hill & Lent, 2006) and has been applied to teacher education. Microskills training is the method familiar to the present author, as both learner and teacher, including workshops with Ivey himself. The method uses a hierarchy of culturally-tuned skills, starting with attending behaviour and basic listening skills such as using open and closed questions and reflecting feelings, through a number of other stages and on to complex skill integration that varies according to different theoretical frameworks, contexts and cultures. Important features of training are skills modelling (which is more effective than instruction and feedback) and the use of more than one teaching method (Hill & Lent, 2006). Active listening skills (listening for meaning) have been identified as especially important for teachers (Walters, Garii, & Walters, 2009). Learners using a variant of the Ivey method that adds microskills in a more explicitly cumulative way improved significantly in all microskills compared with a control group (Kuntze, van der Molen, & Born, 2009).

A microskills-based course for Greek Cypriot in-service teachers on communicating with parents has been developed (Symeou *et al.*, 2012). It includes four weekly three-hour sessions, plus a fifth session after four more weeks. It includes theory and practice about parent–teacher collaboration, and role play, discussion and reflection in the context of the parent-teacher conference. Between the fourth and fifth sessions, teachers organise two conferences (with the same parent) at their school, and keep a structured diary about these and any other significant issues concerning communications with parents. These diaries form the basis for reflection and discussion in the final session. Evaluating the course with more than a hundred teachers, Symeou *et al.* (2012) developed a questionnaire with six factors: reflection of feelings; verbal tips to encourage parents to elaborate; nonverbal communication; facial expressions during communication; accurately paraphrasing the meaning of the discussion; and sharing of information. Except for 'facial expressions' and 'sharing of information', teachers' ratings of the usefulness of these factors and the amount they used them increased significantly. They also gained a greater sense of professionalism. Although the study had weaknesses in lacking a control group and relying on teacher self-report, the pre-test to post-test improvements suggested that the program has promise.

The *LAFF don't CRY* method focuses on training teachers' active listening skills (McNaughton & Vostal, 2010). The LAFF mnemonic stands for: Listen, empathise and communicate respect; Ask questions and permission for note-taking; Focus on the issues; Find a first step. CRY stands for behaviours to avoid: Criticising others not present; Reacting hastily and making undeliverable promises; Yakety-yak-yak (unfocused chat). Parents from various cultural backgrounds blind-rated video role-play interactions of those trained or not trained in the method, and considered the trained teachers by far the best communicators.

The Simulated Interaction Model

This approach, from the field of medicine, has been adapted for use with teachers (Dotger *et al.*, 2010). Based on the theory that cognition is context-dependent, it aims to bridge the gap between course-based theory and practice in schools. The method originally focused on communication with parents, though it was later expanded to other contexts. It was derived from the medical education practice of training individuals to act as 'standardised patients' who present trainees with certain problems that they must address in terms of diagnosis and treatment. The original teacher version, a semester-length course, trains individuals to act as 'standardised parents', who present in various ways (e.g., varying in race, presenting issue, emotional tone and nonverbal demeanour). Each trainee is given information about the simulated parent's 'child' in advance, and then role-plays the part of the child's class teacher, interacting with the 'parent'. This is followed by reflection with the supervisor on an audio and video record of the interaction, prompted by a semi-structured interview. Meanwhile, the 'parent' completes a checklist, providing feedback from their perspective. Finally, all students meet with the supervisor for a group feedback session, also aimed at preparation for the next case, of which six in all are used. The researchers found that teachers initially struggled, but significantly improved, in applying their theoretical knowledge within interviews to address matters such as inclusion, multiculturalism and ethical issues.

Although Dotger et al. (2010) argue that the program is inexpensive, they offer an alternative for when resources are limited (Walker & Dotger, 2012), based on vicarious learning – observing videos of simulated parent–teacher conferences. Learners reflect on differences between two approaches to the same problem (more structured versus more responsive). The method contributes to an evaluation of whether a trainee is ready to engage with families. The candidates agreed with expert observers that the more responsive approach was more effective. However, it is telling that the students had a high level of initial self-efficacy for engaging with families that was not matched by their actual ability. It is interesting, in this regard, that Jordanian education students are less supportive of communication training if they have lower grade point averages or are in their first year of study (Ihmeide et al., 2010). Both these studies demonstrate that those who have a lot to learn often lack insight into their limitations, and may therefore not appreciate the need for specific training in communication skills. Learner readiness therefore needs to be carefully considered.

Using parents' names

Casual encounters with parents occur most frequently in preschool and primary settings, offering regular opportunities to build positive relationships; addressing parents by name is a powerful way to suggest a willingness to enter into a relationship with them. It may be overlooked or avoided for reasons of busyness or the embarrassment of making errors (Ingvarsson & Hanley, 2006). Using parents' names can make them feel important, recognised and welcome (Rolfe & Armstrong, 2010). Three out of four preschool teachers increased their use of parents' names when they brought their children to school, after computerised training in recalling parents' names (Ingvarsson & Hanley, 2006); simply knowing this competence would be assessed and supervisor modelling of the behaviour were not sufficient, and prior to the training the teachers rarely used parents' names. This was in a cultural context where the informal use of parents' forenames was appropriate. It would presumably be less challenging to memory in cultures where family names that are the same as the children's are used. Other methods for memorising names might be useful, though their effectiveness remains untested in the school context (see http://mnemotechnics.org/wiki/MemorizingNames_and_Faces).

Other ways of communicating with parents

Signs welcoming parents to the school, newsletters, report cards, communication books, and school websites have all been identified as ways of engaging parents. These important one-way methods may be effective when two-way communication is not possible. However, two-way interactions through meetings, phone calls and (with a delay) email are regarded as essential for true partnership. School systems vary in their use. In the Greek Cypriot system, for example, teachers must timetable a weekly session where parents can come and talk to teachers (Symeou et al., 2012). Graham-Clay (2005) points out the importance of early efforts by teachers to communicate with parents about any developing issues – the traditional report card should not be the first communication parents receive about a problem.

Hints for Internet-based communications are discussed by Mitchell, Foulger, and Wetzel (2009), while Graham-Clay (2005) details a range of methods for communicating with parents. In brief, she emphasises the importance of care and professionalism in preparing materials, and of making communications thoughtful and planned. Parents often favour the convenience of email, sometimes even for relatively complex and sensitive issues such as behavioural and peer relationship difficulties (Thompson & Mazer, 2012), though teachers need to be sensitive about which matters require face-to-face communication. While communications with parents are often problem-based, relationships can be built by communicating about positive events – a note or call about a child's achievement, or a positive passing comment about a child or a parent's parenting skill can pay dividends (Rolfe & Armstrong, 2010). This parallels the commonly advocated parenting tip of 'catching your child being good'.

The broader context

An ecological approach reminds us that teacher communication skills are neither learned nor utilised in a vacuum. Both initial and in-service teacher education take place in a complex web of legislative and agency requirements. Efforts to address teacher communication skills may come up against the 'crowded curriculum'. Also, teachers in different countries may have very different experiences of, and attitudes towards, professional development. For example, parent–teacher collaboration in the United States has legislative backing, while poor in-service training provision in Turkey means that teachers are not motivated to attend (Bayrakcı, 2009).

Cultural factors will also play into parent–teacher relationships. Communication training should be culturally and cross-culturally sensitive. There may be culturally bound behavioural norms and expectations in face-to-face communication regarding matters such as use of personal space and eye contact, for example. More broadly, there will be cultural expectations of teachers and parents about their respective roles. For example, in Greece, teachers are still regarded as the authorities on children's education, and although parents find them friendly, cultural expectations developed in former times continue to impede collaboration (Antonopolou, Koutrouba, & Babalis, 2011).

The school culture and leadership practices must also be considered. Parent–teacher partnerships are influenced by matters such as such as trust, 'turf' issues, differing expertise and scope of responsibility (File, 2001). A recent US case study (Lareau & Muñoz, 2012) showed systematic conflict between parents and the school, with power struggles between the parent–teacher organisation and the school principal, who had very different views about the running of the school. The principal's response to parental complaints about the unfriendliness of the front-office person (the first point of contact for parents entering the school) was, "I don't need warm and fuzzy, I need efficiency and I need responsibility, and that's what this person represents." The authors noted that research on parent–teacher conflicts tends to treat these as temporary and possible to be addressed through good communication. Their study, however, demonstrated the importance of structural influences. Another US example is a study on parents' experiences of reporting bullying to the school (Brown et al., 2013). Ten out of eleven parents reported serious failures of communication with school personnel and ongoing resistance from school officials to act effectively to protect their child. There were procedural difficulties such as a lack of clarity of the lines of communication for reporting bullying, and a failure of schools to call parents back. Parents often gained a sense that their child, the victim, was the problem. They eventually faced a choice between removing their child from the school or letting the bullying continue, resulting in what one mother described as a "living hell" for her daughter. Laws, programs and policies on school bullying will remain ineffective if the school culture is more concerned with protecting the school than the children.[1]

In-service education

Parent–teacher collaboration should continue to be addressed through in-service education, as an aspect of lifelong learning. Recommendations by Coolahan (2002) include: a combination of school on-site and off-site aspects; teacher participation in agenda-setting; a use of experiential and collaborative methods; peer facilitation; targeting and thorough planning, evaluation and dissemination. To this can be added university–school partnerships that enable in-service education efforts to draw upon, and contribute to, research into teacher education, in the interests of developing better evidence-based practice.

Participation in in-service education is often considered in teacher promotion (Coolahan, 2002), but not everywhere: in the Greek Cypriot system, where in-service education is voluntary, certificates of attendance do not count for teacher evaluation or promotion (Symeou *et al.*, 2012). Although self-motivation is desirable, it seems self-evident that school systems should also be seen to actively support and value in-service education.[2]

Technicist versus humanistic approaches

Concerns were raised in England in the 1990s that a 'technicist' approach to teacher education (emanating from government) was replacing a professional approach (Coolahan, 2002). Dickson (2007), from a Scottish perspective, similarly contrasted competing discourses about professional knowledge in the form of technical-rational approaches and broader values-based approaches. Giles (2010) contrasts technicist and behaviourist approaches with a more humanistic approach, based on 'pathic knowledge', which "feels atmosphere, reads faces and feels the mood of different situations" (Giles, 2010, p. 1512). While raising the importance of such issues for teacher education, he offers no suggestions for imparting such attributes. The proposition of this chapter is that addressing communication skills in teacher education using established and well-evaluated methods such as microskills training would be a good start, even though it runs the risk of being considered as too 'technicist'.

In the field of psychotherapy, it is recognised that basic microskills are only the start, with more complex layers of skill and understanding needed for appreciating the bigger picture (e.g., Ridley, Kelly, & Mollen, 2011). For experienced teachers, reflective practice may offer a familiar way of casting light on such issues. The Simulated Interaction Model offers one systematic way of doing this. Such reflective practice may also facilitate the linking of teachable basic communication skills with the more slippery 'sensibilities' such as 'tact' and 'nous' identified by Giles (2010). Reflective practice also gives an opportunity to consider how structural issues are influencing one's professional practice with parents. Another route to insight might be via mindfulness (an accepting focus on one's current feelings, thoughts and sensations): Burrows (2011) has described how teachers have improved their relationships with students and colleagues through mindfulness practice. Considering a 'professional' approach to communication training as an alternative to a 'technicist' one seems to present a false choice. Various methods discussed here offer evidence-based technical skills training that can be implemented in full consideration of the professional context and personal growth.

Conclusion

Various models are available for incorporating oral communication skills training into teacher education, in both pre-service and in-service contexts. The effective use of such skills, in conjunction with other methods of engaging parents and a consideration of broader contextual issues, has the potential to enhance parent–

teacher partnerships. While we already have a strong enough basis for further action on developing teacher-parent communication skills, a wealth of research opportunities exists in examining how far parent-teacher partnerships are able to contribute to the ultimate goal of benefiting children's mental health and wellbeing.

Notes

1 For a graphic illustration of the abject failure of some US schools to support bullied children and their families, as well as poor teacher communication skills with concerned parents, see the documentary film *Bully* (Hirsch [director], 2013; reviewed at http://dcfilminstitute.org/film-review-bully/).
2 Two useful books to assist teachers in communicating with parents and building partnerships are: Epstein, J. L., and Associates (2009): *School, family and community partnerships* (Thousand Oaks, CA: Corwin); and Dyches, T. T., Carter, N. J., & Prater, M. A. (2012): *A teacher's guide to communicating with parents* (Boston: Pearson). A book with a more specific mental health focus is Lines, C., Miller, G. E., & Arthur-Stanley, A. (2011): *The power of family-school partnering* (Routledge). All these books have US authors.

References

Antonopolou, K., Koutrouba, K., & Babalis, T. (2011). Parental involvement in secondary education schools: The views of parents in Greece. *Educational Studies, 37*(3), 333–344.

Askell-Williams, H., & Lawson, M. J. (2011). A framework that builds bridges between teachers' prior knowledge and mental health promotion in schools. In Shute, R. H., Slee, P. T., Murray-Harvey, R., & Dix, K. L. *Mental health and wellbeing: Educational perspectives.* Adelaide: Shannon Research Press, pp. 155–164.

Australian Institute for Teaching and School Leadership (AITSL) (2011). *Accreditation of initial teacher education programs in Australia.* Carlton South, Victoria: Ministerial Council for Education, Early Childhood Development and Youth Affairs.

Baker, S. B., Daniels, T. G., & Greeley, A. T. (1990). Systematic training of graduate-level counsellors: Narrative and meta-analytic reviews of 3 major programs. *Counseling Psychologist, 18*(3), 355–421.

Bayrakcı, M. (2009). In-service teacher training in Japan and Turkey: A comparative analysis of institutions and practices. *Australian Journal of Teacher Education, 34*, Article 2. Accessed 13.08.2014 at http://ro.ecu.edu.au/ajte/vol34/iss1/2

Bronfenbrenner, U., & Morris, P. A. (1998). The ecology of developmental processes. Ch. 17 in R. M. Lerner (Ed.), *Handbook of child psychology: Theoretical models of human development, 5th edn, Vol. 1.* New York: Wiley, pp. 993–1028.

Brown, J. R., Aalsma, M. C., & Ott, M. A. (2013). The experiences of parents who report youth bullying victimization to school officials. *Journal of Interpersonal Violence, 28*, 494–518.

Burrows, L. (2011). Practising relational mindfulness in school communities. In Shute, R. H., Slee, P. T., Murray-Harvey, R., & Dix, K. L. *Mental health and wellbeing: Educational perspectives.* Adelaide: Shannon Research Press, pp. 213–223.

Coolahan, J. (2002). Teacher education and the teaching career in an era of lifelong learning. OECD Education Working Papers. Accessed 13.08.2014 at www.oecd.org/edu/workingpapers

Cox, D. D. (2005). Evidence-based interventions using home-school collaboration. *School Psychology Quarterly, 20*(4), 473–497.

Dickson, B. (2007). Defining and interpreting professional knowledge in an age of performativity: A Scottish case-study. *Australian Journal of Education, 32*(4), Article 2. Accessed 15.04.2015 at http://ro.ecu.edu.au/ajte/vol32/iss4/2

Dotger, B. H., Dotger, S. C., & Maher, M. J. (2010). From medicine to teaching: The evolution of the Simulated Interaction Model. *Innovations in Higher Education, 35*, 129–141.

Dotger, B. H., Harris, S., Maher, M., & Hansel, A. (2011). Exploring the emotional geographies of parent–teacher candidate interactions: An emerging signature pedagogy. *The Teacher Educator, 46*(3), 208–230.

Epstein, J. L. (2013). Ready or not? Preparing future educators for school, family, and community partnerships. *Teaching Education, 24*(2), 115–118.

File, N. (2001). Family–professional partnerships: Practice that matches philosophy. *Young Children, 56*(4), 70–74.

Giles, D. (2010). Developing pathic sensibilities: A critical priority for teacher education programmes. *Teaching and Teacher Education, 26*, 1511–1519.

Graham-Clay, S. (2005). Communicating with parents: Strategies for teachers. *School Community Journal, 16*, 117–129.

Hill, C. E., & Lent, R. W. (2006). A narrative and meta-analytic review of helping skills training: Time to revive a dormant area of inquiry. *Psychotherapy: Theory, Research, Practice, Training, 43*(2), 154–172.

Hirsch, L. (Director). (2013). *Bully* [Motion picture]. Anchor Bay Entertainment.

Ihmeide, F. M., Al-Omari, K. A., & Al-Dababneh, A. A. (2010). Attitudes toward communication skills among student-teachers in Jordanian public universities. *Australian Journal of Teacher Education, 35*(4). Article 1. Accessed 13.08.2014 at http://ro.ecu.edu.au/ajte/vol35/iss4/1

Ingvarsson, E. T., & Hanley, G. P. (2006). An evaluation of computer-based programmed instruction for promoting teachers' greetings of parents by name. *Journal of Applied Behavior Analysis, 39*, 203–214.

Ivey, A. E. (1988). *Intentional interviewing and counselling: Facilitating client development.* (2nd edn). Pacific Grove, CA: Brooks/Cole.

Joint Consortium for School Health (JCSH) (2010). *Schools as a setting for promoting positive mental health: Better practices and perspectives.* British Colombia: JCSH.

Kuntze, J., van der Molen, H. T., & Born, M. P. (2009). Increase in counselling communication skills after basic and advanced microskills training. *British Journal of Educational Psychology, 79*, 175–188.

Lareau, A., & Muñoz, V. L. (2012). "You're not going to call the shots": Structural conflicts between the principal and the PTO at a suburban public elementary school. *Sociology of Education, 85*(3), 201–218.

Masters, G. (2012). *Enhancing the quality of teaching and learning in Australian schools.* Submission to the Senate Inquiry on Teaching and Learning. Accessed 17.12.2013 at www.acer.edu.au/documents/Masters_submission_to_Senate_Inquiry.pdf

McConaughy, S. H., Kay, P. J., & Fitzgerald, M. (1999). The Achieving, Behaving, Caring project for preventing ED: Two-year outcomes. *Journal of Emotional and Behavioral Disorders, 7*(4), 224–239.

McNaughton, D., and Vostal, B. R. (2010). Using active listening to improve collaboration with parents: The LAFF Don't CRY Strategy. *Intervention in School and Clinic, 45*(4), 251–256.

Mitchell, S., Foulger, T. S., & Wetzel, K. (2009). Tips for involving families through Internet-based communication. *Young Children, 64*, 5.

Ridley, C. R., Kelly, S. M., & Mollen, D. (2011). Microskills training: Evolution, reexamination, and call for reform. *The Counseling Psychologist, 39*, 800–824.

Rolfe, S. A., & Armstrong, K. J. (2010). Early childhood professionals as a source of social support: The role of parent–professional communication. *Australasian Journal of Early Childhood, 35*(3), 60–67.

Slee, P. T., Lawson, M. J., Russell, A., Askell-Williams, H., Dix, K. L., Owens, L., Skrzypiec, G., & Spears, B. (2009). *KidsMatter evaluation final report.* Adelaide: Centre for Analysis of Educational Futures, Flinders University.

Symeou, L., Roussounidou, E., & Michaelides, M. (2012). "I feel much more confident now to talk with parents": An evaluation of in-service training on teacher–parent communication. *School Community Journal, 22,* 65–87.

Thompson, B., & Mazer, J. P. (2012). Development of the parental academic support scale: Frequency, importance, and modes of communication. *Communication Education, 61*(2), 131–160.

Walker, J. M. T., & Dotger, B. H. (2012). Because wisdom can't be told: Using comparison of simulated parent-teacher conferences to assess teacher candidates' readiness for family-school partnership. *Journal of Teacher Education, 63,* 62–75.

Walters, L. M., Garii, B., & Walters, T. (2009). Learning globally, teaching locally: Incorporating international exchange and intercultural learning into pre-service teacher training. *Intercultural Education, 20* (1–2), 151–158.

7

PROFESSIONAL EDUCATION FOR TEACHERS AND EARLY CHILDHOOD EDUCATORS ABOUT MENTAL HEALTH PROMOTION

Helen Askell-Williams and Rosalind Murray-Harvey

Teachers and early childhood educators face new challenges as mental health promotion initiatives are increasingly introduced into schools and early childhood education and care centres. This chapter draws upon extant theoretical frameworks and recent Australian research to identify the essential components of high quality professional education for staff. An emergent conceptual model is proposed that captures elements not identified in previous work.

The challenge

In many countries, schools and early childhood education and care (ECEC) centres are strategic settings for mental health promotion initiatives. This relatively new endeavour brings design, implementation and sustainability challenges. One key challenge is to provide high-quality learning for teachers and ECEC educators, who are unlikely to have been introduced to mental health promotion during their pre-service or in-service education. Efforts must therefore turn towards developing effective mental health professional education for teachers and ECEC educators. With the needs of practitioners, policy makers and professional education providers in mind, our aim in this chapter is to identify the essential components of professional education that will enable high-quality learning in this area.

Background

Schools and ECEC centres and mental health promotion

Community awareness that mental health is an essential component of overall health is growing. The World Health Organization (WHO, 2013) reports that around 20 per cent of the world's children and adolescents have mental disorders or problems. Fourteen percent of Australian children and adolescents have been identified with mental health problems (Sawyer, Miller-Lewis, & Clark, 2007), and the Council of Australian Governments' *National Action Plan for Mental Health 2006–2011* and the *Roadmap for National Mental Health Reform 2012–2022*, for example, identify promotion, prevention and early intervention for positive mental health as essential actions. Prince *et al.*'s (2007) paper "No health without mental health" highlights the catch-cry for health promoting institutions such as the WHO. Importantly, Prince *et al.* pointed out the reciprocal interactions between mental health, physical health and the social determinants of health.

A pragmatic response of policy-makers has been to turn to schools and ECEC centres as preferred settings for broad-scale mental health promotion. This adds *mental* health to the health promoting schools model that has formerly been more focused upon physical health initiatives. School-based mental health promotion initiatives include components such as building positive communities, enhancing young people's social and emotional competencies, supporting parenting, and assisting referrals and early intervention for young people at risk of developing mental health problems (Graetz *et al.*, 2008). These components aim to build competence (Fledderus, Bohlmeijer, Smit, & Westerhof, 2010), foster individual and social resources (Kobau *et al.*, 2011) and help young people to achieve, "a state of complete physical, mental and social well-being and not merely the absence of disease or infirmity" (WHO, 2013, p. 1). For example, the Australian Commonwealth Department of Health and Ageing funds the *MindMatters* (for secondary schools), *KidsMatter Primary* and *KidsMatter Early Childhood* mental health promotion initiatives in all Australian states and territories. Similar programs exist in the UK, such as the Social and Emotional Aspects of Learning initiative, and in the United States, such as the Collaborative for Academic, Social and Emotional Learning programs.

Implications for professional education

Askell-Williams and Lawson (2013) reported a potential range of new areas of knowledge and expertise that teachers might require when working in the domain of mental health promotion, namely:

- increasing adolescents' knowledge about difficulties arising with mental health disorders, such as depression and anxiety;
- developing students' social and emotional capabilities;
- recognising and responding to students demonstrating early signs of mental health problems;
- providing parenting information and support;
- working collaboratively in multi-disciplinary case management teams;
- promoting student-teacher relationships to foster students' psychological health and wellbeing.

A substantial amount of literature addresses teachers' professional knowledge. For example, Shulman (1987) proposed a set of categories, such as content knowledge, pedagogical content knowledge and knowledge of learners and their character-istics. This theorising has underpinned investigations about the types of knowledge that teachers need in order to engage with students in high-quality ways (e.g., Fenstermacher & Richardson, 2005; Grossman, 1995).

Meanwhile, other authors have addressed the professional learning needs of teachers. For example, from an extended program of research, Desimone (2009) proposed five core components of good-quality professional education: (a) focus on content knowledge; (b) opportunities for active learning; (c) coherence with other learning activities; (d) the duration of the activity; and (e) collective participation of teachers from the same school, grade or subject.

However, some authors have expressed concerns about the designs of professional education programs, such as curriculum fragmentation, surface and transmissionist approaches to learning, and failure to acknowledge and accommodate teachers' prior knowledge and expertise (Borko, 2004; Little, 1993). Gore (2014) stressed the necessity for professional education programs to provide teachers with the opportunity to work together to observe, discuss and review authentic teach-ing practices, and to be guided by robust frameworks based upon best available knowledge. Furthermore, recognition of the importance of the early childhood years (Mustard, 2006), and the associated importance of ECEC educators' work, highlights that little is known about the professional learning needs of ECEC educators.

Professional education programs in Australian mental health promotion initiatives

Professional education has been implemented on a large scale in Australia's government-funded mental health promotion initiatives for educational settings mentioned earlier. They include, as a key feature, professional education for staff about four core components, namely:

- building a positive school/centre community;
- providing regular social and emotional education for all children;
- working with parents and carers to support parenting/caring;
- early intervention for children with mental health difficulties.

For example, during pilot testing of *KidsMatter*, staff professional education was delivered sequentially over two years, with approximately six months allocated to each of the four components. Typically, one facilitator was allocated per state, each assuming responsibility for around ten sites. During each six-month period, each facilitator would provide one or more professional education sessions to the staff in their group, through face-to-face delivery, telephone support, access to resources, and site visits. Beyond the pilot phases, the programs provide ongoing, though less intensive, professional education programs, supported by project officers.

The authors are part of a team that evaluated the Australian programs during 2005–2012 (see Askell-Williams, Lawson, Murray-Harvey, & Slee, 2005; Slee *et al.*, 2009; Slee, Murray-Harvey, *et al.*, 2012). Data were collected from: 100 *KidsMatter Primary* schools (1,397 participating staff); 111 *KidsMatter Early Childhood Centres* (1,194 participating staff); teachers and students from three classrooms in South Australia who were working with the *MindMatters* module *Understanding Mental Illness;* and teachers attending a reference-group workshop in Queensland. The evaluators used questionnaires, focus groups, face-to-face interviews and written feedback forms, from teachers, ECEC educators and leadership staff.

These large data sets provided the opportunity to collate, analyse and synthesise data about staff experiences with professional education about mental health promotion. Our re-analysis of these existing data underpins the remaining discussion.

Overview of data analysis and synthesis

We conducted several readings of the transcripts and iteratively discussed the allocation of text to themes. The five core components of professional education proposed by Desimone (2009) provided an initial framework for our thematic analysis, but it became apparent that Desimone's framework did not adequately represent our data. Accordingly, we adapted her work to devise a conceptual model (Figure 7.1) that elaborated the structural and functional components of professional education.

The 'Structural' components represent pre-determined program aspects. Under the heading of 'Content', we grouped participants' responses about their knowledge and skills, self-efficacy, and coherence of the content with other programs. Responses about program timing and duration and about program facilitation were grouped under 'Delivery'.

'Functional' components reflect the ways in which the programmed components provided learning opportunities. Participants commented about discussing and sharing ideas with colleagues ('Collaboration'), and engaging with content through role-plays, being provided with examples and relevant materials, and hands-on practice ('Active learning'). 'Professional practices' encompasses indicators of how the professional education impacted on work practices. Some staff commented on reflection (on actions), others mentioned developing insights about their roles and responsibilities (professional identity), while others noted changes in their attitudes and instructional practices when working with families, children, and colleagues.

A limitation of this type of analysis is that it does not capture all participants' responses, or response frequencies. Rather, we rely upon our deep familiarity with the data set in combination with our knowledge of the educational settings in which participants worked. Although this qualitative approach limits generalisability, it is

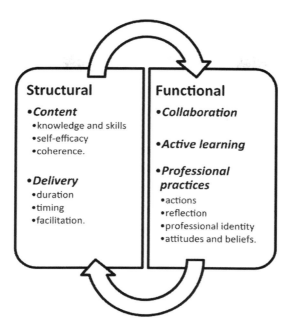

FIGURE 7.1 Structural and Functional components of professional education

This figure is an adapted version of the figure that originally appeared in Askell-Williams, H. & Murray-Harvey, R. (2015). *Sustainable professional learning for early childhood educators: Lessons from an Australia-wide mental health promotion initiative.* Journal of Early Childhood Research: DOI: 10.1177/1476 718X15570958. Reproduced with permission.

a strength with respect to developing a fine-grained understanding of the key issues and commonalities across the three initiatives. This has the potential to inform future theoretical frameworks for the interpretation of data and the design of new initiatives.

What did we learn about teachers' professional education experiences?

Structural components of professional education

Content: knowledge, skills and self-efficacy

Teacher knowledge frameworks (e.g., Desimone, 2009; Shulman, 1987) place content-knowledge centrally, and this is relevant to the curriculum area of mental health promotion. In addition, Darling-Hammond, Wei, Andre, Richardson, & Orphanos (2009) emphasised that teachers' knowledge of children and their characteristics is crucial: this applies equally well in the field of mental health promotion.

Our respondents clearly appreciated the opportunity to acquire new knowledge, thus demonstrating metacognitive awareness about what they did not previously know, what they had learned, and how much more they needed to learn. Staff acknowledged that professional education is invaluable, and found it empowering to know that their thinking and practices were in accord with the best available knowledge. However, some staff were frustrated about revisiting knowledge they felt they already had, or programs that their site already delivered:

> *I didn't feel that the actual content of that professional development was as relevant to our needs as it could've been. I think we would have been better served by . . . moving more quickly to choose the program that we wanted and then having more time and support to develop the skills to deliver the actual program.*

Broadly based professional education must be sensitive to community cultural needs. For example, Slee, Skrzypiec, Dix, Murray-Harvey, & Askell-Williams (2012) drew attention to distinctions between the concepts of 'social and emotional wellbeing' used in Aboriginal or Torres Strait Islander settings and the term 'mental health' used in non-Indigenous settings. The Slee, Skrzypiec, *et al.* report highlighted specific areas requiring attention in such settings, including the need to have programs that:

- empowered educators;
- aligned with the Aboriginal and Torres Strait Islander people's sense of family and community;
- improved understanding in the areas of the four components.

Slee, Skrzypiec *et al.* also recommended key elements of professional education to increase its impact, including:

- delivery: more informal with more 'conversations' and 'yarning' (discussing, having your say);
- content: less 'jargon';
- context: more attuned to the local conditions;
- material resources: greater representation of Aboriginal and Torres Strait Islander people and community settings.

A challenge for nationwide programs is how to tailor professional education to individual site and staff needs. If a school already delivers strong social and emotional education programs, the standard professional education program may need to be re-designed. If the community has particular cultural needs, then negotiations with the community about how to best meet these needs are essential.

Content: coherence

Some sites took steps to integrate the professional education content with other programs, creating coherence with other learning activities and mandated requirements. However, participants noted the difficulty of addressing all of the requirements of the 'crowded' curriculum:

> *The social and emotional learning program we thought we might implement, was not supported by the staff and once again the crowded curriculum played a big role in that decision.*

Staff need to be cognisant of many system-level requirements, such as the Australian National Curriculum, the National Safe Schools Framework and the Early Years Learning Framework. Managing time and resources to accommodate such curriculum demands is essential to prevent staff from feeling overwhelmed by each new imperative.

Delivery: duration and timing

There were many comments about the limitations of time, highlighting the need felt by staff to access professional education, and the value they placed on it. A typical three-hour session per component (sometimes delivered as two or more shorter sessions) is inadequate, based on the research literature (e.g., Darling-Hammond *et al.*, 2009) and reflected in comments such as:

> *It was a bit rushed, because we did it after work or stuff like that. We only had a short period of time and I think that lessons should probably be a bit longer and to get a full understanding of topics.*

Many staff struggled with sessions delivered at the end of a working day. Inevitably, site and staff learning priorities, staffing timetables and costs will directly impact upon session scheduling. For example, releasing staff for training creates a large financial impost, or takes time away from other priorities. Staff turnover also necessitates ongoing education. Where staff turnover is high, this is a substantial issue.

Delivery: facilitation

Overwhelmingly, positive feedback was received about the quality of the facilitators' delivery of the program. Comments included the value of 'being led through the components' and 'learning from a skilled teacher'. The provision of expert facilitators is expensive, and therefore potentially unsustainable: alternative approaches are needed, such as further developing the capabilities of selected local staff, who can, in turn, facilitate the learning of staff at their own sites.

Functional components of professional education

Collaboration

Opportunities for collaboration were valued and, in staff's opinion, provided the cornerstone of their learning experiences. Such opportunities emerged as the most-frequently cited benefit of face-to-face learning sessions:

> *I appreciate the opportunity to discuss points as a whole staff team (particularly as staff are part time) and the 'hands on' approach, not just listening, and sharing with other staff, feeling like we are all in this together.*

Collaborative learning is a particular challenge in the ECEC sector, where it is not traditional, and is costly, to incorporate professional education into work schedules. One solution, online content delivery, might not address the collaborative feature of the professional education that our participants found especially beneficial. Gore's (2014) extended research demonstrates the importance of teacher-to-teacher observations and discussions about professional practice. Several theoretical frameworks for e-learning have been proposed to address such pedagogical issues (e.g., see Tucker, Halloran, & Price, 2013), but the effectiveness of online professional education about mental health promotion in educational settings is currently unknown.

Active learning

Teachers and ECEC educators, faced with extreme time challenges, express needs for professional education to be relevant to their immediate practices. This can sometimes conflict with the aims of program developers, who may wish to begin with background theory. Achieving a balance between theory and practice, keeping in mind participants' backgrounds, is an important consideration. Participants' comments indicated that workshops typically began with a didactic, theoretical approach, but included, or were followed by, experiences that engaged staff in active learning. This is consistent with social constructivist theories that identify effective learning environments as relational, interactive and cognitively engaging (e.g., Bransford, Brown, & Cocking, 2000).

Professional practices: actions

Many staff indicated that the professional education had a direct influence upon their practices, leading to increased awareness and new strategies for working with children, other staff and parents/carers. For example, Table 7.1 summarises results from the *KidsMatter Primary* and *KidsMatter Early Childhood* evaluations in response to questions about the practical impact of the professional education.

TABLE 7.1 Staff responses about the impact of the *KidsMatter* professional education

Questionnaire items	% selecting "Strongly Agree"
Primary school teachers' responses (N = 716)	
The professional education relating to *KidsMatter (Primary)* has:	
– enhanced my knowledge about students' mental health	62
– improved the way I interact with students	49
– increased my level of commitment to promoting student wellbeing	63
– helped me to foster student wellbeing through my practices as a teacher	61
ECEC educators' responses (N = 445)	
The professional education relating to *KidsMatter (Early Childhood)* has:	
– enhanced my knowledge about children's mental health	77
– improved the ways I interact with children	73
– improved the ways I interact with parents	72
– increased my level of commitment to promoting children's mental health and wellbeing	76
– helped me to foster children's mental health and wellbeing in my work	79
– helped me to respond to children who are experiencing social, emotional or behavioural difficulties	77

(Collated from Slee *et al.*, 2009; Slee, Murray-Harvey, *et al.*, 2012).

Arguably, though, relatively short periods of engagement with professional education may have little impact upon staff capabilities to translate knowledge and theory into practice, and to change their long-held attitudes, beliefs and conceptions (e.g., see Argyris & Schön, 1974). People form strong intuitive beliefs, based on everyday experiences, which influence how they interpret and process new information (Vosniadou, 2013). This may be particularly so in the field of mental health, with its history of secrecy and stigma. Staff will need extended opportunities for dialogue and safe practice, to take risks, refine new skills in a supported environment, and experience substantial encouragement within a supportive culture endorsed by site leaders.

Professional practices: reflection

Reflections on practice need to be theoretically guided in order to contribute to sustainable changes (Kreber & Cranton, 2000). Otherwise, reflection remains surface-level re-telling, rather than in-depth re-conceptualising. The opportunity and impetus for reflection was regarded by participants as important, captured by feedback such as:

> I think the main thing that I got out of it was that I'm using reflective practice more . . . sometimes I'll get home at the end of the day and I'll remember maybe an issue, like children [not] getting along. And I'll think, maybe I could have dealt with that in a different way or I could have stopped and been a bit more focused on what was happening.

Professional practices: professional identity and attitudes

Professional identity and changing attitudes and beliefs about mental health emerged as important outcomes of the professional education, enabling staff to develop a sense of clarity about their roles and responsibilities. Staff indicated that their engagement with mental health promotion initiatives had led them to reconfirm or reconsider their professional roles and responsibilities for promoting young people's mental health. However, not all staff considered mental health promotion their responsibility. A teacher involved in the *MindMatters* secondary program pointedly captured this sentiment:

> From one faculty I had four members who said, "This is not our area of teaching: How can you expect us to deal with any of this?"

Another aspect of professional identity is the imperative to engage with professional learning. In particular, compared with teachers, for ECEC educators, in-service professional education may bring new, perhaps welcome but perhaps unwelcome, additional demands. Programs need to consider the wide variation in staff background knowledge and qualifications and motivation to attend, and learn from, professional education.

Conclusions

The evaluations of *MindMatters, KidsMatter Primary* and *KidsMatter Early Childhood* informed policy decisions to support ongoing national roll-outs of mental health promotion programs in Australia. Similar programs are being delivered internationally. This chapter contributes to discussions about the educational needs of adult learners located in different types of educational settings who are responsible for promoting the mental health of the young people in their charge.

The structural and functional components of professional education were salient for respondents, who provided clear indications about the importance and influence of constructs such as building knowledge, collaboration, and active learning. Challenges in achieving good-quality professional learning include differentiation to meet individual staff and whole-site needs, and delivery modes and schedules.

A useful area for future research will be the efficiency and efficacy of combining online delivery of content with locally facilitated opportunities for collaborative and interactive learning, including discussions and activities such as professional observations, mentoring and feedback, and planning for teaching and learning.

An additional issue is the influences of different micro-, meso- and macro-system components on staff approaches to, and opportunities for, learning. Issues such as staff prior knowledge, beliefs, turnover, part-time employment, qualification levels, and the integration of professional education into staff work schedules are clear points of difference between the school and ECEC centres, and between different sites (e.g., metropolitan, rural, remote). Opfer and Pedder (2011) noted such complexities as being substantially unaccounted-for components of professional education designs. However, if such difficulties are not addressed, mental health promotion initiatives that are proven to be successful in small, well-resourced trials are unlikely to achieve their expected outcomes when up-scaled to larger populations.

References

Argyris, C., & Schön, D. A. (1974). *Theory in practice: Increasing professional effectiveness*. San Francisco: Jossey-Bass.

Askell-Williams, H., & Lawson, M. J. (2013). Teachers' knowledge and confidence for promoting positive mental health in school communities. *Asia-Pacific Journal of Teacher Education, 41*, 126–143.

Askell-Williams, H., Lawson, M. J., Murray-Harvey, R., & Slee, P. T. (2005). An investigation of the implementation of a MindMatters teaching module in secondary school classrooms. *Report to the MindMatters consortium of the Australian Principals Association Professional Development Council*. Flinders University, Adelaide. Adelaide: Centre for the Analysis of Educational Futures, Flinders University.

Borko, H. (2004). Professional development and teacher learning: Mapping the terrain. *Educational Researcher, 33*, 3–15.

Bransford, J. D., Brown, A. L., & Cocking, R. R. (2000). *How people learn (Expanded edn.)*. Washington, DC: National Academy Press.

Darling-Hammond, L., Wei, R. C., Andre, A., Richardson, N., & Orphanos, S. (2009). Professional learning in the learning profession: A status report on teacher development in the United States and abroad: National Staff Development Council and The School Redesign Network at Stanford University.

Desimone, L. M. (2009). Improving impact studies of teachers' professional development: Toward better conceptualizations and measures. *Educational Researcher, 38*, 181–199.

Fenstermacher, G. D., & Richardson, V. (2005). On making determinations of quality in teaching. *Teachers College Record, 107*, 186–213.

Fledderus, M., Bohlmeijer, E. T., Smit, F., & Westerhof, G. J. (2010). Mental health promotion as a new goal in public mental health care: A randomized controlled trial of an intervention enhancing psychological flexibility. *American Journal of Public Health, 100*, 2372–2378.

Gore, J. (2014, 3–5 August). *Towards quality and equity: The case for quality teaching rounds*. Paper presented at the Quality and Equity Conference: What does the research tell us? Adelaide.

Graetz, B., Littlefield, L., Trinder, M., Dobia, B., Souter, M., Champion, C., . . . Cummins, R. (2008). KidsMatter: A population health model to support student mental health and well-being in primary schools. *International Journal of Mental Health Promotion, 10*(4), 13–20.

Grossman, P. L. (1995). Teachers' knowledge. In L. W. Anderson (Ed.), *International encyclopedia of teaching and teacher education* (2nd edn., pp. 20–24). Tarrytown, NY: Pergamon.

Kobau, R., Seligman, M. E., Peterson, C., Diener, E., Zack, M. M., Chapman, D., & Thompson, W. (2011). Mental health promotion in public health: Perspectives and strategies from positive psychology. *American Journal of Public Health, 101*(8), e1–e9.

Kreber, C., & Cranton, P. (2000). Exploring the scholarship of teaching. *The Journal of Higher Education, 71*, 476–495.

Little, J. W. (1993). Teachers' professional development in a climate of educational reform. *Educational Evaluation and Policy Analysis, 15*, 129–151.

Mustard, J. F. (2006). Experience-based brain development: Scientific underpinnings of the importance of early child development in a global world. *Paediatrics and Child Health, 11*, 571–572.

Opfer, V. D., & Pedder, D. (2011). Conceptualizing teacher professional learning. *Review of Educational Research, 81*, 376.

Prince, M., Patel, V., Saxena, S., Maj, M., Maselko, J., Phillips, M. R., & Rahman, A. (2007). No health without mental health. *The Lancet, 370*, 859–877.

Sawyer, M. G., Miller-Lewis, L. R., & Clark, J. J. (2007). The mental health of 13–17 year-olds in Australia: Findings from the national survey of mental health and well-being. *Journal of Youth and Adolescence, 36*, 185–194.

Shulman, L. S. (1987). Knowledge and teaching: Foundations of a new reform. *Harvard Education Review, 57*, 1–22.

Slee, P. T., Lawson, M. J., Russell, A., Askell-Williams, H., Dix, K. L., Owens, L., . . . Spears, B. (2009). KidsMatter primary evaluation final report. Accessed 13.07. 2014 at www.kidsmatter.edu.au/early-childhood/about/evaluation

Slee, P. T., Murray-Harvey, R., Dix, K. L., Skrzypiec, G., Askell-Williams, H., Lawson, M. J., & Krieg, S. (2012). KidsMatter Early Childhood Evaluation. Accessed 18.07.2014 at www.kidsmatter.edu.au

Slee, P. T., Skrzypiec, G., Dix, K. L., Murray-Harvey, R., & Askell-Williams, H. (2012). *KidsMatter early childhood evaluation in services with high proportions of Aboriginal and Torres Strait islander children*. Adelaide, South Australia: Shannon Research Press.

Tucker, B., Halloran, P., & Price, C. (2013). *Student perceptions of the teaching in online learning: An Australian university case study*. Paper presented at the Research and Development in Higher Education conference: The Place of Learning and Teaching, Auckland, New Zealand.

Vosniadou, S. (Ed.). (2013). *International Handbook of Research on Conceptual Change* (2nd edn.). London: Routledge.

World Health Organization (WHO). (2013). Mental health: A state of well-being. Accessed 15.04.2015 at www.who.int/features/factfiles/mental_health/en/index.html

SECTION 4

The challenges and opportunities of new technologies

8

PSYCHOLOGICAL WELLBEING AND THE USE OF THE INTERNET IN ADOLESCENCE

Antonella Brighi , Sandra Maria Elena Nicoletti and Annalisa Guarini

Rather than seeing information and communication technologies as dangerous for young people's mental health, we propose the adoption of a more articulated vision of risk pathways. The two relational experiences offered by the online and the offline dimensions should not be considered as dichotomous but as integrated. The online and offline environments represent social worlds placed along a continuum that requires a restructuring and reorganization of relations, nested in a complex system.

The challenge

Information and communication technologies (ICTs) and social media are rewriting how we socially interact, calling for a redefinition and reassessment of social boundaries and the relationships that operate within and around them. The border between offline and online behaviors is becoming increasingly indistinct, especially for adolescents, and new technologies are now to be considered among the crucial contexts of experience for psycho-social wellbeing. The current opinion among policy makers, educators, teachers and parents is that ICTs may be dangerous for growing adolescents, since the time spent online reduces opportunities for face-to-face interaction, without providing appropriate guidelines for facilitating social relations. ICTs may be used in dangerous ways (e.g., cyberbullying and cybercrime) with a negative impact on social interactions and learning, but the 'knee-jerk reaction' often reported in the case of cyber-incidents is to exclude technologies, impose filters, and/or restrict the use of ICTs, at least in educational settings. This short-sighted action can only increase conflict between adolescents and adults and, overall, may limit a deeper understanding of the contribution that Internet communication makes to adolescents' development and mental wellbeing. The virtual context, in fact, is a crucial scenario for understanding the dynamics of socialization and communication involved in the construction of views, values and patterns of behavior that define and influence adolescents' lifestyle, and, consequentially, psychological wellbeing. Research on risk processes has replaced simplistic models of developmental risk with a more systemic and integrated consideration of the interplay between risk and protective factors in different fields of expertise. For example, research on cyberbullying highlights the strong continuity between being a victim offline, at school, and online (Hinduja & Patchin, 2012) and the role of poor family and peer relationships (Brighi, Guarini, Melotti, Galli, & Genta, 2012; Sourander *et al.*, 2010) as predictors of both victimization and aggression online. The offline relational context (family, school, peer group) seems a powerful predictor of what happens online, and vice versa. Moreover, maladjusted adolescents generally present a complex set of intertwined problems, which may be summarized as an overall 'risky lifestyle'. Thus, we need to widen our analysis of developmental trajectories, both maladaptive and adaptive, to the online dimension, trying to understand the processes and mechanisms that may distinguish it from the offline relational context.

Background

Psychological wellbeing in adolescence: a multidisciplinary approach

Adolescence is a critical developmental period with long-term implications for health and wellbeing. While it represents a challenging period for some, research points out that many adolescents meet in a constructive way the developmental tasks typically identified for this period of the life-span, with a positive impact on wellbeing. The main developmental challenges consist of the construction of a personal sense of identity, the achievement of sexual maturity, the establishing of intellectual and emotional autonomy and a moral system independent from parents and other adults, increased impulse control and behavioral maturity, and the creation of stable and productive peer relationships. These salient developmental tasks are contextualized by prevailing sociocultural and historically embedded expectations.

During the transition into and out of adolescence, how can optimal development and wellbeing be supported? The answer requires a multidisciplinary and multifactorial perspective, open to several influences, ranging from the sociocultural to the biological. The interplay among individual, contextual and developmental resources may outline very different pathways, which may result in happiness and success with later tasks, or in failure leading to unhappiness, societal disapproval and difficulty with later tasks. Within this framework, wellbeing is conceived as multidimensional, determined by the positive interaction among physical, psychological and social features of health and one's own perceived quality of life. It consists of "positive self-perceptions and evaluation of one's position in life and in cultural context, values and beliefs, expectations, worries, fears, performances" (Albiero, 2012, p. 19).

Since the meaning of developmental transitions and their impact on adolescents' health is heavily influenced by proximal social and relational contexts as well as distal sociocultural ones, it is necessary to consider the contexts wherein adolescents live, in order to understand what can promote wellbeing. In this sense, it becomes crucial to consider how ICTs shape adolescents' social experience, since the Internet is a significant part of adolescents' lives, with an important role in their activities, their sources of information and guidance, their social relationships, and broadly speaking, their wellbeing.

The context of peer relations, in offline and online worlds

Developing positive peer relationships and maintaining friendships is crucial in helping adolescents to deal with developmental tasks such as forming identity, developing social skills and self-esteem and establishing autonomy. Peer relationships create context characterized by mutual assistance, confrontation and self-experimentation through other peers' perspectives. Not surprisingly, some authors assume that peer relationships increase adolescents' wellbeing and interpersonal competence and play a unique role with respect to later adjustment. Perceived social support, such as the perception of being valued and cared for by others, predicts a positive global self-worth and is a crucial factor for psychological wellbeing, especially during adolescence (Sarason, Pierce, & Sarason, 1990).

The sense of 'connectedness' provided by social networks buffers negative life events and outcomes, whereas lack of close friends and peer rejection contribute significantly to poor mental health, such as depression and negative self-views, and major psychiatric disorders (Joiner, 1997). The relationship and mutual reinforcement between experiences of rejection and social isolation from peers, cognitive-affective evaluations such as loneliness and low self-esteem and depressed feelings, can be explained by the 'vulnerability-stress' depression model (Beck and Clark, 1988). This proposed that negative stressful events, such as peer rejection, could be internalized in maladaptive self-schemas, leading to an increased risk of depression. Moreover, a review of the literature reveals that low self-esteem and depressive symptoms are consistently associated in adolescence (MacPhee & Andrews, 2006).

In recent years, ICTs have assumed an important role in building and consolidating relationships among adolescents. Given the strict link between peer-group relationships and healthy adolescent development, understanding the relation between Internet use and psychological wellbeing is essential. Internet use introduces new modalities of communication in comparison with offline relationships. Anonymity and the lack of audio/visual cues (facial expressions, gaze, body language) in social networking sites can promote the creation of online relationships and enhance self-disclosure. The 'disinhibition effect' has been described along the two polarities of 'benign disinhibition' and 'toxic disinhibition' (Suler, 2004). The former happens when people online "reveal secret emotions, fears, wishes or they show unusual acts of kindness and generosity" (p. 321), while the latter appears when people use rude language, criticize or display anger, or explore the dark side of the Internet such as pornography and violence. *Benign disinhibition* allows the opportunity to understand and explore oneself, while *toxic disinhibition* is "a blind catharsis, [. . .] a way to remove unsavory needs and wishes" (ibid.). Adolescents use the Internet as an anonymous playground, where they may share personal thoughts, feelings, and experiences (Gross, 2004). Self-disclosure is important for developing high-quality friendships because it may indicate the dimension and the degree of trust in a specific interaction partner, and ultimately may foster the formation and maintenance of relationships.

Internet use: time

Given the extent of adolescents' Internet use, some authors were concerned that it displaced activities important for development, such as physical activities and social interactions with peers that occur in face-to-face contexts. The data from our Italian sample (N=3002 students; N=934 middle school students, mean age=12 years; range 11–15 years and N=2068 secondary school students; mean age=15.3 years; range 14–20 years, Guarini, Brighi, & Genta, 2013) showed that in a normal working day students used the Internet from 20 minutes to 1 hour (22 percent), 1–2 hours (27.5 percent) and 2–3 hours (18.5 percent). Some students used it for a very long period of the day: 3–5 hours (10.6 percent) and more than 5 hours (9.1 percent). Time increased from middle to secondary school. Adolescents declared that they used the Internet mainly alone. If they chose to share with someone, they preferred a friend, followed by brothers/sisters. Internet use with parents was present in middle schools, but decreased in secondary schools.

Some research suggested that increased Internet use is associated with declining psychological wellbeing (Kraut *et al.*, 1998) and a reduction of social ties among adolescents (Sanders, Field, Diego, & Kaplan, 2000). The most-frequent users are more likely to report lower levels of attachment to friends and have a worse perception of the quality of family relationships (Brighi, Guarini, *et al.*, 2012). Sanders and colleagues found that greater use of the Internet was associated with weaker relationships with peers and parents, although the directionality of this relationship could not be clearly determined. However, other studies have not shown a strong connection between time online and psychological wellbeing (e.g., loneliness and depression) (Gross, Juvonen, & Gable, 2002), and the quality and quantity of face-to-face relationships (Kraut *et al.*, 2002). In fact, use of the Internet can improve existing relationships and facilitate the construction of new social networks (Valkenburg & Peter, 2007) especially for isolated teenagers, since online interaction is a relatively safe context that does not require the social skills needed in face-to-face interaction. It is noteworthy that Internet connectedness patterns may differ as a function of the nature of the social environment, of family social status and other environmental factors, such as the rate of Internet adoption by peers. In fact, as the proportion of friends using the Internet increased, the more likely the user was to intensify online communication, suggesting a strong effect of peer groups on the likelihood of connecting to the Internet (Jung, Kim, Lin, & Cheong, 2005).

As Valkenburg and Peter (2007) suggest, Internet time cannot alone explain the controversial association with social ties and mental wellbeing. The differences among the studies may be explained by several quantitative and qualitative changes in Internet use:

> In the early stages of the Internet, adolescents' online contacts were clearly separated from their offline contacts. As a result, the time invested in online contacts reduced the time that could be invested in offline contacts. In the past few years, however, the strict separation between online and offline contacts no longer exists, at least among adolescents; new technologies, such as IM, encourage communication with existing friends. As a result, adolescents' online and offline contacts now progressively seem to overlap.
>
> (p. 268)

This highlights the importance of considering the range of activities that adolescents carry out on in the Internet, since they may be meeting very different psychological needs.

Internet use: activities

Communication, entertainment and information seeking are three of the most important uses of media. Gross (2004) highlighted that teens spend their time online mainly in private conversation with instant-messaging and social networking; visiting websites and sending email are also popular, showing an online multitasking attitude. Our research confirmed that the main activities reported by Italian adolescents were the use of social networks and instant messages, followed by watching movie websites (see Figure 8.1, Guarini *et al.*, 2013). Adolescents performed other activities less frequently, such as sending/receiving email, watching Web TV, looking for information about news and schools, buying things and online gaming. More rarely, adolescents upload their personal details reporting information about diets, sex, health, politics, sexual orientation and religion.

Analysing the patterns of activities for Italian adolescents, some clusters emerged: social networking (social networks, chat, emails); information seeking (information concerning school topics, politics, news, online shopping); information seeking on 'sensitive' topics (sexuality, sexual identity, diets); use of multimedia content and products (downloading videos, movies, music, watching Web TV, online gaming).

The research suggested that adolescents find opportunities on the Internet for role experimentation, identity play and establishment of connections. Using social networking sites, adolescents may meet new people, be in contact with friends, exchange information and develop intimate relationships as well, even if these relationships are different from the nuances of face-to-face interaction. Wellman and Haythornthwaite (2002) stated that the communicative use of media allows connectedness by overcoming spatial and temporal constraints. In this regard, being

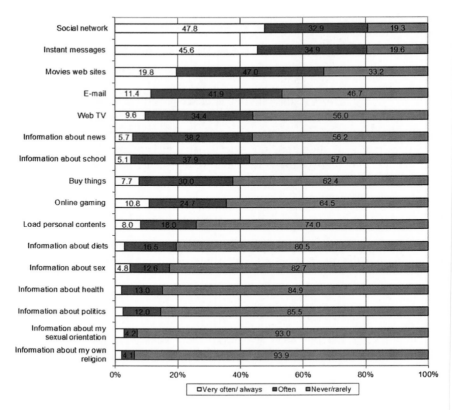

FIGURE 8.1 Activities carried out by adolescents on the Internet

Adapted from Guarini, A., Brighi, A., & Genta, M. L. (Eds) (2013). *Stili di vita online e offline degli adolescenti in Emilia-Romagna*. Quaderni del Corecom Emilia-Romagna. Corecom Emilia-Romagna.

part of online social groups gives the opportunity to feel understood and appreciated and avoid threats or negative stimuli such as loneliness and social isolation.

Moreover, self-disclosure seems to be positively related to the number of online friends and to satisfaction with online friendship: larger networks are associated with greater life satisfaction and perceived social support (Manago, Taylor, & Greenfield, 2012), though this relationship may not hold, or even become negative, for individuals with a particularly large number of online friends (Kim & Lee, 2011). When it occurs, loneliness in online environments may be attributable to the absence of social cues, which is associated with decreases in psychological wellbeing and perceived social support or to Internet addiction.

Given these mixed findings, some authors proposed personality as an important mediator between Internet use and wellbeing. Kraut *et al.* (2002) found a significant relationship between personality traits and the impact of Internet use on wellbeing. Extrovert adolescents, in contrast with introverts, use the Internet to 'augment' their social networks, keeping in touch with friends and meeting new people, while introverts tend to surf anonymously, 'seeking connectedness', in attempting to avoid social isolation. It would not be surprising to find some introverted adolescents experimenting through online interaction to enhance their self-confidence and feeling of belongingness to a group. The point, therefore, is to see whether these new social skills may be transferred into offline interactions as this transfer may be difficult: socially isolated individuals may find that virtual communication gratifies their need for a sense of belonging because it can be easily accessed by those lacking social competence (Kim, LaRose, & Peng, 2009). However, the social use of media may not gratify this need completely, especially if this need is based on the desire to escape social isolation:

> You might have begun your online life in a spirit of compensation. If you were lonely and isolated, it seemed better than nothing. But online you're slim, rich, and buffed up, and you feel you have more opportunities than in the real world. So, here too, better than nothing can become better than something, or better than anything. Not surprisingly, people report feeling let down when they move from the virtual to the real world.
>
> (Turkle, 2011, p. 12)

This failure can foster a vicious circle of problematic media use: social isolation can motivate lonely individuals to find media use as a proxy for face-to-face interactions, but media use cannot completely gratify their needs, which motivates them to increase their media use (Caplan, 2003; Kim *et al.*, 2009). Media can mainly contribute increasing efficiency of connection, but may not be a suitable means to build emotional bonds (Ahn & Shin, 2013). This phenomenon is well described by Turkle (2011) in her book *Alone Together*, wherein she suggests that digital connections may offer the illusion of companionship without the demand of friendship: "We are increasingly connected to each other but oddly more alone: in intimacy, new solitude" (p. 19).

Internet use: risk and positive behaviors

In our research (Guarini *et al.*, 2013) students were asked to indicate whether several statements were true or false for them concerning their experience while using the Internet. Some considered themselves experts in computer use (41.3 percent), some published their creations on the net (21.2 percent) and some managed their own blog and/or website (21.9 percent). These adolescents benefit from the positive potentialities of the Internet (Brighi, Fabbri, Guerra, & Pacetti, 2012), using it for increasing social support and facilitating the formation of new relationships. However, some revealed risky behavior patterns: in all, 37.6 percent declared getting bored if they could not connect to the Internet for just a day, 17 percent spent all their spare time on the PC, and 23 percent said that it would be better that no one knew what they did online. Moreover, 10 percent claimed not to sleep at night because they were using the Internet, and said they felt better in the virtual than the real world (16.4 percent). These results point to a possible risk for mental health: several studies, in fact, have outlined the potentially addictive properties of the Internet for those adolescents who use it overly, who can no longer control their behavior online and may develop symptoms of *compulsive Internet use* or *Internet addiction* (Young, 1998) or *problematic Internet use* (Caplan, 2003). These terms define a technological addiction syndrome, which consists of symptoms such as loss of control over behavior, conflicts (internal and interpersonal), absorption with the Internet, use of the Internet to modify one's mood, and withdrawal symptoms. The *DSM-5* (American Psychiatric Association, 2013) has included 'gaming disorder' among psychiatric conditions that require further research, but not 'Internet addiction', which remains a controversial construct in scientific literature. Internet addiction, therefore, is not a psychiatric diagnosis, but a potentially pathological behavioral pattern that can be related to adverse outcomes in adolescence, such as: problems with identity formation (Kim *et al.*, 2012); changes in the structure of the developing brain (Lin *et al.*, 2012); impaired cognitive functioning (Park *et al.*, 2011); poor academic performance and engagement in risky activities (Tsitsika *et al.*, 2011); poor dietary habits (Kim *et al.*, 2010); and low quality of interpersonal relations (Milani, Osualdella, & Di Blasio, 2009). Moreover, Internet addiction seems to be related to depression, insomnia, obsessive-compulsive disorder and suicidal ideation, and alcohol and drug use (Cheung & Wong, 2011). Addicted Internet adolescents also have low emotional stability, low extraversion (or introversion), and low agreeableness (van der Aa *et al.*, 2009).

Solutions

The research evidence discussed in this chapter regarding Italian adolescent ICT use presents a puzzling picture. To summarize the possibilities and risks implied in the interaction between offline and online socialization processes, two different perspectives have been outlined: the 'displacement hypothesis', and the 'rich-get richer' or 'augmentation hypothesis' (Valkenburg & Peter, 2007). The first postulates that media use may consume a substantial amount of time, sacrificing other valuable activities without providing appropriate functions for facilitating social relations, thereby limiting actual social relations (Kraut *et al.*, 2002); such displacement often leads users to have a negative sense of subjective wellbeing (Stepanikova, Nie, & He, 2010). From this point of view, the Internet replaces offline social life with the online one, as online friendships are a social compensation for adolescents who have difficulties in building intimate relationships in the offline context. On the contrary, the 'augmentation hypothesis' posits that individuals often use media to develop and enhance social relations (Valkenburg & Peter, 2007; 2009).

Our suggestion, therefore, is to consider multiple aspects of adolescents' Internet activity and its overall meaning at specific times of development. The relation between the Internet and adolescents' wellbeing, in fact, is not simplistically reducible to the polarities of 'displacement' or 'augmentation', nor to the amount of time spent online. Therefore, it calls for a complex and nuanced approach, wherein the whole of an individual's personal and social potentialities and risk factors are closely intertwined, since use of the Internet may be a response to very different psychological and developmental needs. For these reasons, it will be important to design future studies that will help us to determine which teens will benefit from online communication, and which may be harmed. Only if we understand individual differences will we be able to design interventions that target different subgroups of adolescents.

The integration of information technology with everyday social life has created a complex phenomenon whereby social contexts, information channels and network properties interact. The virtual arena is at the same time socially embedded, but operates under autonomous technical rules. So, ICT use is both social and technological; it contains both positive potentials and negative threats to the quality of adolescents' development, in a continuum with everyday life and communication. The boundaries between offline and online are less and less meaningful, as ICTs and social structure mutually affect each other in various ways.

Conclusion

Our discussion implies three consequences. First, adolescents must be helped to learn how to develop precautionary behaviors and attitudes regarding the disclosure of intimate and personal information, especially with strangers; since most new online contacts rely on the transitivity of friendship, it is important to empower peers to share social norms against abusive behaviors online.

Second, the quality of relational offline context should be taken into consideration, as a proximal protective or risk factor for what happens online; evidence from many studies has shown how positive offline peer relations may transfer online, fostering a feeling of connectedness and belonging, thus reducing problematic behaviors both offline and online (Hinduja & Patchin, 2012).

Third, promoting healthy and positive relationships, both online and offline, must be the core of our educative aims. This claim contrasts with Italian and European University curricula for teachers, with little provided in the way of education on topics concerning ICTs and their impact on socialization, social norms, group functioning and psychological wellbeing. International literature (Li, 2008) shows that teachers report personal experiences with cyberbullying interventions, but at the same time claim insufficient skills and knowledge to coordinate or actively participate in a cyberbullying intervention. School leaders and teachers should acquire a systemic view of the potentialities and risks of ICTs in their schools, and realize how to use these tools in order to promote a positive climate in the school and, more broadly, to foster adolescents' wellbeing.

Acknowledgements

Our research has received funding from the Corecom Emilia Romagna to dott. Guarini and dott. Brighi, in the framework of a project entitled "Stili di vita online e offline degli adolescenti in Emilia Romagna" (*Online and offline adolescents' lifestyles in the Emilia Romagna Region*).

References

Ahn, D., & Shin, D. H. (2013). Is the social use of media for seeking connectedness or for avoiding social isolation? Mechanisms underlying media use and subjective well-being. *Computers in Human Behavior, 29*, 2453–2462.

Albiero, P. (Ed.) (2012). *Il benessere psicosociale in adolescenza. Prospettive multidisciplinari*. Roma: Carocci.

American Psychiatric Association (2013). *Diagnostic and Statistical Manual of Mental Disorders, Fifth Edition* (DSM-5).Washington, DC: APA.

Beck, A. T., & Clark, D. (1988). Anxiety and depression: An information processing perspective. *Anxiety Research, 1*, 23–36.

Brighi, A., Fabbri, M., Guerra, L., & Pacetti, E. (2012). ICT and relationships: Promoting positive peer interactions. In A. Costabile & B. A. Spears (Eds.), *The impact of technology on relationships in educational settings*. London and New York: Routledge, pp. 45–54.

Brighi, A., Guarini, A., Melotti, G., Galli, S., & Genta, M. L. (2012). Predictors of victimization across direct bullying, indirect bullying and cyberbullying. *Emotional and Behavioural Difficulties, 17*, 375–388.

Caplan, S. E. (2003). Preference for online social interaction: A theory of problematic Internet use and psychosocial well-being. *Communication Research, 30*, 625–648.

Cheung, L. M., & Wong, W. S. (2011). The effects of insomnia and Internet addiction on depression in Hong Kong Chinese adolescents: An exploratory cross-sectional analysis. *Journal of Sleep Research, 20*(2), 311–317.

Gross, E. F. (2004). Adolescent Internet use: What we expect, what teens report. *Applied Developmental Psychology, 25*, 633–649.

Gross, E. F., Juvonen, J., & Gable, S. L. (2002). Internet use and well-being in adolescence. *Journal of Social Issues, 58*, 75–90.

Guarini, A., Brighi, A., & Genta, M. L. (2013). *Stili di vita online e offline degli adolescenti in Emilia-Romagna*. Quaderni del Corecom Emilia-Romagna. Corecom Emilia-Romagna.

Hinduja, S., & Patchin, J. W. (2012). *School Climate 2.0: Preventing cyberbullying and sexting one classroom at a time*. Thousand Oaks, CA: Sage.

Joiner, Jr., T. E. (1997). Shyness and low social support as interactive diatheses, and loneliness as mediator: Testing an interpersonal-personality view of depression. *Journal of Abnormal Psychology, 106*, 386–394.

Jung, J.-Y., Kim, Y.-C., Lin, W.-Y., & Cheong, P. H. (2005). The influence of social environment on Internet connectedness of adolescents in Seoul, Singapore and Taipei. *New Media & Society, 7*(1), 64–88.

Kim, J., & Lee, J. R. (2011). The Facebook paths to happiness: Effects of the number of Facebook friends and self-presentation on subjective well-being. *Cyberpsychology, Behavior, and Social Networking, 14*(6), 359–364.

Kim, J., LaRose, R., & Peng, W. (2009). Loneliness as the cause and the effect of problematic Internet use: The relationships between Internet use and psychological well-being. *CyberPsychology & Behavior, 12*(4), 451–455.

Kim, Y., Park, J. Y., Kim, S. B., Jung, I.-K., Lim, Y. S., & Kim, J.-H. (2010). The effects of Internet addiction on the lifestyle and dietary behavior of Korean adolescents. *Nutrition Research and Practice, 4,* 51–57.

Kim, Y. R., Son, J. W., Lee, S. I., Shin, C. J., Kim, S. K., Ju, G., *et al.* (2012). Abnormal brain activation of adolescent Internet addict in a ball-throwing animation task: Possible neural correlates of disembodiment revealed by fmri. *Progress in Neuro-Psychopharmacology and Biological Psychiatry, 39*(1), 88–95.

Kraut, R., Patterson, M., Lundmark, V., Kiesler, S., Mukopadhyay, T., Scherlis, W. (1998). Internet paradox: A social technology that reduces social involvement and psychological well-being? *American Psychologist, 53*(9), 1017–1031.

Kraut, R., Kiesler, S., Boneva, B., Cummings, J., Helgeson, V., & Crawford, A. (2002). Internet paradox revisited. *Journal of Social Issues, 58,* 49–74.

Li, Q. (2008). A cross-cultural comparison of adolescents' experience related to cyberbullying. *Educational Research, 50*(3), 223–234.

Lin, F., Zhou, Y., Du, Y., Qin, L., Zhao, Z., Xu, J., *et al.* (2012). Abnormal white matter integrity in adolescents with Internet addiction disorder: A tract-based spatial statistics study. *PLoS ONE, 7*(1).

Manago, A.M., Taylor, T., Greenfield, P.M. (2012). Me and my 400 friends: The anatomy of college students' Facebook networks, their communication patterns, and well-being. *Developmental Psychology, 48*(2), 369–380.

MacPhee, A. R., & Andrews, J. J. (2006). Risk factors for depression in early adolescence. *Adolescence, 41*(163), 435–466.

Milani, L., Osualdella, D., & Di Blasio, P. (2009). Quality of interpersonal relationships and problematic Internet use in adolescence. *CyberPsychology & Behavior, 12*(6), 681–684.

Park, M.-H., Park, E. J., Choi, J., Chai, S., Lee, J.-H., Lee, C., et al. (2011). Preliminary study of Internet addiction and cognitive function in adolescents based on IQ tests. *Psychiatry Research, 190*(2–3), 275–281.

Sanders, C., Field, T., Diego, M., & Kaplan, M. (2000). The relationship of Internet use to depression and social isolation among adolescents. *Adolescence, 35,* 237–242.

Sarason, B. R., Pierce, G. R., & Sarason, I. G. (1990) Social support: The sense of acceptance and the role of relationships. In Sarason, B. R., Sarason, I. G., & Pierce, G. R. (Eds.), *Social support: An interactional view.* New York: Wiley, pp. 97–128.

Sourander, A., Brunstein-Klomek, A., Helenius, H., Ikonen, M., Lindroos, J., Luntamo, T., & Koskelainen, M. (2010). Psychosocial risk factors associated with cyberbullying among adolescents: A population-based study. *Archives of General Psychiatry, 67*(7), 720–728.

Stepanikova, I., Nie, N. H., & He, X. (2010). Time on the Internet at home, loneliness, and life satisfaction: Evidence from panel time-diary data. *Computers in Human Behavior, 26,* 329–338.

Suler, J. (2004). The online disinhibition effect. *CyberPsychology & Behavior, 7,* 3.

Tsitsika, A., Critselis, E., Louizou, A., Janikian, M., Freskou, A., Marangou, E., *et al.* (2011). Determinants of Internet addiction among adolescents: A case-control study. *The Scientific World Journal, 11,* 866–874.

Turkle, S. (2011). *Alone together: Why we expect more from technology and less from each other.* New York: Basic Books.

Valkenburg, P. M., & Peter, J. (2007). Preadolescents' and adolescents' online communication and their closeness to friends. *Developmental Psychology, 43,* 267–277.

Valkenburg, P. M., & Peter, J. (2009). Social consequences of the Internet for adolescents: A decade of research. *Current Directions in Psychological Science, 18,* 1–5.

van der Aa, N., Overbeek, G., Engels, R. C. M. E., Scholte, R. H. J., Meerkerk, G. J., & van den Eijnden, R. J. J. M. (2009). Daily and compulsive Internet use and well-being in adolescence: A diathesis-stress model based on Big Five personality traits. *Journal of Youth and Adolescence, 38*, 765–776.

Wellman, B., & Haythornthwaite, C. (2002). *The Internet in everyday life*. London: Blackwell Publishers Ltd.

Young, K. S. (1998). Internet addiction: The emergence of a new clinical disorder. *CyberPsychology & Behavior, 1*, 237–244.

9

THE USE OF TECHNOLOGY TO SUPPORT YOUNG PEOPLE WITH MENTAL HEALTH ISSUES IN SCHOOLS

Cathy Richards and Jennifer Hughes

There are various barriers to young people's help-seeking for mental health difficulties. School-based e-resources have the potential to give better access to mental health information, services and support for adolescents. However, much remains to be done to ensure that such resources are safe, effective and confidential.

The challenge

Globally, about one in four young people aged 13 to 24 experiences a mental health disorder. In turn, this is likely to cause significant impairment in social and academic functioning (e.g., Weems & Stickle, 2005). Seeking and receiving timely and appropriate mental health care can lower the risk of developing severe or extended episodes of common mental health disorders such as anxiety and depression (Rickwood, Deane, & Wilson, 2007). However, too few young people access specialist help, with various barriers to help-seeking identified. How can schools best raise awareness of mental health problems and encourage productive help-seeking in their pupils? This chapter considers the role of new technologies in supporting young people with mental health issues in schools.

Background

Common barriers to young people's help-seeking for mental health issues include stigma, confidentiality, trust in the provider, accessibility of resources (especially in rural locations) and problems recognising symptoms (Gulliver, Griffiths, & Christensen, 2010). Notably, Chandra and Minkovitz (2007) found an increase in stigmatised views when students had less knowledge about mental health. Furthermore, a preference for self-reliance is one of the most important barriers (Gulliver *et al.*, 2010), while another is 'not knowing where to go for help', with pupils reporting a lack of resources available at their school to answer their questions (Bowers, Manion, Papadopoulos, & Gauvreau, 2013). Some evidence also suggests that young people perceive positive past experiences, and social support and encouragement from others, as aids to the help-seeking process (Gulliver *et al.*, 2010). The availability of self-help materials is also a potential facilitator.

In the context of limited access to, and the high cost in providing, traditional face-to-face mental health services, there is growing interest in providing mental health interventions in schools (Attwood, Meadows, Stallard, & Richardson, 2012), including through e-mental health resources. While this presents challenges, an unparalleled advantage is that schools are places through which the majority of adolescents can be reached.

Although young people often fail to consult professionals with respect to their worries about mental health problems, they do use the Internet. Importantly, this is the only such resource accessed equally by boys and girls (Gould, Harris Munfakh, Lubell, Kleinman, & Parker, 2002); other sources of help and information (e.g., the GP or written material) are more likely to be utilised by girls. Williams and Pow (2007) found that Scottish teenage boys placed less importance than girls on knowledge about mental health problems and were more likely to think they already knew enough. Therefore, a challenge for schools will be how to create a curiosity in boys so that they want to find out more.

School-based interventions have typically been provided in two main ways: universally, in order to promote emotional resilience and prevent the development of mental health disorders; and in a targeted way, focusing upon those at increased risk of developing mental health problems or already displaying mild/moderate problems. A characteristic of more effective interventions includes focusing on positive mental health (not problems), starting early, and operating for a lengthy period of time (Weare, 2013). However, Vostanis, Humphrey, Fitzgerald, Deighton, and Wolpert (2013) showed that UK schools rarely use evidence-based approaches and default to using targeted approaches alone. Especially in a mainstream school setting, this gives rise to the problem of stigma, often a side-effect of well-intentioned mental health work; hence it is important to take a balanced universal/targeted approach (Weare, 2013).

Addressing the challenge and opportunities

Awareness of barriers to productive help-seeking is necessary for schools to find creative solutions for facilitating getting help to young people. It seems reasonable to suggest that Internet-based resources are well positioned to overcome concerns about stigma and confidentiality and to allow for greater availability and accessibility of mental health information and resources, especially as pupils are entirely comfortable with using such media, with which they have grown up. In addition, there is a range of platforms and media for the accessing and delivery of ICT-based mental health interventions, notably, information provision via websites, self-help

CD-ROMS, smartphone apps, interactive gaming and computerised cognitive behavioural therapy (cCBT).

Good-quality mental health information from reliable e-health sources may help overcome barriers to help-seeking in young people and improve awareness of common symptoms related to mental health problems. Websites can also provide basic evidence-based self-help and signpost young people to sources of professional help. However, Reavley and Jorm (2011) reported that there continues to be significant variation in their quality.

One of the most evaluated school-based programmes is the *FRIENDS for Life* programme (Barrett & Ollendick, 2004), a brief cognitive-behavioural intervention, which has demonstrated a reduction in anxiety and depressive symptoms in several studies conducted in the UK, Australia, Mexico, Germany and Sweden (e.g., Ahlen, Breitholtz, Barrett, & Gallegos, 2012) with gains maintained after three years (Barrett & Pahl, 2006). Importantly, the most recent evaluation showed high fidelity to the group leader manual (delivered by classroom teachers), which suggests the promise of manualisation for transfer to other settings (Ahlen *et al.*, 2012).

For schools, it is a significant challenge to identify evidence-based sources of information and self-help materials. An example of a solution is a bibliotherapy resource developed in Lothian in Scotland and launched in 2008: the *Healthy Reading* intervention, comprising a range of books and resources such as websites, CDs and DVDs to help young people and their parents/carers cope with mental health issues. The *Healthy Reading* scheme offers reliable information, practical advice and self-help guidance on a range of mental health issues, and is available through school and public libraries. Training has been offered to local library and school library staff to support the use of these resources.

User and stakeholder perceptions of the scheme were overwhelmingly positive: 86 per cent of the prescribers stated that they would use the scheme in the future, while users reported that the resources made them feel less isolated, facilitated an understanding of their psychological difficulty and provided useful advice for overcoming it. However, evaluation of the scheme (Richards, Gunning, & Prescott, 2012) indicated several barriers inhibiting its uptake, including a lack of awareness and knowledge of the resources and the potential barrier of using a public library. So any resources need to be consistently promoted across settings in a school: in classrooms, sports changing rooms and the school toilets! An idea that arose from a consultation led by young people about mental health in schools in Edinburgh was that there should be one website/helpline actively promoted, its role being to direct pupils to appropriate evidence-based self-help resources and help lines, and so on.

Web-based resources in school

The presentation of psycho-educational material about wellbeing through a multimedia format increases its accessibility to children and adolescents in general.

It can also benefit young people who live in rural and/or remote areas where access to a computer may be more readily available than to specialist mental health services.

Examples of e-health resources included in the *Healthy Reading* scheme are two computer-based resources aimed at providing easily accessible information on anxiety and depression (Young, Richards, & Gunning, 2012). The websites www.depressioninteenagers.co.uk and www.stressandanxietyinteenagers.co.uk are aimed at young people and those caring for them, offering CBT-based self-help and signposts for further help. The two websites are available through two domains along with a CD-ROM containing the same content, a copy of which was provided free to every secondary school in Scotland. The website had been made accessible to young people through recommendations from health care and educational professionals. The qualitative evaluation indicated that the majority of users found the website easy to navigate and thought that the information was easy to understand and trustworthy.

> *I thought that when it went on to the 'four in a row' game, every time you put a counter in, you got a tip on what to do to relax. I think that worked really well, and it's really simple so it's like; 'go home, watch a funny DVD', 'text a friend you've not seen in ages'.*
>
> *The CD would be really useful around exam time.*
>
> *I thought the CD was really good. Personally I think it would be useful for someone who isn't really sure about the symptoms or anything. So if you had been stressed I think it would be good. If I was worried about a friend then I would recommend the CD.*
>
> *I think it will come in handy around exam time because there are some things in the CD which I feel around that time.*

The development of both websites included testing with pupils aged 12–16 in a school setting. Published research looking at help-seeking on the Internet/from IT applications has not focused upon the different ways in which adults and young people use interactive resources, nor has it explored gender differences. So this study was able to add to the established knowledge base.

In the second stage of testing, following the introduction of a new game, there was a significant increase in the number of young people who rated this as the most useful section of the CD-ROM. Similarly, we added more personal stories with a solution-focused approach in light of feedback from young people. The perception of the adults showed no significant change, suggesting that adults and young people interact with this resource in a very different way, with young people most frequently choosing to gather information via the games, and adults preferring the more information-heavy parts of the resource. The resource was designed to be accessible for both young people and the adults caring for then, so the different styles of information presentation seem to increase the likelihood of both age-groups accessing information in an interesting and relevant way. The differences between adults and young people highlight the importance of consulting with young people in designing and marketing resources.

Gender

Given boys' and girls' different approaches to help-seeking, it is important to find ways of appealing to both. A clue to this was also found in the evaluation of the websites/CD-ROMS described above: the girls were significantly more likely to describe the CD-ROM as very useful and were almost twice as likely as boys to state that they would use it again. This difference in attitude is important as lack of accurate information is likely to impact on boys' ability to make informed choices about help-seeking and self-help if they experience mental health problems. Given that the suicide rate for young men is unacceptably high, it is important to continue to seek to develop targeted mental health information and promotional information that is likely to appeal to boys and to continue the whole school approach to optimise the likelihood of boys receiving accurate, helpful information. Boys showed a clear preference for the areas of the site that included games, while the girls preferred the personal stories. School staff could be encouraged to direct boys to those parts of e-mental health resources with which they are most likely to engage.

Online web-based cCBT

Computerised Cognitive Behaviour Therapy (cCBT) programmes offer the potential to make evidence-based interventions more accessible for children and young people. cCBT refers to the delivery of interventions based on CBT via computer technology with or without support from a coach/clinician and accessed via a CD-ROM or the Internet. Online interventions offer practical advantages over face-to-face treatment as they are accessible at any time and can preserve anonymity, so barriers associated with stigma and difficulty accessing services are reduced. Research into the use of cCBT for the treatment of anxiety and depression in children and adolescents is limited, but pilot studies have shown positive results regarding the treatment of anxiety through such programmes (e.g., *Cool Teens* CD-ROM, Cunningham *et al.*, 2009; *Think, Feel, Do* CD-ROM, Stallard, Richardson, Velleman, & Attwood, 2011). Preliminary outcomes demonstrated reductions in core symptoms. Abeles *et al.* (2009) conducted a case series of the programme *Stressbusters* with adolescents aged 12–16 with depression and found significant reductions in depression and anxiety, with improvements in global functioning and cognitions. O'Kearney, Kang, Christensen, and Griffiths (2009) used the programme *MoodGym* with a non-clinical population aged 15–16 and found a reduction in the number of those classed as at high risk for depression. Equally, a therapist-guided Internet intervention for the treatment of childhood anxiety, *BRAVE for children-ONLINE*, has produced promising outcomes with 75 per cent of participants free from primary anxiety disorders at six-month follow-up (March, Spence, & Donovan, 2009). The treatment group received regular support through email to maintain motivation and programme adherence.

Attwood *et al.* (2012) demonstrated that cCBT provided as a universal or targeted health intervention in schools is viable and may result in immediate therapeutic benefits for emotional problems in children and adolescents. The study was limited by a small sample size and absence of follow-up assessments but highlighted the potential for the use of cCBT as a structured school-based intervention that requires limited training and can be delivered by mental health non-professionals. Notably, the findings support previous work demonstrating that children and adolescents are satisfied with cCBT, often as much as face-to-face interventions (Cunningham *et al.*, 2009). Parents also tend to be positive towards the use of cCBT with children and can identify a number of benefits (Stallard, Velleman, & Richardson, 2010). However, child mental health professionals consider cCBT more effective as a supported intervention for mild and moderate problems rather than as a stand-alone intervention for more significant disorders (Stallard *et al.*, 2010). These resources do offer a good resource to schools which, with consistent promotion, could improve awareness and effective self-help in pupils.

Gaming

Increased attention is being given to the potential to leverage video game technologies to promote health-related behaviours (Papastergiou, 2009). An Internet resource based on mental health educational materials delivered as an online gaming programme, *Reach Out Central*, for young people (aged 16–25 years) has been evaluated for its ability to increase mental health literacy and help-seeking and reduce stigma (Shandley, Austin, Klein, & Kyrios, 2010). The gaming format is intended to allow for real-life scenarios through the process of role play for users to consider solutions to common problems and encourage practice of the skills introduced. Outcomes from the open trial revealed improvements in mental health literacy and help-seeking intentions, with significantly greater effect with female participants (Shandley *et al.*, 2010). Positive outcomes have also been demonstrated for another cCBT gaming resource *SPARX* (Merry *et al.*, 2012).

Apps and social networking

Apps – software specifically designed for and available on smartphones and tablets – have been enthusiastically embraced by the general public. Furthermore, smartphone apps are now found in almost every facet of conventional medicine including severe mental illness. They are increasingly recognised by policy-makers as a potential medium for self-management of health interventions (Ackerman *et al.*, 2010). Smartphone apps designed for self-assessments can help people assess and monitor symptoms and can also be programmed to auto-detect distress and, where appropriate, offer one-touch contact to a support hotline (Luxton, McCann, Bush, Mishkind, & Reger, 2011). Importantly, games are among the most frequently downloaded and used apps on the app markets. This trend could be extended to the downloading of behavioural health apps (Papastergiou, 2009). The unique capabilities of smartphones compared with traditional games consoles have the potential to improve the game experience by mixing real-world behaviours with software emulations. For example, a number of health apps combine GPS, compass and real-world viewing capabilities that overlay computer-generated information and stimuli to create augmented-reality experiences. Given the number of evidence-based interventions that include difficult real-world excursions for clients, there is high potential for engaging mental health apps that provide game motivations for desired behaviours. Kauer, Mangan, and Sanci (2014) found that adolescents will monitor their daily moods, stresses and other mental health factors with a mobile phone programme in order to share this information with their doctor. Apps for behavioural activation, exercise, and treatment of Obsessive Compulsive Disorder and anxiety could prove useful, but more research is needed.

However, the opportunity for app use can only be realised if they offer content and tools of appropriate quality. To date this is not the case for similar apps targeting smoking cessation, weight loss or asthma (e.g., Huckvale, Car, Morrison, & Car, 2012) and this should prompt caution in encouraging staff, health professionals and policy makers to think about their imminent introduction to the mental health arena. Apps are, and will remain, a rapidly evolving field, but the issues of content assessment, technology reliability and safety will also persist. The software poses a unique risk to patient confidentiality: one study found that 55 per cent of apps tested sent information such as demographics and contact information to other companies (Thurm & Kane, 2010). Currently, no oversight or standards for health-related smartphone apps exist and there is still a lack of published research. So while this is a rapidly developing area, the data-protection issues and variability in terms of safety of these resources might mean that as yet schools might want to hold back from very actively promoting them, though it is likely that evidence and guidance will improve rapidly.

The use of interactive tools such as forum, chat and message boards are often included in e-health interventions, but the important question of monitoring or mediation arises and how this is realised in light of the resource required. Similarly, social networking sites have both the potential to be health promoting and/or harmful. There have been many stories reported in the press of young people being encouraged to harm themselves/being bullied online.

The *Risk Awareness Management Programme (RAMP)* has produced a very helpful guide for those designing e-mental health platforms: *Delivering mental wellbeing online – A guide to the provision of safe and secure mental health*, which may be helpful for schools (info@rampguide.net).

Ongoing challenges

Stallard *et al.* (2010) conducted a review to assess the attitudes of adolescents and their parents towards computers and the Internet as a medium for the delivery of mental health interventions. Three-quarters of respondents expressed a preference to meet with a therapist face-to-face as opposed to using an unguided computer-based intervention. However, the help-seeking preferences of adolescents may be accounted for by previous negative experiences in relation to receiving unreliable information from such resources (Conlon, Power, Cleary, Guerin, & Fitzpatrick, 2010).

One problem for ICT-based interventions is drop-out; this appears to be more likely using computer mediated self-help resources than with traditional face-to-face services. For example, Christensen, Griffiths, Mackinnon, and Brittliffe (2006) found that only 7 per cent of spontaneous users of *MoodGym* progressed beyond module 2, and 40 per cent of these did not attempt any of the module assessments.

Security considerations are an often overlooked and underfunded aspect of the development, delivery and evaluation of e-mental health interventions, although they are often crucial to the overall success of any eHealth project (Bennett, Bennett, & Griffiths, 2010). The credibility and reliability of service delivery relies on a high standard of data security, especially given the highly stigmatised nature of mental illness. However, the increasing popularity and availability of e-mental health interventions over the past decade has prompted psychological societies across the world to develop specialised guidelines for psychologists engaged in such activities (e.g., British Psychological Society Professional Practice Board, 2009). These developments promote professional and ethical practices and are important for the protection of consumers of e-mental health interventions. However, the realisation of ethical standards is complicated in the realm of e-delivery. In particular, protection of consumer privacy and confidentiality, a central principle of professional psychological services, evolves into wide-ranging technical and nontechnical security considerations that need to be addressed. Notably, there are no statistics on the overall prevalence of different types of security breaches in the domain of e-health or e-mental health.

A final concern is how to offer Internet access to safe and reliable websites whilst reducing access to harmful sites such as those that are pro-anorexia, or promote self-harm and suicide and expose vulnerable young people to bullying and other abuse.

Conclusions

E-resources made available through schools have the potential to address shortfalls in young people's access to help for mental health problems. There is nevertheless a range of challenges to the use of such technology that need to be addressed to ensure effectiveness, online safety and confidentiality.

References

Abeles, P., Verduyn, C., Robinson, A., Smith, P., Yule, W., & Proudfoot, J. (2009). Computerized CBT for adolescent depression ('Stressbusters') and its initial evaluation through an extended case series. *Behavioural and Cognitive Psychotherapy*, *37*, 151–165.

Ackerman, M. J., Filart, R., Burgess, L. P., Lee, I., & Poropatich, R. K. (2010). Developing next generation telehealth tools and technologies: Patients, systems, and data perspectives. *Telemedicine Journal and E-Health*, *16*, 93–95.

Ahlen, J., Breitholtz, E., Barrett, P., & Gallegos, J. (2012). School-based prevention of anxiety and depression: A pilot study in Sweden. *Advances in School Mental Health Promotion*, *5*(4), 246–257.

Attwood, M., Meadows, S., Stallard, P., & Richardson, T. (2012). Universal and targeted computerised cognitive behavioural therapy (Think, Feel, Do) for emotional health in schools: Results from two exploratory studies. *Child and Adolescent Mental Health*, *17*(3), 173–178.

Barrett, P. M., & Ollendick, T. M. (2004). *Handbook of interventions that work with children and adolescents: Prevention and treatment*. New York: Wiley.

Barrett, P. M., & Pahl, K. M. (2006). School-based intervention: Examining a universal approach to anxiety management. *Australian Journal of Guidance & Counselling*, *16*, 55–75.

Bennett, K., Bennett, A. J., & Griffiths, K. M. (2010). Security considerations for E-mental health interventions. *Journal of Medical Internet Research*, *12*(5):e61.

Bowers, H., Manion, I., Papadopoulos, D., & Gauvreau, E. (2013). Stigma in school-based mental health: Perceptions of young people and service providers. *Child and Adolescent Mental Health*, *18*(3), 165–170.

British Psychological Society Professional Practice Board (2009). *The provision of psychological services via the internet and other non-direct means*, 2nd edn. Leicester: British Psychological Society.

Chandra, A., & Minkovitz, C. (2007). Factors that influence mental health stigma among 8th grade adolescents. *Journal of Youth and Adolescence*, *36*(6), 763–774.

Christensen, H., Griffiths, K. M., Mackinnon, A. J., & Brittliffe, K. (2006). Online randomized controlled trial of brief and full cognitive behaviour therapy for depression. *Psychological Medicine*, *36*(12), 1737–1746.

Conlon, A., Power, M., Cleary, D., Guerin, S., & Fitzpatrick, C. (2010). Help-seeking among Irish adolescents: Where would they turn? *Advances in School Mental Health Promotion*, *3*(3), 5–12.

Cunningham, M. J., Wuthrich, V. M., Rapee, R. M., Lyneham, H. J., Schniering, C. A., & Hudson, J. L. (2009). The cool teens CD-ROM for anxiety disorders in adolescents, a pilot care series. *European Child and Adolescent Psychiatry*, *18*(2), 125–129.

Gould, M. S., Harris Munfakh, J. L., Lubell, K., Kleinman, M., & Parker, S. (2002). Seeking help from the internet during adolescence. *Journal of the American Academy of Child and Adolescent Psychiatry*, *41*(10), 1182–1189.

Gulliver, A., Griffiths, K. M., & Christensen, H. (2010). Perceived barriers and facilitators to mental health help-seeking in young people: A systematic review. *BMC Psychiatry*, *10*, 113.

Huckvale, K., Car, M., Morrison, C., & Car, J. (2012). Apps for asthma self-management: A systematic assessment of content and tools. *BMC Medicine*, *10*, 144.

Kauer, S. D., Mangan, C., & Sanci, L. (2014). Do online mental health services improve help-seeking for young people? A systematic review. *Journal of Medical Internet Research*, *16*(3), e66.

Luxton, D. D., McCann, R. A., Bush, N. E. Mishkind, M. C., & Reger, G. M. (2011). mHealth for mental health: Integrating smartphone technology in behavioral healthcare. *Professional Psychology: Research and Practice*, *42*(6), 505–512.

March, S., Spence, S. H., & Donovan, C. L. (2009). The efficacy of an internet-based cognitive-behavioural therapy intervention for child anxiety disorders. *Journal of Paediatric Psychology*, *34*, 474–487.

Merry, S. N., Stasiak, K., Shepherd, M., Frampton, C., Fleming, T., & Lucassen, M. F. G. (2012). The effectiveness of SPARX, a computerised self help intervention for adolescents seeking help for depression: Randomised controlled non-inferiority trial. *BMJ*, *344*: e2598.

O'Kearney, R., Kang, K., Christensen, H., & Griffiths, K. (2009). A controlled trial of a school-based internet program for reducing depressive symptoms in adolescent girls. *Depression and Anxiety*, *26*(1), 65–72.

Papastergiou, M. (2009). Exploring the potential of computer and video games for health and physical education: A literature review. *Computers & Education*, *53*(3), 603–622.

Reavley, N. J., & Jorm, A. F. (2011). The quality of mental disorder websites: A review. *Patient Education and Counseling*, *85*, 273–277.

Richards, C., Gunning, M., Prescott, N., (2012). Healthy reading for children, young people and families in East Lothian, *Clinical Psychology Forum*, *234*, 39–44.

Rickwood, D. J., Deane, F. P., & Wilson, C. J. (2007). When and how do young people seek professional help for mental health problems? *Medical Journal of Australia*, *187*(7 Suppl): S35–S39.

Shandley, K., Austin, D., Klein, B., & Kyrios, M. (2010). An evaluation of 'Reach Out Central': An online gaming program for supporting the mental health of young people. *Health Education Research*, *25*(4), 563–574.

Stallard, P., Velleman, S., & Richardson, T. (2010). Computer use and attitudes towards computerised therapy amongst young people and parents attending child and adolescent mental health services. *Child and Adolescent Mental Health*, *15*(2), 80–84.

Stallard, P., Richardson, T., Velleman, S., & Attwood, M. (2011). Computerized CBT (Think, Feel, Do) for depression and anxiety in children and adolescents: Outcomes and feedback from a pilot randomized controlled trial. *Behavioural and Cognitive Psychotherapy*, *39*(3), 273–284.

Thurm, S., & Kane, Y. I. (2010). Your apps are watching you. *Wall Street Journal*. Retrieved 27.11.15 from http://online.wsj.com/article/SB10001424052748704694004576020083703574602.html

Vostanis, P., Humphrey, N., Fitzgerald, N., Deighton, J., & Wolpert, M. (2013).How do schools promote emotional well-being among their pupils? Findings from a national scoping survey of mental health provision in English schools. *Child and Adolescent Mental Health, 18*, 151–157.

Weare, K. (2013). Child and adolescent mental health in schools. *Child and Adolescent Mental Health*, *18*(3), 129–130.

Weems, C. F. & Stickle, T. R. (2005). Anxiety disorders in childhood: Casting a nomological net. *Clinical Child & Family Psychology Review*, *8*(2), 107–134.

Williams, B. & Pow, J. (2007). Gender differences and mental health: An exploratory study of knowledge and attitudes to mental health among Scottish teenagers. *Child and Adolescent Mental Health*, *12*(1), 8–12.

Young, M., Richards, C., & Gunning, M. (2012). Online mental health resources for teenagers: An evaluation of two websites developed for adolescents. *Advances in School Mental Health Promotion*, *5*(4), 277–289.

10

USING ONLINE ENVIRONMENTS TO BUILD SCHOOL STAFF CAPACITY TO ADDRESS STUDENT WELLBEING

Amy Barnes, Natasha Pearce, Donna Cross, Laura Thomas and Phillip T. Slee

Teachers and school executive teams are often required to address health and wellbeing issues affecting students' learning – issues that may have traditionally been considered the domain of families. Limited time and resources for professional learning may lead teachers to feel they lack sufficient knowledge and skills to adequately address the challenges facing children and young people, and may ultimately lead to a school culture that does not (or students perceive that it does not) adequately care for students. Data from three longitudinal research projects forming part of a program of cyber-safety research suggest that the professional development of school staff can be enhanced with carefully developed and delivered online learning resources, though these have yet to be fully exploited.

The challenge

In their formal and informal provision of pastoral care in the school environment, all teachers and school executive teams are required to address health and wellbeing issues affecting student learning. However, a limited awareness of their specific role in contributing to students' wellbeing, as well as competing demands and few resources for professional learning, means many teachers feel they lack sufficient knowledge and skills to address the ongoing and nascent challenges facing young people (Barnes *et al.*, 2012).

The impact of peer bullying on students' social and emotional wellbeing, and its recent emergence in cyber contexts, presents school staff with particularly complex and difficult issues. Limited staff capacity to prevent and resolve such incidents is a significant barrier to schools' success in implementing cyberbullying interventions, and may contribute to a school culture that tolerates bullying (Cross *et al.*, 2015a). This chapter will describe comprehensive research conducted since 2008 to determine Australian teachers' necessary and preferred modes of capacity building, including online professional learning, to support students' wellbeing in relation to bullying.

Background

Cyberbullying

Schools' primary goals are to educate and develop academic competencies among children and adolescents, yet teachers and other staff are frequently confronted by health and wellbeing issues affecting young people's learning outcomes. A lack of time, support and relevant knowledge, training or resources is likely to limit staff's capacity to consistently and adequately promote student wellbeing. In particular, the increasing centrality of digital technology in the lives of young people poses unique challenges, with greater opportunities for both positive and negative peer interactions in cyber contexts.

In Australia, mobile phones are owned by 22 per cent of children aged 9–11 years and 73 per cent of those aged 12–14 (Australian Bureau of Statistics, 2012), as well as by over 90 per cent of Australians aged 15 years or more (Australian Communications and Media Authority, 2010). The number of Australian children and young people with household Internet access has grown to 96 per cent of households (Australian Bureau of Statistics, 2014). As access to these technologies has increased, 'cyberbullying' has emerged as a particularly damaging form of psychological covert aggression (Cross *et al.*, 2009). Cyberbullying occurs when an individual or group uses Information and Communication Technologies (ICT) to intentionally and repeatedly harm a person, who finds it hard to stop this bullying from continuing (Smith *et al.*, 2008). Such behaviours include sending nasty or threatening messages via the Internet or mobile devices, posting images or videos of others without their consent, and deliberately excluding or impersonating others in online settings (Cross *et al.*, 2009).

In contrast to face-to-face bullying, the limits of cyberbullying are difficult to define. For instance, a single image or message can be forwarded to innumerable people, while an aggressor can remain unidentified by using multiple profiles, thus maintaining anonymity and making it harder for the victim to defend themselves or escape. Furthermore, cyberbullying behaviours can change and assume new forms according to different interactional settings, highlighting both the overt and covert nature of these behaviours (Spears, Kofoed, Bartolo, Palermiti, & Costabile, 2011). In Australia, a national study found that over one-quarter (27 per cent) of Australian students aged 8–14 years were bullied, and 9 per cent bullied others, on a frequent basis (every few weeks or more often) (Cross *et al.*, 2009).

Those targeted by bullying and cyberbullying, and those who cyberbully others, are at heightened risk of mental health issues (including low self-esteem, depression, anxiety, and suicidal ideation), psychosomatic symptoms and poorer physical health, absenteeism and reduced academic achievement, substance abuse, and other antisocial behaviours (e.g. Kowalski & Limber, 2013; Landstedt & Persson, 2014). Finally, witnesses to bullying can also experience harm; their likelihood of reporting symptoms of depression, anxiety and interpersonal sensitivity is heightened (Rivers, Noret, Poteat, & Ashurst, 2009). Bullying therefore significantly impacts upon young people's social and emotional wellbeing, as well as their capacity for learning, and is thus of concern to all school community members.

School staff nevertheless face challenges in detecting cyberbullying behaviours and knowing how to respond. Staff may have limited access, for example, to young people's online spaces, and students who experience cyberbullying often tell no one for fear of having their computers or mobile phones confiscated (Patchin & Hinduja, 2006). Students may also believe that adults will be unable to help, or that their intervention will exacerbate the bullying (Bauman & Del Rio, 2006). When school staff do become aware of concerning behaviours, they may struggle to determine whether these behaviours should be considered cyberbullying and how best to resolve the situation (Bauman & Del Rio, 2006). Given cyberbullying occurs across both home and school environments, it is difficult for staff to know when and how they should intervene (Shariff, 2005).

Further, many Australian teachers feel unskilled to address student cyberbullying, with fewer than 10 per cent of secondary school staff reporting they feel very skilled, and 50 per cent feeling not at all or poorly skilled to do so (Barnes *et al.*, 2012). This is concerning, as self-efficacy to address bullying is associated with the likelihood of effective intervention (Bradshaw, Sawyer, & O'Brennan, 2007). A lack of appropriate responses to bullying may lead young people to perceive that their school does not care for their safety and wellbeing.

School capacity to address cyberbullying

Bullying behaviours are complex social phenomena; school-based interventions therefore require a systematic approach to create a culture that promotes positive relationships and builds social skills at all levels of the school community. This approach includes: clear policies and procedures for promoting social skills and preventing/managing bullying behaviours; social and emotional focused student learning; activities that build positive relationships between students, teachers and families; a physical environment organised to promote positive behaviours and provide engaged teacher supervision; and robust partnerships with parents, support services and the wider community (Pearce, Cross, Monks, Waters, & Falconer, 2011).

School capacity to implement this whole-school approach is influenced by individual, organisational, community, and system-level factors (Domitrovich *et al.*, 2008). Contextual factors including school and classroom climates, leadership and decision-making structures and personal expertise, as well as school characteristics such as size, location, student mobility and physical environment, contribute to the likelihood of teachers prioritising student wellbeing and being confident to take appropriate actions. Further, community or system-level factors such as government and community policies and financing, and the perceived complexity and adaptability of intervention strategies (Durlak & DuPre, 2008), may also affect school capacity to address student wellbeing. In Australia, the National Safe Schools Framework (NSSF) provides significant support and resources to address bullying in all forms, but as the Cross, Epstein, Hearn, Slee, *et al.* (2011) study demonstrated, there are significant shortfalls in school and staff awareness and use of this resource. At the individual level, factors including teachers' levels of skill and competency, their professional characteristics (e.g., experience and education), their perceptions of the likely benefits and challenges of change to school practices, and whether these changes are compatible with current school values may influence their willingness to implement a bullying prevention program (Rogers, 2010).

While working with Australian schools to implement bullying prevention programs, the authors identified a need to improve capacity among individual staff, and at the whole-school level, to enhance student wellbeing by reducing bullying.

New perspectives and responses

Three longitudinal research projects comprising part of an extensive program of cyber-safety research were conducted by the authors over six years. These three-to-five-year projects included the *Strong Schools Safe Kids* project; the *Cyber Friendly Schools Project*; and the *Cyber Strong Schools* project.

Data from the *Friendly Schools* and *Supportive Schools* suite of research studies (Child Health Promotion Research Centre, 2008; Cross *et al.*, 2010; Cross *et al.*, 2012), conducted by some of the authors in 2000–2007, identified that while schools and teachers were keen to promote student social and emotional learning and reduce bullying, they often lacked the pre-service and in-service professional learning to adequately teach and provide support in this area. Supporting resources, such as the *Friendly Schools* curriculum, were necessary but not sufficient to secure effective implementation. Teachers required more training than was typically available or that they were able to attend. Consequently, teachers often 'cherry-picked' learning activities related to their levels of expertise, rather than implementing all those necessary for positive behaviour change in students.

The following case studies therefore describe in more detail the key learnings that informed the development of online professional learning for school staff.

Strong Schools Safe Kids Project (SSSK)

This is a longitudinal, multi-site case-study research project, involving seven schools (2010–2014). The project focused on developing capacity at the individual, school and system level to deliver a whole-school approach called *Friendly Schools Plus*, designed to address students' social and emotional learning and bullying in Australian schools.

The *Friendly Schools Plus* (FS+) approach was developed based on findings from four randomised control longitudinal studies involving over 12,000 students (one targeting early childhood, two targeting primary school students, and one targeting secondary school students). Empirical and process findings from these studies and several others, including a large seven-year project focusing on Aboriginal students' needs (Coffin, Larson, & Cross, 2010), was used to refine the FS+ resources. The result was a universal, school-based intervention targeting students aged 5–15 years, and their teachers and families. The intervention aimed to prevent bullying in school environments by enhancing students' social and emotional learning through comprehensive implementation of whole-school evidence-based policy and practice.

The development of *FS+* has, from its outset, featured implementation supports such as training, coaching, planning and assessment tools aiming to build school and teacher implementation capacity. However, despite these supports, study schools still reported capacity and implementation challenges, such as difficulty modifying their policies and practices to include cyberbullying or in managing bullying incidents.

The *SSSK* project utilised qualitative methodology, with case-study schools as naturalistic settings observed to determine how they used a systematic implementation process and capacity-building resources (enhanced and tested as part of the *SSSK* project) to assess their strengths and needs, to select evidence-based practices and to implement change to enhance social and emotional learning and reduce bullying. Regular *SSSK* project feedback loops between the case-study schools and the researchers identified key factors affecting the quality of policy and practice implementation. This feedback contributed to the re-development and refinement of a five-stage implementation process (Figure 10.1). School executive teams were responsible for facilitating this process and selecting strategies aligned with their school's strengths and needs.

During the *SSSK* study, however, it was evident that school executive teams faced continuing challenges in building school capacity, particularly in helping staff prepare for changes to current practice, and providing timely (often 'in the moment') access to support tools. Professional learning support was therefore needed. However, whilst face-to-face trainings are an effective way to build understandings and competencies, barriers to Australian teachers accessing face-to-face professional learning are significant (e.g., the high costs of teacher relief). In the *SSSK* project, school executive teams attended face-to-face training and were then responsible for taking these learnings back to their teaching staff. However, they reported difficulties in transferring this knowledge in a format that was feasible, memorable and valued by staff.

Members of the case-study schools suggested online environments as an alternative, cost-effective mechanism to deliver professional learning and support. These environments would allow flexibility in access and delivery, being available whenever staff were ready to learn and put skills into action. In response to this demand, the *SSSK* project's capacity-building tools were transformed into an online implementation management system to guide school executive teams through the five-stage process, as well as to collate school practice assessment and student and staff survey data. These online tools provided schools with timely access to training and resources for facilitating staff engagement, and allowed teams to plan, monitor and review progress and success via a *Friendly Schools* website (www.friendly schools.com.au).

FIGURE 10.1 The five-stage implementation process for *Strong Schools Safe Kids*

Maintaining the currency of information was found to be both a challenge and opportunity in the online delivery of professional learning. The dynamic nature of online environments means they can be updated regularly, but this process requires ongoing monitoring and funding to ensure resources are maintained and up to date. To ensure currency and sustainability, the *SSSK* project and the *FS+* research teams work in partnership with a purveyor (publishing company Hawker Brownlow Education Pty Ltd), who provide the platform and ongoing support to deliver resources and training supports to schools commercially.

Whilst the *SSSK* project thus provided a broad whole-school approach and tools to build schools' and teachers' capacity to address bullying, it became evident during the project that the area of greatest need among schools and teachers was cyber-safety and *cyberbullying-specific* capacity supports for teachers. This cyber-specific need was addressed on two levels; first via an extensive series of formative research projects culminating in a randomised control intervention trial, the *Cyber Friendly*

Schools Project (*CFSP*). The *CFSP* was then expanded with a teacher capacity-building project called the *Cyber Strong Schools* project. Both projects are described as follows.

Cyber Friendly Schools Project (CFSP)

This was a group randomised controlled trial conducted from 2010 to 2012. It assessed the impact of a whole-school cyberbullying prevention and intervention program on cyber-victimisation and perpetration among 3,400 adolescents from 35 randomly selected schools (Cross, Epstein, Hearn, & Waters, 2011). Both control and intervention schools implemented the *Friendly Schools* resources, with emphasis on cyberbullying. In the intervention condition, the *CFSP* whole-school intervention strategies focused on: enhancing teaching and learning about pro-social behaviours through curriculum; assisting staff to implement strategies related to their school's organisational context; providing a consistent understanding of cyberbullying with strategies to support and develop students' social relationships and peer support; policy development and implementation (e.g. mobile phone, IT policy) involving the school community; attention to school ethos and culture development; strategies to support students' social and emotional development; positive behaviour-management strategies; and school-home-community links. In addition, schools in the intervention group received the online whole-school (including parents) and student-level resources in Grades 8 and 9 (aged 13–14 years).

The three years of formative research indicated that teachers had limited skills and capacity to teach cyber-safety to their students, often seeking external parties to deliver this content. Further, teachers did not have the time required to enhance their skills and knowledge to what they thought was the requisite level. Accordingly, the *CFSP* intervention was designed to require only limited teacher expertise. The classroom resources, for example, were developed so that students could complete these in a self-directed manner. Student leaders (one to two years older than the study cohort) were also recruited and trained to support school staff to promote and implement whole-school level strategies, and face-to-face training was provided to pastoral care staff.

The *CFSP* intervention was associated with small but significant declines from Grade 8 to Grade 9 in the proportion of students being cyberbullied and those cyberbullying others, compared to the comparison schools (Cross *et al.*, 2015b). However, the major process finding was that teachers did not provide sufficient time for students to access the online activities (on average, schools implemented three of the nine modules of activities) due to a crowded curriculum, but also because of a lack of confidence to engage with resources in this area. Similarly, the whole-school teams, though supported by student cyber leaders, implemented only minor changes to school policies and practices. Hence, it appeared that schools continued to struggle with insufficient skills and support to implement bullying prevention strategies. The *CFSP* teachers reported they needed more accessible, personal and practical opportunities to develop expertise in the cyber environment to enhance their teaching in this area. This became the research goal of the *Cyber Strong Schools* project conducted in 2012–2013.

Cyber Strong Schools project

The *Cyber Strong Schools* (*CSS*) project developed a resource targeting teachers, with variable computer literacy, to build their capacity to implement student-focused cyber-safety programs in the classroom. The project was highly formative and engaged stakeholders, school staff and students to identify critical factors for building staff capacity to actively engage in the positive uses of ICT. The design enabled validation of resource content to confirm its relevance, practicality and usefulness to school staff, and ensured the content was tested with and could be easily accessed by school staff.

Phase 1 involved formal consultation with stakeholders, and collection of descriptive and observational data to identify the strengths and needs of teachers and other school staff. This included: a) teachers completing online surveys and participating in interviews; b) focus groups with government and non-government agencies; and c) extensive observational research with students. The major outcome was an outline of the key content to be included in the online resource and how this content linked to support provided by other agencies. This informed the content and delivery mechanisms for the online teacher cyber-safety capacity-building resource.

During Phase 2, the online resource was developed and various hard-copy iterations checked with school staff and students to ensure their usefulness and feasibility. Professional expertise in designing online resources was also obtained to ensure the resource was appropriate for an online environment. The final version was then developed by these experts into an online resource.

Phase 3 comprised the formal pilot testing of the resource in its online format with teachers. All teacher reviewers were asked to trial and provide feedback on specific sections in the context of the overall resource, to ensure all of the resource was piloted effectively. Interestingly, a major finding of this development and dissemination process was that the content was found to be relevant to all adults who spend time with young people, including parents.

Following this pilot process, the online resource was modified and disseminated through the *Friendly Schools* website. The final version of the *CSS* project, available in the teacher section at www.friendlyschools.com.au, included online capacity-building resource modules targeting school staff knowledge and competences, whole-school policies and practices, and professional challenges that may emerge for educators when interacting with social media, as well as providing background information about young people's use of social media, and a student leadership/staff support package to encourage young people to become school leaders in the reduction of cyber harms.

Benefits and challenges of online learning environments

While professional learning enables school staff to learn and enhance their skills to support student wellbeing, particularly important when addressing student behaviours associated with online and cyber environments, the opportunities and challenges associated with such environments expand and change rapidly. Teachers' access to professional learning to enhance and update their knowledge is often limited, however, by heavy workloads, competing demands, the poor availability and high cost of training, or a lack of support from school executive teams. As discussed above, such challenges can be addressed using online learning environments, which provide flexible and timely access to information.

As noted by Duncan-Howell (2010), staff can adjust the time spent in online environments according to other demands, and school staff may have flexibility to access only those portions of information related to their immediate interests or concerns, helping ensure the content of the learning material is relevant and useful (Duncan-Howell, 2010; Fishman *et al.*, 2013). Ongoing access to online material also allows staff to review and re-engage with information, and focus on issues of most relevance at a particular time (Fishman *et al.*, 2013). Learning, skill development and problem solving can thus occur quickly and in an engaging manner, particularly if the online environment is interactive and provides opportunities for discussion (Duncan-Howell, 2010).

The comparative effectiveness of face-to-face and online professional learning appears to support the value of online learning for school staff. In a study of secondary school teachers involved in face-to-face or online professional development, those in both conditions demonstrated improvements in self-efficacy to teach and knowledge of their teaching material, and in both conditions this professional development extended to improved student learning outcomes (Fishman *et al.*, 2013). Importantly, the researchers identified considerable variety in the extent to which teachers in the online condition spent time engaging with the material, but such differences were not significantly associated with student outcomes. This suggests that participants engaged with online material only as required, reducing the amount of time spent on learning that was not currently relevant or needed (Fishman *et al.*, 2013). Teachers in the online condition were also more likely to refer back to professional development materials when teaching, emphasising the value of making online professional learning available and accessible in a flexible and timely manner.

Empirical data to establish the effectiveness of online learning for school staff is currently limited, however, so it is unclear whether such positive findings extend to other professional learning programs and contexts (Moon, Passmore, Reiser, & Michaels, 2014). Further, online learning environments may offer limited opportunities for engaging with other teachers and developing a sense of collegiality – characteristics identified as highly important to school staff (Duncan-Howell, 2010). Nevertheless, the opportunities provided by online learning environments may balance out this loss of peer engagement (Fishman *et al.*, 2013). Further, the inclusion of online opportunities for networking and coaching-style discussion may help to mitigate the loss of face-to-face contact with instructors and peers, even extending this contact by providing opportunities to engage with school staff who would otherwise be inaccessible due to location or time restraints.

Conclusion

There is a clear need for targeted and responsive online professional learning resources for school staff to build and maintain relevant knowledge and skills to meet the needs of children and young people, particularly in relation to bullying and cyberbullying. Online learning environments offer dynamic and flexible opportunities for learning and have garnered much interest from educators and other adult learners as a place to meet their spontaneous and/or sustained learning needs.

It should nevertheless be remembered that whilst teacher capacity-building and professional learning are essential to support quality implementation of school practices, these alone are insufficient to ensure positive impact on student wellbeing (Fixsen, Naoom, Blase, Friedman, & Wallace, 2005; Roberts-Gray, Gingiss, & Boerm, 2007). A proactive approach to building school capacity that targets leadership, competencies and organisational supports is required to assist teachers, parents, students and the broader community to implement student wellbeing and bullying prevention strategies, and to overcome existing barriers to the implementation of research evidence into real-world practice.

References

Australian Bureau of Statistics (2012). *Children's participation in cultural and leisure activities, Australia, Apr 2012*. Cat. no. 4901.0. Canberra: ABS.

Australian Bureau of Statistics (2014). *Household use of information technology, Australia, 2012–13*. Cat. no. 8146.0. Canberra: ABS.

Australian Communications and Media Authority (2010). *Trends in media use by young people: Insights from the Kaiser Family Foundation's Generation M2 2009 (USA), and results from the ACMA's Media and communication in Australian families 2007*. Canberra: Australian Communications and Media Authority (ACMA).

Barnes, A., Cross, D., Lester, L., Hearn, L., Epstein, M., & Monks, H. (2012). The invisibility of covert bullying among students: Challenges for school intervention. *Australian Journal of Guidance and Counselling, 22*(2), 206–226.

Bauman, S., & Del Rio, A. (2006). Preservice teachers' responses to bullying scenarios: Comparing physical, verbal, and relational bullying. *Journal of Educational Psychology, 98*(1), 219–231.

Bradshaw, C. P., Sawyer, A. L., & O'Brennan, L. M. (2007). Bullying and peer victimization at school: Perceptual differences between students and school staff. *School Psychology Review, 36*(3), 361–382.

Child Health Promotion Research Centre (2008). *A randomised trial to reduce bullying and other aggressive behaviours in secondary schools, final report*. Perth: Edith Cowan University.

Coffin, J., Larson, A., & Cross, D. (2010). Bullying in an Aboriginal Context. *Australian Journal of Indigenous Education, 39*(1), 77–87.

Cross, D., Epstein, M., Hearn, L., Slee, P. T., Shaw, T., Monks, H., & Schwartz, T. (2011). National safe schools framework: Policy and practice to reduce bullying in Australian schools. *International Journal of Behavioural Development, 35*(5), 398–404.

Cross, D., Epstein, M., Hearn, L., & Waters, S. (2011). *Cyber Friendly Parents' Project: Final report to the Telstra Foundation*. Perth, Western Australia: Edith Cowan University, Child Health Promotion Research Centre.

Cross, D., Monks, H., Hall, M., Shaw, T., Pintabona, Y., Erceg, E., Hamilton, G., Roberts, C., Waters, S., & Lester, L. (2010). Three-year results of the Friendly Schools whole-of-school intervention on children's bullying behaviour. *British Educational Research Journal, 37*(1), 105–129.

Cross, D., Shaw, T., Barnes, A., Monks, H., Pearce, N., & Epstein, M. (2015a). Evaluating the capacity of Australian school staff to recognise and respond to cyberbullying behaviours. *Les dossiers des Sciences de l'Education, 33*, 91–108.

Cross, D., Shaw, T., Hadwen, K., Cardoso, P., Slee, P., Roberts, C., Thomas, L., Barnes, A. (2015b) Longitudinal impact of the Cyber Friendly Schools intervention on adolescents' cyberbullying behavior. Aggressive Behavior. DOI: 10.1002/ab.21609. Accessed 03.02.2016 at http://onlinelibrary.wiley.com/doi/10.1002/ab.21609/full

Cross, D., Shaw, T., Hearn, L., Epstein, M., Monks, H., Lester, L., & Thomas, L. (2009). *Australian Covert Bullying Prevalence Study (ACBPS)*. Western Australia: Report prepared for the Department of Education, Employment and Workplace Relations (DEEWR).

Cross, D., Waters, S., Pearce, N., Shaw, T., Hall, M., Erceg, E., Burns, S., Roberts, C., & Hamilton, G. (2012). The Friendly Schools Friendly Families programme: Three-year bullying behaviour outcomes in primary school children. *International Journal of Educational Research, 53*, 394–406.

Domitrovich, C. E., Bradshaw, C. P., Poduska, J. M., Hoagwood, K., Buckley, J. A., Olin, S., Romanelli, L. H., Leaf, P. J., Greenberg, M. T., & Ialongo, N. S. (2008). Maximizing the implementation quality of evidence-based preventive interventions in schools: A conceptual framework. *Advances in School Mental Health Promotion, 1*(3), 6–28.

Duncan-Howell, J. (2010). Teachers making connections: Online communities as a source of professional learning. *British Journal of Educational Technology, 41*(2), 324–340.

Durlak, J. A., & DuPre, E. P. (2008). Implementation matters: A review of research on the influence of implementation on program outcomes and the factors affecting implementation. *American Journal of Community Psychology, 41*(3–4), 327–350.

Fishman, B., Konstantopoulos, S., Kubitskey, B. W., Vath, R., Park, G., Johnson, H., & Edelson, D. C. (2013). Comparing the impact of online and face-to-face professional development in the context of curriculum implementation. *Journal of Teacher Education, 64*(5), 426–438.

Fixsen, D. L., Naoom, S. F., Blase, K. A., Friedman, R. M., & Wallace, F. (2005). *Implementation research: A synthesis of the literature*. Tampa, FL: National Implementation Research Network, Louis de la Parte Florida Mental Health Institute, University of South Florida.

Kowalski, R. M., & Limber, S. P. (2013). Psychological, physical, and academic correlates of cyberbullying and traditional bullying. *Journal of Adolescent Health, 53*(1), S13–S20.

Landstedt, E., & Persson, S. (2014). Bullying, cyberbullying, and mental health in young people. *Scandinavian Journal of Public Health*, Published online, DOI 10.1177/1403 494814525004, 1–7.

Moon, J., Passmore, C., Reiser, B. J., & Michaels, S. (2014). Beyond comparisons of online versus face-to-Face PD. Commentary in response to Fishman *et al.*, "Comparing the impact of online and face-to-face professional development in the context of curriculum implementation". *Journal of Teacher Education, 65*(2), 172–176.

Patchin, J. W., & Hinduja, S. (2006). Bullies move beyond the schoolyard: A preliminary look at cyberbullying. *Youth Violence and Juvenile Justice, 4*(2), 148–169.

Pearce, N., Cross, D., Monks, H., Waters, S., & Falconer, S. (2011). Current evidence of best practice in whole-school bullying intervention and its potential to inform cyber-bullying interventions. *Australian Journal of Guidance and Counselling, 21*(1), 1–21.

Rivers, I., Noret, N., Poteat, V., & Ashurst, N. (2009). Observing bullying at school: The mental health implications of witness status. *School Psychology Quarterly, 24*(4), 211–223.

Roberts-Gray, C., Gingiss, P. M., & Boerm, M. (2007). Evaluating school capacity to implement new programs. *Evaluation and Program Planning, 30*, 247–257.

Rogers, E. M. (2010). *Diffusion of innovations.* New York: Simon and Schuster.

Shariff, S. (2005). Cyber-dilemmas in the new millennium: School obligations to provide student safety in a virtual school environment. *The McGill Journal of Education, 40*(3), 467–487.

Smith, P. K., Mahdavi, J., Carvalho, M., Fisher, S., Russell, S., & Tippett, N. (2008). Cyberbullying: Its nature and impact in secondary school pupils. *Journal of Child Psychology and Psychiatry, 49*(4), 376–385.

Spears, B. A., Kofoed, J., Bartolo, M. G., Palermiti, A., & Costabile, A. (2011). Positive uses of social networking sites: Youth voice perspectives. In A. Costabile & B. Spears (Eds.), *The impact of technology on relationships in educational settings* (pp. 7–21). London: Routledge.

SECTION 5
Targeted interventions

11

MENTAL HEALTH PROMOTION AND STUDENTS WITH DISABILITIES

The need for targeted interventions

Jane M. Jarvis and Julie M. McMillan

This chapter discusses key issues and challenges related to supporting mental health promotion for students with disabilities and special educational needs in Australian schools. We present a multi-tiered framework connecting school-wide approaches to mental health promotion, positive behaviour support, and academic learning that has shown considerable promise internationally, and consider how such a framework might be applied to support positive mental health outcomes for students in Australian schools, with a focus on students with disabilities.

The challenge

Schools are uniquely placed to lay the foundations for positive mental health and to respond to early signs of mental health difficulties in children and young people, particularly through sustained, whole-school approaches that combine universal and targeted interventions (Weare & Nind, 2011). In Australia, whole-school mental health promotion typically represents a preventive, ecological approach, which is consistent with the World Health Organization's (WHO) definition of mental health as more than simply the absence of disease or difficulty, but "a state of well-being in which the individual realises his or her own abilities, can cope with the normal stresses of life, can work productively and fruitfully, and is able to make a contribution to his or her community" (2004, p. 1). Universal interventions aim to enhance the capacity of all children and young people to effectively navigate challenges through a focus on social-emotional learning and wellbeing, developing personal psychological resources such as resilience, and fostering safe and supportive school communities (Slee, Dix & Askell-Williams, 2011).

Within whole-school approaches, supporting positive mental health outcomes for students with disabilities and special educational needs is emerging as a significant challenge for Australian schools and educators. There is growing evidence that individuals with disabilities are at heightened risk of developing mental health difficulties (e.g., McMillan & Jarvis, 2013), but until recently they have been overlooked as an at-risk population. There is a need for increased attention to the specific mental health needs of students with disabilities in school mental health promotion, and for the development of an Australian evidence base of effective practices.

To what extent are Australian schools and education systems equipped to understand and support the mental health needs of students with disabilities and special educational needs? The challenge is complex and multifaceted. Addressing the challenge entails recognising the inextricable links between teaching and learning, behaviour support, and student wellbeing (Jarvis, 2011); efforts to promote student wellbeing and positive mental health must articulate with efforts to build excellence in teaching and learning and positive behaviour support in a context of school-wide inclusive practices. Traditionally, these areas tend to be treated in isolation using different intervention models by professionals from different fields of expertise (Eber, Weist, & Barrett, 2013). Achieving an effective, coherent approach will involve careful consideration of issues including staffing, professional learning, teaching practices, models of special education service delivery, models of mental health intervention, and integration between multiple services and supports.

Background

Mental health is influenced by complex interactions between personal and environmental factors over time. Students with disabilities are by no means a homogeneous group, and the relationship between disability and mental health outcomes varies widely both within and between specific disability groups. While the federal *Disability Discrimination Act* employs a deliberately broad definition of disability that includes psychiatric, physical, sensory and intellectual disability, schools and education systems in Australia have employed more restrictive definitions in determining eligibility for additional funding and disability support. Discrepant definitions and data-collection methods across Australia and internationally make it difficult to accurately document and compare outcomes for students with disabilities.

From 2015, all Australian schools will be required to report against a common definition of disability, encompassing categories of physical (including neurological), cognitive, sensory and social-emotional disability. Currently, the term 'disability' is used in most jurisdictions to encompass students with intellectual and developmental disabilities, autism spectrum disorders, speech and/or language disabilities, and physical and sensory disabilities, while those with specific learning difficulties such as dyslexia, dyscalculia and non-verbal learning disability, and those with emotional and behavioural disorders, usually do not meet eligibility criteria for disability support in schools. In this chapter, we use the phrase 'students with disabilities and special educational needs' to encompass both those students currently considered to have a disability according to more restrictive eligibility-based definitions, and those who are not, but are likely to have identifiable needs for additional educational support.

Approximately one in twelve Australian children (8.3 per cent) are identified as having a disability, and close to 90 per cent of those are educated full time or close to full time in mainstream schools (Australian Institute of Health and Welfare, 2008). In addition, between 10 per cent and 25 per cent of school-age children experience learning disabilities or specific learning difficulties, depending on the definition used (Westwood, 2011). There is growing evidence that individuals with disabilities are more likely than those without disabilities to experience mental health difficulties; the pattern of increased risk begins to emerge from a young age, continues into adulthood, and has been documented across disability types (MAC: SWD, 2007). For example, an evaluation of the *KidsMatter Primary Mental Health Initiative* in South Australian schools found students with an identified disability to have a one in three chance of experiencing mental health problems, compared to a one in eight chance for students without a disability, while for students with more than one disability the risk increased to one in two (Dix, Shearer, Slee, & Butcher, 2010). Similarly, a national evaluation of *KidsMatter Early Childhood* showed that young children without a disability had a one in six chance of experiencing mental health difficulties, while those with a disability had a one in four chance; for young children with more than one disability, the risk increased to one in two (Dix, Jarvis, & Slee, 2013).

Research has highlighted a range of factors associated with mental health outcomes for students with disabilities, including individual temperament, family circumstances, quality of relationships with educators, exposure to bullying and ostracism, quality of peer interactions and relationships, experiences of abuse, capacity to communicate effectively, community and educator attitudes, quality of educational supports and services, and access to effective early intervention (McMillan & Jarvis, 2013). Students with disabilities that affect their educational achievement may be at particular risk. Educational achievement has long been recognised as fundamental to positive post-school outcomes such as employment, access to community and health services, and social and emotional wellbeing, whereas poor educational achievement has been associated with poverty and social exclusion, which are recognised as strong predictors of mental health difficulties. Some students with disabilities may be marginalised by mainstream educational systems due to a combination of learning difficulties and the social, emotional and behavioural difficulties associated with their disability, placing them at increased risk for poor mental health outcomes.

The relationship between disability and mental health is not straightforward, and having a disability is not an inevitable pathway to mental health difficulties. It is important to acknowledge each individual's range of strengths, interests and opportunities for positive growth given an enabling set of circumstances. Further, contextualised research is needed to move beyond documenting increased risk to better understand the combined impact of personal and environmental factors for students of different ages and in different disability groups in Australian schools.

However, it is essential for educators to acknowledge the potentially heightened need for targeted mental health support for students with disabilities and special educational needs, and to apply this knowledge in the design of school-based mental health initiatives.

Addressing the challenge: The Integrated Systems Framework

Consistent with a preventive, ecological approach to mental health promotion, contemporary research emphasises the use of naturalistic resources within schools to implement and sustain effective, integrated supports that address learning, behaviour and mental health (Atkins, Hoagwood, Kutash, & Seidman, 2010). There is a growing recognition of the need for improved mental health outcomes for all students, including those considered at risk and those with indicated mental health difficulties.

In the United States, the OSEP Technical Assistance Center on Positive Behavioral Interventions and Supports (PBIS) and the Center for School Mental Health (CSMH) have recognised the need for an integrated model which addresses the reciprocal nature of academic achievement and social, emotional and behavioural difficulties for all students. The two centres have recently collaborated to develop the Interconnected Systems Framework (ISF) for school mental health (Barrett, Eber, & Weist, 2012). A recently published monograph on the ISF described an impressive collaborative effort between school systems, researchers and practitioners in implementing established frameworks of school-wide positive behaviour intervention and supports (SWPBIS) and school mental health (SMH) (Barrett, Eber, & Weist, 2013). A shared agenda is executed through cross-system leadership, characterised by a common language and approach to addressing school and community needs (Barrett, Eber, & Weist, 2013). This monograph is the first of its kind to bring together disciplines to address the mental health needs of all students, including those with disabilities and special needs in a multi-tiered system of supports.

Consistent with other ecological approaches, foundational principles of the ISF reflect a shift from treating the individual with the goal of symptom reduction, to improving functioning by examining the learning context and environmental impact on emotional health, behaviour and learning, and promoting collaboration between families, schools, mental health and community services. The shared agenda for all stakeholders is represented in a three-tiered system of mental health promotion, prevention and intervention (Figure 11.1). Tier I involves universal approaches aimed at preventing occurrences of problems and promoting positive mental health. Tier II, targeted prevention, is aimed at preventing risk factors (targeted selective) or early-onset problems (targeted-indicated) from progressing. Tier III is aimed at reducing the intensity and duration of symptoms that may be associated with disorder (indicated) or difficulty.

Interconnected Systems Framework for School Mental Health

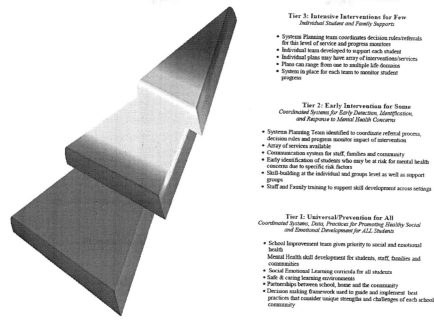

Tier 3: Intensive Interventions for Few
Individual Student and Family Supports

- Systems Planning team coordinates decision rules/referrals for this level of service and progress monitors
- Individual team developed to support each student
- Individual plans may have array of interventions/services
- Plans can range from one to multiple life domains
- System in place for each team to monitor student progress

Tier 2: Early Intervention for Some
Coordinated Systems for Early Detection, Identification, and Response to Mental Health Concerns

- Systems Planning Team identified to coordinate referral process, decision rules and progress monitor impact of intervention
- Array of services available
- Communication system for staff, families and community
- Early identification of students who may be at risk for mental health concerns due to specific risk factors
- Skill-building at the individual and groups level as well as support groups
- Staff and Family training to support skill development across settings

Tier I: Universal/Prevention for All
Coordinated Systems, Data, Practices for Promoting Healthy Social and Emotional Development for ALL Students

- School Improvement team gives priority to social and emotional health
  Mental Health skill development for students, staff, families and communities
- Social Emotional Learning curricula for all students
- Safe & caring learning environments
- Partnerships between school, home and the community
- Decision making framework used to guide and implement best practices that consider unique strengths and challenges of each school community

FIGURE 11.1 Interconnected Systems Framework for School Mental Health

Reprinted with permission from the OSEP Technical Assistance Center for Positive Behavioral Interventions and Support (www.pbis.org/school/school_mental_health/default.aspx)

The majority of literature on school-wide mental health has addressed implementation of universal behaviour support, universal SMH programming and tertiary-level intensive intervention (e.g., Bayer *et al.*, 2009; Hawken, Adolphson, Macleod, & Schumann, 2009). However, there is a growing base of evidence in the form of meta-analyses to support Tier II targeted prevention programs as a critical component of effective school-wide approaches (e.g., Atkins *et al.*, 2010; Franklin, Kim, Ryan, Kelly, & Montgomery 2012; Green, Howes, Waters, Maher, & Oberkaid, 2005; Tennant, Goens, Barlow, Day, & Stewart-Brown, 2007; Weare & Nind, 2011). This level of intervention may be particularly relevant to students with disabilities and special educational needs, given the evidence for disability as a risk factor for mental health difficulties. Research on specific Tier II interventions is discussed in the next section.

Conceptually, school-wide mental health programs such as *KidsMatter* in Australia mirror this ecological, multi-tiered framework in that they incorporate components of universal preventive efforts, family and community partnerships, building positive school climate and identifying students experiencing mental health difficulties to facilitate access to more intensive early intervention, such as through referral to external agencies. However, frameworks such as *KidsMatter* do not explicitly distinguish targeted (Tier II) interventions for students likely to be at risk of developing difficulties to the same extent as the ISF, which may be an area for future development particularly relevant to students with disabilities and other at-risk groups. Evaluation of the *KidsMatter Primary* program revealed that while a universal focus on social and emotional learning was most readily adopted by participating schools, they spent the least time on Component 4, which relates to identifying students experiencing difficulties (Slee *et al.*, 2009). This may suggest that there is further scope to develop teachers' capacity to recognise students at risk and provide effective, increasingly targeted supports, both in the program framework and its implementation by schools. In addition, programs such as *KidsMatter* focus primarily on mental health promotion, with less systematic focus on integrating mental health promotion with school-wide efforts to promote positive student behaviour and manage challenging behaviour, or to provide effective, inclusive academic curriculum and instruction with escalating interventions for students in need.

The ISF is based on the three-tiered Response to Intervention (RtI) model of prevention and intervention and combines PBIS and SMH into one interconnected multi-tiered system of promotion, prevention and intervention for academic, social, emotional and behavioural learning.

Targeted prevention

Systematic reviews have documented evidence that the most-effective school mental health programs include consistent, long-term support for mental health promotion, targeted prevention, and intensive intervention (Reddy, Newman, De Thomas, & Chun, 2009; Weare & Nind, 2011). Meta-analyses have consistently found that programs combining long-term, whole-school mental health promotion with more targeted prevention have greater effects on the social, behavioural and emotional health of children and youth, and researchers have called for a redress of the balance between universal mental health promotion and targeted prevention (e.g., Green *et al.*, 2005; Weare & Nind, 2011).

Reflecting the ecological model, targeted prevention should be evidence-based, flexible in response to the needs of students identified by the school, and grounded in the link between academic learning, and social, emotional and behavioural competence. Evidence-based Tier II interventions commonly used in schools include effective instruction and classroom management (Atkins *et al.*, 2010), *Check and Connect* (Todd, Campbell, Meyer, & Horner, 2008), *First Step to Success* (Loman, Rodriguez, & Horner, 2010) and social skills development (Reddy *et al.*, 2009), and these are described below. One of the most potent Tier II preventive approaches for behavioural difficulties involves consistent classroom management practices that are systematically planned and implemented by staff and directly linked to universal Tier I efforts (Atkins *et al.*, 2010; Franklin *et al.*, 2012).

Check and Connect programs aim to improve student engagement through promoting positive interactions between students and school staff and reinforcing prosocial and academic engagement (Anderson, Christenson, Sinclair, & Lehr, 2004; Hawken, 2006), and include the *Behaviour Education Program* and *Check in-Check Out* (CICO). Checking involves systematic assessment of engagement, behaviour and academic progress with regular evaluation to ensure a prompt response to signs of difficulty. The 'Connect' component involves developing a personal connection with a monitor who maintains persistence (with students and families), positive expectations, continuity and consistency over time (Anderson *et al.*, 2004). Students check in and check out of school daily with a monitor to ensure they are prepared for the day and to share a daily report of their progress, and the monitor works with a support team to evaluate student progress, monitor the plan as needed, and decide when the student is ready to transition out of the intervention (Hawken, 2006). The effectiveness of *Check and Connect* programs in improving student behaviour and academic engagement has been supported by a body of research evidence (Todd *et al.*, 2008).

First Steps to Success (FSS) is a collaborative home and school program aimed at improving behavioural and academic outcomes for young children (K-3) who demonstrate behaviours of concern, through early screening, school-based intervention and parent/home intervention (Loman *et al.*, 2010). The young child is supported to develop social skills and improve interactions with teachers and peers as well as increasing successful engagement in learning. Detailed descriptions for implementation of FSS can be found in Rodriguez, Loman and Horner (2009). Similarly, the *Fast Track Program* is a multimodal approach focused on academic, behavioural and family support for students of all ages whereby intervention involves both teachers and parents. The *Fast Track Program* has been found to be dually effective in improving prosocial behaviour and academic achievement (Tennant *et al.*, 2007).

Numerous social skills instructional programs aimed at improving prosocial peer interactions for children at risk have been found to be effective at both the targeted Tier II level and the indicated Tier III level. In a meta-analysis of the effectiveness of Tier II and III programs for students with emotional disorders, Reddy *et al.* (2009) found that prevention studies aimed at improving social skills produced moderate effects, while intervention studies produced large effects on social skills improvement. Similarly, a systematic review by Arbesman, Bazyk and Nochajski (2013) found strong evidence that social skills programs improved social inter-action and peer acceptance for children involved in Tier II targeted prevention and were effective for a range of at-risk children and youth. The above descriptions of programs are by no means exhaustive, and documented case examples of targeted prevention programs can be found in the ISF monograph (Barrett *et al.*, 2013).

The value of consensus and shared vision across professional disciplines (mental health, education, behavioural support and special education), within a frame-work that represents shared knowledge and practices, is embodied in the ISF.

Competition for resources among promotion, prevention and intervention services within schools is removed through the multi-tiered, interconnected system designed to address the needs of all children, including those with heightened risk of developing difficulties, such as children and youth with disabilities and special needs. While pilot studies in multiple states and school settings in the United States lend support to the ISF, there is no published research on the model in Australian settings.

Further considerations

In order for school-wide, integrated approaches to mental health promotion to be effective, researchers have highlighted key factors such as strong school leadership, fidelity to intervention models (Slee *et al.*, 2009), and support for teachers to develop more sophisticated "cognitive schemata" related to the content and pedagogy of mental health promotion (Askell-Williams & Lawson, 2013, p. 139). To effectively address the mental health needs of students with disabilities within whole-school approaches, further issues may also warrant consideration. These include the need to support teachers' capacity to provide effective, inclusive teaching practices for students with disabilities and special needs, and the need for qualified, school-based educators with expertise in the area of disability and special education to recognise specific student needs, lead intervention efforts, and collaborate with school-based and external mental health professionals.

Researchers have noted a lack of content knowledge, pedagogical knowledge, and self-efficacy related to mental health promotion among up to half of classroom teachers, prior to engagement with a well-designed, school-wide mental health program (Askell-Williams & Lawson, 2013). Research similarly highlights pre-service and practising teachers' perceived lack of knowledge and self-efficacy for teaching students with disabilities and special educational needs in mainstream settings (e.g., Forlin, 2001). Since effective implementation of targeted interventions requires knowledge and skill related to both mental health and disability, it is easy to see how the intersection between the two might create significant challenges for teachers, especially in the absence of well-designed school-wide approaches. For example, in a recent Australian study of teachers and parents of children with Autism Spectrum Disorders, social-emotional learning, mental health and behavioural support emerged as the areas in which teachers felt least confident and skilled in supporting students (McMillan & Papatraianou, 2014).

At the universal level of prevention, school-wide mental health initiatives often refer to the importance of building supportive, inclusive learning environments, but to do so requires considerable knowledge and skill on the part of classroom teachers to support academic progress and achievement for students with disabilities and special needs, in the context of strong school and system leadership for inclusive practices. Kauffmann and Badar (2014) suggest that a general focus on physical *inclusion* as the central issue for students with disabilities in schools is misguided when the primary focus should be on the provision of the most effective possible *instruction* to ensure that students with disabilities can access and make progress within a framework of high-quality curriculum; they note that disability requires a clear instructional response from educators and not only inclusive attitudes, a sense of valuing diversity, and efforts to foster a sense of belonging for students from diverse backgrounds. In this way, focusing on teachers' capacity to design and implement excellent classroom instruction for diverse students, with opportunities for more focused, intensive or specialised supports for small groups or individuals as needed, is an essential component of efforts to promote student wellbeing and positive mental health outcomes.

Achieving genuine inclusion with a layer of Tier II targeted intervention relies on knowledgeable, school-based personnel to support classroom teachers and to design, monitor and tailor flexible interventions. In some cases, interventions might be implemented by teacher aides who are employed in a growing number of Australian schools to support students with disabilities in or out of the classroom. However, while teacher aides may be effective in program implementation, Giangreco (2013) cautions that an over-reliance on teacher aides as primary educators of students with disabilities at the expense of employing qualified special education teachers has little defensible foundation "from a conceptual, theoretical or data-based perspective" as an effective model of special education (p. 24).

In the context of multi-tiered interventions with targeted support for students with disabilities and special needs, qualified special education teachers are well placed to design, implement and monitor interventions related to both mental health and academic outcomes. These include interventions related to self-regulation, social skills, communication, behaviour, and specific aspects of academic learning. In addition, special education teachers can play a key role in supporting classroom teachers' understanding and practices related to students with disabilities; the coordination of multiple services and supports; and the development of systems to monitor student progress and evaluate the effectiveness of interventions at the classroom and school level. In the area of mental health promotion and intervention, the effectiveness of specialist teachers is likely to be further enhanced where there are opportunities to collaborate with school-based, qualified mental health professionals such as counsellors and school psychologists. Further research is needed into the effectiveness of current collaborative models and practices between classroom teachers, special education teachers, teacher aides and mental health personnel in Australian schools.

Conclusion

Children and young people with disabilities are at heightened risk of developing mental health difficulties, and this should be considered in the design of whole-school efforts to promote mental health and wellbeing. Well-designed interventions should incorporate multi-tiered opportunities to build mental health-related competencies, provide supportive communities, target students at risk and respond early to students with identified difficulties. For students with disabilities and special educational needs in particular, it is essential that efforts to promote mental health are integrated with school-wide approaches to behavioural and academic support, and that qualified personnel work in partnership to design, monitor and evaluate tailored interventions at all levels.

References

Anderson, A. R., Christenson, S. L., Sinclair, M. F., & Lehr, C. A. (2004). Check & Connect: The importance of relationships for promoting engagement with school. *Journal of School Psychology, 42*(2), 95–113.

Arbesman, M., Bazyk, S., & Nochajski, S. M. (2013). Systematic review of occupational therapy and mental health promotion, prevention, and intervention for children and youth. *American Journal of Occupational Therapy, 67*(6), e120–e130.

Askell-Williams, H., & Lawson, M. J. (2013). Teachers' knowledge and confidence for promoting positive mental health in primary school communities. *Asia-Pacific Journal of Teacher Education, 41*(2), 126–143.

Atkins, M. S., Hoagwood, K. E., Kutash, K., & Seidman, E. (2010). Toward the integration of education and mental health in schools. *Administration and Policy in Mental Health, 37,* 40–47.

Australian Institute of Health and Welfare (AIHW). (2008). *Disability in Australia: Intellectual disability* (AIHW Bulletin no. 67). Canberra, Australia: Author. Retrieved November 19, 2015 from www.aihw.gov.au/publication-detail/?id=6442468183

Barrett, S., Eber, L., & Weist, M. (2012). *Development of an interconnected systems framework for school mental health.* Retrieved May 17, 2013 from http://pbis.org/school/school_mental_health/default.aspx

Barrett, S., Eber, L., & Weist, M. (2013). Advancing education effectiveness: Interconnecting school mental health and school-wide Positive Behavior Support. *OSEP Center for Positive Behavioural Interventions and Supports.*

Bayer, J., Hiscock, H., Scalzo, K., Mathers, M., McDonald, M., Morris, A., Birdseye, J., & Wake, M. (2009). Systematic review of preventive interventions for children's mental health: What would work in Australian contexts? *Australian and New Zealand Journal of Psychiatry, 43,* 695–710.

Dix, K. L., Jarvis, J. M., & Slee, P. T. (2013). *KidsMatter and young children with disability.* Adelaide, Australia: Shannon Research Press.

Dix, K., Shearer, J., Slee, P., & Butcher, C. (2010). *KidsMatter for students with a disability: Evaluation report.* Adelaide, Australia: MAC: SWD.

Eber, L., Weist, M., & Barrett, S. (2013). An introduction to the Interconnected Systems Framework. In S. Barrett, L. Eber, & M. Weist, *Advancing education effectiveness: Interconnecting school mental health and school-wide Positive Behavior Support.* OSEP Center for Positive Behavioural Interventions and Supports.

Forlin, C. (2001). Inclusion: Identifying potential stressors for regular class teachers. *Educational Research, 43,* 235–245.

Franklin, C. G., Kim, J. S., Ryan, T. N., Kelly, M. S., & Montgomery, K. L. (2012). Teacher involvement in school mental health interventions: A systematic review. *Children and Youth Services Review, 34*(5), 973–982.

Giangreco, M. F. (2013). Teacher assistant supports in inclusive schools: Research, practices and alternatives. *Australasian Journal of Special Education, 37,* 93–106.

Green, J., Howes, F., Waters, E., Maher, E., & Oberkaid, F. (2005). Promoting the social and emotional health of primary school-aged children: Reviewing the evidence base for school-based interventions. *International Journal of Mental Health Promotion, 7*(3), 30–36.

Hawken, L. S. (2006). School psychologists as leaders in the implementation of a targeted intervention: The Behavior Education Program. *School Psychology Quarterly*, *21*, 91–111.

Hawken, L. S., Adolphson, S. L., Macleod, K. S., & Schumann, J. (2009). Secondary-tier interventions and supports. In W. Sailor, G. Dunlap, G. Sugai, & R. Horner (Eds.), *Handbook of positive behavior support* (pp. 395–420). Springer US.

Jarvis, J. M. (2011). Promoting mental health through inclusive pedagogy. In R. H. Shute, P. T. Slee, R. Murray-Harvey, & K. L. Dix (Eds.), *Mental health and wellbeing: Educational perspectives* (pp. 237–248). Adelaide, Australia: Shannon Research Press.

Kauffman, J. M., & Badar, J. (2014). Instruction, not inclusion, should be the central issue in special education: An alternative view from the USA. *Journal of International Special Needs Education*, *17*(1), 13–20.

Loman, S. L., Rodriguez, B. J., & Horner, R. H. (2010). Sustainability of a targeted intervention package: First step to success in Oregon. *Journal of Emotional and Behavioral Disorders*, *18*(3), 178–191.

McMillan, J. M., & Jarvis, J. M. (2013). Mental health and students with disabilities: A review of literature. *Australian Journal of Guidance and Counselling*, *23*(Special Issue 2), 236–251.

McMillan, J. M., & Papatraianou, L. (2014, July). *Supporting students in key indicators of autism spectrum disorder: Variations between educators' and parents' perceptions.* Paper presented at the Autism in Education Conference, Sydney.

Ministerial Advisory Committee: Students with Disabilities. (MAC: SWD) (2007). *Mental health and students with a disability.* Adelaide, Australia: Government of South Australia. Retrieved November 19, 2015 from www.decd.sa.gov.au/docs/documents/1/MentalHealthandChildrenan.pdf

Reddy, L. A., Newman, E., De Thomas, C. A., & Chun, V. (2009). Effectiveness of school-based prevention and intervention programs for children and adolescents with emotional disturbance: A meta-analysis. *Journal of School Psychology*, *47*(2), 77–99.

Rodriguez, B. J., Loman, S. L., & Horner, R. H. (2009). A preliminary analysis of the effects of coaching feedback on teacher implementation fidelity of First Step to Success. *Behavior Analysis in Practice*, *2*(2), 11.

Slee, P. T., Dix, K., & Askell-Williams, H. (2011). Whole-school mental health promotion in Australia. *The International Journal of Emotional Education*, *3*(2), 37–49.

Slee, P. T., Lawson, M. J., Russell, A., Askell-Williams, H., Dix, K. L., Owens, L., Skrzypiec, G., & Spears, B. (2009). *KidsMatter Primary Evaluation Final Report.* Centre for Analysis of Educational Futures, Flinders University of South Australia.

Tennant, R., Goens, C., Barlow, J., Day, C., & Stewart-Brown, S. (2007). A systematic review of reviews of interventions to promote mental health and prevent mental problems in children and young people. *Journal of Public Mental Health*, *6*(1), 25–32.

Todd, A. W., Campbell, A. L., Meyer, G. G., & Horner, R. H. (2008). The effects of a targeted intervention to reduce problem behaviors: Elementary school implementation of Check In-Check Out. *Journal of Positive Behavior Interventions*, *10*(1), 46–55.

Weare, K., & Nind, M. (2011). Mental health promotion and problem prevention in schools: What does the evidence say? *Health Promotion International*, *26*(1), 29–69.

Westwood, P. (2011). *Commonsense methods for students with special educational needs* (6th Edn.). London: Routledge.

World Health Organization. (WHO). (2004). *Promoting mental health: Concepts, emerging evidence, practice. Summary report.* Retrieved November 19, 2015 from www.who.int/mental_health/evidence/en/promoting_mhh.pdf

12

ISSUES OF BULLYING AND AUTISM SPECTRUM DISORDER

Alison Wotherspoon, Phillip T. Slee, Verity Bottroff, Jon Martin and Barbara Spears

Educating children with Autism Spectrum Disorder (ASD) in mainstream schools places them at very high risk of experiencing bullying. Bullying prevention initiatives tailored for children with ASD are in the very early stages of development. Programs need to be targeted at students with ASD and the broader school community, and should consider the experiences of parents of children with ASD, who may also experience bullying. A recently produced video resource package to support interventions is described.

The challenge

Across the globe, the inclusion and mainstreaming of children with disabilities in schools means that it is timely to investigate the wellbeing of vulnerable groups, such as children diagnosed with Autism Spectrum Disorder (ASD), and the risk and protective factors for the victimisation they experience as students.

In Australia, it has been reported that 82 per cent of children with ASD 'have difficulty' at school, the majority having problems with communication, learning and fitting in socially (Australian Bureau of Statistics, 2009). A major challenge is the systematic development, implementation, evaluation and dissemination of programs that specifically address the issues that young people with ASD face in schools with regard to bullying. An additional challenge relates to the meaningful inclusion of parents of students with ASD within schools: mothers of children with ASD report that they too experience exclusion and bullying within their child's school community and that this impacts on their wellbeing (Spears, Slee, Owens, & Johnson, 2007). There is a need for school communities and researchers involved with issues of bullying associated with the inclusion of students with ASD to concurrently address the status of their parents within the school community and the role these parents can play within programs to reduce bullying.

Background

Traditionally, the umbrella term of 'Autism Spectrum Disorders' was utilised to cover a number of pervasive developmental disorders, for example, autism and Asperger disorder, and did not operate as a diagnostic category in and of itself. However, under the most recent edition of the American Psychiatric Association's *Diagnostic and Statistical Manual of Mental Disorders* (*DSM-5*) (2013) the range of disorders has been collapsed into one diagnosis of Autism Spectrum Disorder (ASD). Clinically significant disordered development in social communication skills is a core characteristic of ASD, and poor social skills are frequently identified as a core characteristic of individuals who are targeted for bullying. Not surprisingly, then, preliminary research has demonstrated that children with ASD are at greater risk for victimisation than their peers, and more children with ASD are rejected than their peers. In addition, behaviours and characteristics reflecting autism and communication difficulties are significant predictors of variations in victimisation scores. We now examine these issues in more depth.

Bullying and ASD

Bullying is a particularly destructive form of aggression, involving repeated physical or psychological intimidation or attack intended to cause fear, distress or harm, involving an imbalance of power in favour of the perpetrator. An early meta-analytic study established the negative physical and mental sequelae of victimisation (Hawker & Boulton, 2000) with more recent studies confirming this (e.g., Campbell, Spears, Slee, Butler, & Kift, 2012). Bullying others is also identified as a risk factor for suicide (Kim, Leventhal, Koh, & Boyce, 2009) and future criminal behaviour (Olweus, 1999).

The characteristics of individuals who may be the targets of bullying often include poor social skills, such as an inability to understand the subtleties of peer relations, with subsequent difficulty in fitting in (Heinrichs, 2003). Other issues associated with victimisation include learning disability (Jones *et al.*, 2012), lack of friends (Skrzypiec, Slee, Murray-Harvey, & Pereira, 2011), and health-related symptoms (Fekkes *et al.*, 2006). It is precisely these characteristics that are often observed in individuals with ASD, a correlation that is consistent with research findings that individuals with ASD are more at risk of experiencing bullying compared with their peers (Humphrey & Symes, 2010).

The social skills demonstrated by individuals with ASD do, however, vary greatly, as does the range of social difficulties they experience. Individuals with ASD typically have limited knowledge and awareness of many aspects of the social world, appropriate social behaviour and society (Howlin, 2003). They generally have a limited capacity to use prior social knowledge or read social cues, and often have difficulties interpreting subtle non-verbal behaviours (e.g., body language, facial expression). The difficulty in predicting, understanding, interpreting and appropriately responding to the actions, emotions and intentions of others can lead to situations where they misinterpret or fail to perceive the actions and/or intentions of those around them (Jackson, 2002).

Individuals with ASD often present with poor skills in understanding or being aware of the potential consequences of an action or an intention (Bartak, Bottroff, & Zeitz, 2006). Unless explicitly instructed in specific social situations, particularly those where the 'rules' are implied and seem like common knowledge but are not actually taught, individuals with ASD typically present with impaired social judgement. They often need to learn in a structured way, situation by situation, many of the social behaviours that other people acquire incidentally (Brown & Miller, 2003). As they have difficulties using prior knowledge to evaluate novel situations, it cannot be assumed that they will know what to do or how to interpret a new situation based on past experience. It is these difficulties in social situations that can lead to vulnerability regarding peers and, indeed, bullying from peers. Research (e.g., Sterzing, Shattuck, Narendorf, Wagner, & Cooper, 2012) has identified an urgent need for school-based interventions that focus on redressing specific skills development in students diagnosed with ASD and the integration of these students into peer groups.

Heinrichs' (2003) book *Perfect Targets* discusses the issues of bullying experienced by students with Asperger's syndrome. Results from a questionnaire developed by the South Australian Parent Autism Spectrum Disorder in Education Committee (2005) identified bullying as the biggest concern of parents in relation to their child's school experience. One student with ASD stated, "[T]hey are repulsed by me – I know this because they show it all the time . . . they think I am the lowest form of life" (2005, p. 18), while a parent of a student with ASD commented, "[H]e has been bullied on a daily basis and it varies from subtle to severe" (2005, p. 18). These two quotes, selected from many, reflect the intense effect that bullying can have on an individual.

In research by Rigby and Slee (1999) and Slee (2005) of over 25,000 students from more than 60 schools (State, Catholic and independent) in Australia, it was confirmed that in the general population between 1 in 5 and 1 in 7 students report being bullied 'once a week or more'. Bottroff, Slee and Zeitz (2005) administered the Peer Relations Questionnaire (Rigby & Slee, 1995) to 176 South Australian students at one school across years eight and nine. Results indicated that 24 per cent reported being bullied once a week or more, but 47 per cent reported that the students most bullied at school were 'kids with disabilities'. There was a significant correlation between being bullied and feeling unhappy, as well as unsafe, at school. This led to an increase in school absenteeism. Other research (Condron, 1997) of the peer relations experiences of children with learning difficulties in an inclusive classroom in South Australia indicated that there were often significant social difficulties, including bullying, that had a great impact on this student group.

Little (2002) analysed 400 middle-class American mothers' perceptions of peer and sibling victimisation among children aged 4–17 with Asperger syndrome or the closely related Nonverbal Learning Disability, finding that 94 per cent of parents reported that their child had been bullied by a peer at least once in the previous year. Compared with children in the general population, those with Asperger syndrome or Nonverbal Learning Disability were: four times more likely to be bullied; twice as likely to be hit by their peers or siblings; and experienced high levels of peer shunning that increased with age and peaked at high school.

A South Australian study (Cole, 1997) also demonstrated that children with ASD are at greater risk for victimisation than their peers, and more children with ASD were rejected than their peers. In addition, behaviours and characteristics reflecting autism and communication difficulties were significant predictors of variations in victimisation scores. These factors place children with ASD at risk within a mainstream classroom by increasing their vulnerability, acting as precipitating agents and increasing the opportunity for victimisation (Cole, 1997). Amongst a small group of secondary school students, 53 per cent of those with ASD reported being bullied 'once a week' or more (Bottroff et al., 2005). The need for interventions tailored for this population was identified some years ago (Bottroff, 1998).

Macklin's (2004) research indicated that students with ASD identified friends as 'protectors' and that the peer group primarily served a protective function. It was evident that the students with ASD often misunderstood elements of social situations and thus 'masqueraded' in an attempt not to stand out but lacked understanding of what was taking place. This often led to misinterpretation of situations and to difficulties. Bullying and harassment were identified as significant issues, with roles as both target and perpetrator carried out by individuals with ASD.

In a three-year intensive behavioural intervention program conducted with children and adolescents with ASD and challenging behaviours (Bottroff & Zeitz, 2004), 19 of the 20 participants experienced bullying at school (the 20th was home schooled, meaning that 100 per cent of those attending school were bullied). Family members and the individuals with ASD discussed the negative impact of the bullying experience, in the long term as well as the short term.

A qualitative study on covert bullying reported on the impact on family members, noting the plight of parents of children with Asperger's, who had not been given voice previously in the bullying literature (Spears et al., 2007). Parents reported experiencing isolation and exclusion by other parents and within the school system, leading to the recommendation that an investigation of the literature and research be undertaken, with a view to highlighting the vulnerability of the families, and not just the children, to bullying in our schools.

Solutions

Schools have ready-made populations of students that can be targeted for both general and specific mental health promotion initiatives (Giesen, Searle, & Sawyer, 2007). Increasingly, in Australia and overseas, attention is being given to the possibility of working through schools to improve the mental health and wellbeing of children.

Members throughout the school community need to be made aware of the complex issues for students diagnosed with ASD, and their families, and of the time required to implement appropriate, evidence-based, evaluated, school-wide intervention programs. Students diagnosed with an ASD need appropriate support from staff and students, as well as purpose-designed environments, to learn effectively. All members of the school community need to recognise the highly individualistic nature of a diagnosis of ASD and that a 'one-size-fits-all' approach will be of limited use and effectiveness. There is a clear need for new and ongoing research into how schools can best include children with ASD, and their families, in a significant way, while addressing the complex issues of bullying and its impact on these students.

The research on bullying and the inclusion of students with ASD in their local schools is a recent development. It is perhaps not surprising, therefore, to find an initial research focus on establishing the quantitative figures such as prevalence, nature and outcomes of the bullying (e.g., Sterzing *et al.*, 2012) as well as qualitative data to explore issues such as the strategies students with ASD employ to deal with bullying and what they perceive as likely to be helpful in the future (Slee, Bottroff, & Michaelsen, 2007). Ideally these research results will inform practice, including an emphasis on a whole school approach.

Humphrey and Symes (2010) provided a very valuable perspective in approaching the practical implementation of strategies to assist specific populations of students at risk of bullying. They proposed three levels to consider in developing a positive and safe school environment that includes information and practices: the first is common to all students; the second specific to groups (e.g., students with ASD); and the third level unique to individuals (e.g., a student with ASD who has specific sensory issues). The following discussion of solutions will first consider practices specific to students with ASD (level 2) and then broaden the practice to the total school community (level 1) while acknowledging that all three levels are of equal importance in the development and maintenance of mental health and wellbeing for individuals on the autism spectrum.

Solutions specific to students with an ASD (level 2)

The finding mentioned above that 100 per cent of those with ASD attending school experienced bullying was the impetus for a pilot research project (Webb, 2004) evaluating a bullying prevention program for mainstream primary-aged children with an ASD, with encouraging results. Previously, there had been an absence of evaluative programs designed to assist children with ASD to deal with bullying. Cognitive Behaviour Therapy (CBT) strategies formed the basis of this program as they have been found useful for children with ASD to reduce social anxiety and develop social skills (Groden, LeVasseur, Diller, & Cautela, 2002). A major consideration was for the program to be easily administered in a mainstream school setting, as many CBT approaches are too complex for adaptation to such an active environment (Parsons & Mitchell, 2002).

For students with ASD, incorporating elements such as visual cues, role-playing, social stories and comic-strip conversations may assist in developing concepts associated with the prevention of bullying. In Webb's (2004) program, cognitive understanding underpinned the eight sessions offered, and included strategies that were successful in the intensive intervention program. Visual mapping of connections between concepts (e.g., drawing on a whiteboard, use of action cards, subjects of interest, a video camera) provided a framework for breaking down the interactions between people and assisted students with an ASD to gain an insight into their own actions and the actions, thoughts and feelings of a significant other involved in the same conflict, and how others view a situation. The program achieved greater understanding of bullying and the use of strategies to avoid it.

While most students on the autism spectrum are motivated by a desire to have friends, they may need support to initiate and maintain these friendships. If students with ASD are to be genuinely included in mainstream schools, attention to developing support from classmates is an important goal for schools. Bartak *et al.* (2006) reported on the value of a buddy system, and Bottroff *et al.* (2005) obtained qualitative data in which students with ASD highlighted friends and buddies as a safe haven to stop bullying.

Another major qualitative finding from Bottroff *et al.*'s (2005) research participants was their recommendation that other students should be educated about students with disability/special needs/autism/individuality to *"help me be better understood"* and *"be more patient with me."* Humphrey and Symes (2010) cited the issue of 'diagnosis disclosure' as important in developing peer acceptance and understanding, while acknowledging that more research is required on this issue. Sensitive disclosure of a student's diagnosis with the intention of increasing acceptance of differences is an important part of the 'Circle of Friends' model and Gus (2000) reported on its value for students on the spectrum. A final suggestion from a number of Bottroff and colleagues' research participants that highlighted the theme of a 'safe haven' was the creation of a secure place within the school grounds: *"a safe place for kids to go"*, and in keeping with the ability of students with ASD to think outside of the square: *"make a tease proof dome for everyone who gets bullied regularly"*.

Solutions for the school community (Level 3)

Between 2010 and 2013, an educational resource, *Asperger's and Bullying*, was developed and produced in partnership between academics from three departments at Flinders University (Education, Disability Studies and Screen and Media), in association with Autism SA. Based on an evidence-based model of screen production developed by Wotherspoon (2013), the resource consists of a series of 12 videos, podcasts and interviews and is designed to increase understanding in school communities about the difficulties faced by children with ASD, as well as the challenges encountered by their families and schools. The intended audience includes educators, primary and secondary students, parents, community representatives and other stakeholders concerned with students with an ASD. The content reflects the findings that students with an ASD are at risk of both covert and overt forms of bullying, and that parents of these students can also experience bullying, particularly from other parents within the school community, as well as from teachers. The resource aims to raise awareness in the school community about the issues associated with ASD and bullying, and identifies the need for school communities to become more inclusive environments that support students and families dealing with ASD.

The videos acknowledge that a diagnosis of an ASD, such as Asperger syndrome, with the associated difficulties in social-emotional communication, does not mean that students do not want to share the company of others and develop friendships. They highlight the importance to students with ASD of having positive relationships with teachers, some friends, and buddies who support them. Conversely, it is shown that without the support of teachers and peers, these students feel alone and isolated within the school environment. The resource points out that students with ASD often have a strong desire to learn, and often have particular areas of strength, such as the visual arts and technology.

The resource is intended to stimulate discussion about ASD and bullying for a range of groups within a school setting. The videos and podcasts give voice to parents, a principal and a classroom teacher, as well as individuals with ASD, and challenge stereotypes associated with Asperger syndrome and bullying. They highlight proactive approaches in developing an inclusive school environment and the isolation experienced by parents of children with ASD, and discuss the pressures on teachers and the ways in which they can be supported by school personnel in including a student with Asperger syndrome (Wotherspoon, 2013).

Whilst there is some research regarding the issue of students with an ASD, bullying and peer relations, there is little regarding the impact of this bullying on the caregivers of those children. Spears *et al.* (2007), in their investigation into covert bullying, produced a series of podcasts designed to capture the voice of parents and young people. These podcasts are included in the *Asperger's and Bullying* resource. In the podcasts the parents of children with Asperger's related not only their children's experiences, but also, poignantly, their own as they navigated the schooling system with their children.

These stories highlight the need for attention to this 'at-risk' group of students and their parents at a national level, and this resource builds upon the recommendation from Spears *et al.*'s (2007) report that more research is needed in relation to understanding the broader familial impacts of bullying, particularly those of vulnerable children. The experiences of four mothers of children with Asperger disorder who experienced bullying, in particular, covert bullying, tell stories of their sons/daughters, the impact on the family, proposed strategies for change and how they, as mothers, felt bullied by exclusion from the social supports of the school. The following comment by one of the mothers highlights not only the bullying experienced but also the effects relating to mental health and wellbeing issues (Spears *et al.*, 2007, p. 72).

I have a child who has Asperger's syndrome. I felt that while he went to school that I was bullied as a parent. I was bullied by the Principal at one of my son's schools who kept telling me that the reason things were failing was due to my parenting skills. He didn't realise how hard it was to parent a child with Asperger's. I also got bullied by teachers who would always give me negative feedback about my son and never give me any positive feedback. The teachers also tended to exclude me when there were family picnics. I felt that before my son started school I had a really good self-esteem and after a few years into school I would go to school and just feel physically ill and I lost a lot of my self-esteem which made it much harder to help my son because I didn't believe in myself. I also found that when I went to pick him up at school the other parents wouldn't talk to me and I always felt like they were thinking to themselves, oh there's the parent of that child. As a result, when the kids had birthday parties my son was never invited. If I met them at the shopping centre they would just walk the other way. I also felt that it was quite easy to make friends before my son started school.

The above comments raise a concern requiring further exploration as well as immediate consideration for school communities.

Conclusions

The current, and likely to continue, practice of including and mainstreaming children with disabilities within schools is a potentially positive experience for students with an ASD, but at present rarely is so. With 82 per cent of this vulnerable group experiencing difficulty at school, there is considerable work to be done to make their school experience a safe and educationally productive one. Parents, too, need to be able find schools that offer their children with an ASD positive peer relationships and safe learning environments, and that encourage parents to play an active role in their children's educational experiences.

The impact of bullying in schools on the mental health and wellbeing of young people diagnosed with ASD is significant and there is an ongoing need to trial, implement and evaluate programs for their effectiveness and usefulness. To make significant change will require a commitment by schools to support the wellbeing of students diagnosed with ASD (and their families), within the classroom, playground and wider school community. However, developing effective interventions can be seen as only a preliminary step toward improving the health and wellbeing of populations. Transferring effective programs into real-world settings and maintaining them there is a complicated, long-term process that requires dealing effectively with the successive, complex phases of program diffusion.

References

American Psychiatric Association (2013). *Diagnostic and statistical manual of mental disorders* (Fifth Edition). Washington, DC: American Psychiatric Association.

Australian Bureau of Statistics (2009). Autism in Australia - 4428.0. ABS, Canberra. Accessed 03.02.2016 at www.abs.gov.au/ausstats/abs@.nsf/Lookup/4428.0main+features 62009

Bartak, L., Bottroff, V., & Zeitz, J. (2006). Therapist insights in working with stress in people with autism spectrum disorder. In M. G. Baron, J. Groden, G. Groden, & L. P. Lipsitt (Eds.), *Stress and coping in autism.* Oxford: Oxford University Press, pp. 246–273.

Bottroff, V. (1998). The development of friendships and the puzzle of autism. In K. Rigby & P. Slee (Eds.), *Children's peer relations.* London: Routledge, pp. 91–105.

Bottroff, V., & Zeitz, J. (2004). Intensive intervention programs for individuals with Asperger syndrome and challenging behaviours. *Proceedings of the Biennial Australian Autism Conference, Autism Spectrum: Pathways to Understanding,* October, Canberra.

Bottroff, V., Slee, P., and Zeitz, J. (2005). *Students with Asperger's Syndrome: Victimization and bullying.* Adelaide: Flinders University.

Brown, M., & Miller, A. (2003). *Aspects of Asperger's syndrome: Success in the teens and twenties.* Clifton: Lucky Duck.

Campbell, M., Spears, B., Slee, P. T., Butler, D., & Kift, S. (2012). Victims' perceptions of traditional and cyberbullying, and the psychosocial correlates of their victimisation. *Emotional and Behavioural Difficulties, 17*(3–4), 389–401.

Cole, C. (1997). Victimisation of children with autism spectrum disorder in mainstream schools. Unpublished Honours Thesis. Adelaide: Flinders University.

Condron, J. (1997*). 'I just want to be a friend': The peer relations experiences of children with learning disabilities in an inclusive classroom.* Adelaide: Flinders University.

Fekkes, M., Pijpers, F. I., Fredriks, A. M., Vogels, T., & Verloove-Vanhorick, S. P. (2006). Do bullied children get ill, or do ill children get bullied? A prospective cohort study on the relationship between bullying and health-related symptoms. *Pediatrics, 117*(5), 1568–1574.

Giesen, F., Searle, A., & Sawyer, M., (2007) Identifying and implementing prevention programmes for childhood mental health problems. *Journal of Paediatrics and Child Health, 43*(12), 785–789.

Groden, J., LeVasseur, P., Diller, A., & Cautela, J. (2002). *Coping with stress through picture rehearsal: A how-to manual for working with individuals with autism and developmental disabilities.* Providence, RI: The Groden Center.

Gus, L. (2000). Autism: Promoting peer understanding. *Educational Psychology in Practice, 16,* 461–468.

Hawker, D. S., & Boulton, M. J. (2000). Twenty years' research on peer victimization and psychosocial maladjustment: A meta-analytic review of cross-sectional studies. *Journal of Child Psychology and Psychiatry, 41*(4), 441–455.

Heinrichs, R. (2003). *Perfect targets: Asperger syndrome and bullying (practical solutions for surviving the social world).* Kansas: Autism Asperger Publishing Co.

Howlin, R. (2003). Asperger Syndrome in the adolescent years. In L. Holliday Willey (Ed.), *Asperger Syndrome in adolescence: Living with the ups, the downs, and things in between.* England: Jessica Kingsley.

Humphrey, N., & Symes, W. (2010), Perceptions of social support and experience of bullying among pupils with autistic spectrum disorders in mainstream secondary schools. *European Journal of Special Needs Education, 25*(1), 77–91.

Jackson, L. (2002). *Freaks, geeks and Asperger syndrome.* United Kingdom: Jessica Kingsley.

Jones, L., Bellis, M., Wood, S., Hughs, K., McCoy, E., Eckley, L., Bates, G., Mikton, C., Shakespeare, T., & Officer, A. (2012). Prevalence and risk of violence against children with disabilities: A systematic review and meta-analysis of observational studies. *The Lancet, 380*(9845), 899–907.

Kim, Y. S., Leventhal, B. L., Koh, Y., & Boyce, W. T. (2009). Bullying increased suicide risk: Prospective study of Korean adolescents. *Archives of Suicide Research*, *13*(1), 15–30.

Little, L. (2002). Middle-class mothers' perceptions of peer and sibling victimization among children with Asperger's syndrome and nonverbal learning disorders. *Issues in Comprehensive Pediatric Nursing*, *25*, 43–57.

Macklin, S. (2004). Conceptualising the peer group: A study of adolescent boys with Asperger syndrome. Unpublished Honours Thesis. Adelaide: Flinders University.

Olweus, D. (1999) Sweden. In P. K. Smith, Y. Morita, J. Junger-Tas, D. Olweus, R. F. Catalano, & P. T. Slee (Eds.), *The nature of school bullying*. London: Routledge, pp. 8–27.

Parsons, S., & Mitchell, P. (2002). The potential of virtual reality in social skills training for people with autistic spectrum disorders. *Journal of Intellectual Disability Research*, *46*(5), 430–443.

Rigby, K., & Slee, P. T. (1995). *Manual for the peer relations questionnaire (PRQ)*. Adelaide: University of South Australia.

Rigby, K., & Slee, P .T. (1999). The nature of school bullying: Australia. In P. K. Smith, Y. Morita, J. Junger-Tas, D. Olweus, R. Catalano, & P. Slee (Eds.), *The nature of school bullying: A cross-national perspective*. London: Routledge.

Skrzypiec, G., Slee, P. T., Murray-Harvey, R., & Pereira, B. (2011). School bullying by one or more ways: Does it matter and how do students cope? *School Psychology International*, *32*(3), 288–311.

Slee, P. T. (2005). Bullying in Australia. In M. Tsuchiya & P. Smith (Eds.), *Eliminating bullying in schools – Japan and the World*. Kyoto: Minerva Publishing Co.

Slee, P., Bottroff, V., & Michaelsen, K. (2007). *Autism spectrum disorders, bullying and relationships: A school community approach to intervention*. National Coalition Against Bullying Conference: Promoting Positive Relationships for Safer School Communities (November, Melbourne).

South Australia Parent Autism Spectrum Disorders in Education Committee (2005). *School Satisfaction survey*. Author.

Spears, B. A., Slee, P. T., Owens, L., & Johnson, B. (2007). *Behind the scenes: Insights into the human dimension of covert bullying*. Interim report to the Australian Government Department of Education, Science and Training, Canberra, November 2007. Short report accessed 03.02.2016 at http://safeschoolshub.edu.au/

Sterzing, P. R., Shattuck, P. T., Narendorf, S. C., Wagner, M., & Cooper, B. P. (2012). Bullying involvement and autism spectrum disorders: Prevalence and correlates of bullying involvement among adolescents with an autism spectrum disorder. *Archives of Pediatrics & Adolescent Medicine*, *166*(11), 1058–1064.

Webb, S. (2004). *Bullying and autism spectrum disorders: A practical programme. Link Magazine*, *13*(1), April.

Wotherspoon, A. J. (2013). *Asperger's and bullying: A series of 12 educational videos*. Adelaide: Flinders University.

13

SCHOOL-BASED RESPONSES TO YOUTH SUICIDE

Rosalyn H. Shute

Although youth suicide is a global public health issue, comprehensive theoretical models and evidence-based methods are lacking. After briefly reviewing the available theories, this chapter examines the evidence with regard to school-based prevention programs. Proposals are made for ways of dealing with the inevitable complexity of the issues, and specific suggestions made regarding future school-based efforts.

The challenges

Worldwide, suicide is the second cause of death in those aged 15–29 (World Health Organization, 2014). Although statistically rare, youth suicide is devastating for those left behind when it does occur, and at 'epidemic' rates in certain Indigenous communities around the world (e.g., Mackin, Perkins, & Furrer, 2012). Youth suicidality has been characterised as a global public health issue (Apter, Bursztein, Bertolote, Fleischmann, & Wasserman, 2009). Furthermore, beneath the tip of the completed suicide iceberg is a larger body of emotional distress, suicidal ideation and self-injury among youth that demands an effective response.

However, empirical advances have been hampered by a lack of comprehensive theoretical models (van Orden *et al.*, 2010), while Nock (2012) has bluntly stated that "there currently are no evidence-based methods available for treating or preventing adolescent suicidal self-injury or NSSI [non-suicidal self-injury]" (p. 258). More optimistically, he identifies some promising leads. This chapter briefly considers some theoretical issues, overviews the types of school-based suicide prevention programs, and reviews the evidence for their effectiveness. A view of youth suicide prevention as a complex issue is put forward, and some suggestions made for dealing with this complexity.

Background

Theories of suicide

Durkheim's nineteenth-century sociological approach suggested that suicide resulted from a lack of social integration. This influence remains apparent in both sociological and psychological theories (Mäkinen, 2009; Rudd, Trotter, & Williams, 2009), although there has been no recent sociological 'grand theory' (Mäkinen, 2009). Psychological theories focus on cognition, including Baumeister's escape theory (with various steps leading to a wish to escape unbearable pain), Shneidman's theory of wanting to escape unbearable 'psychache', Williams' theory of over-general memory (difficulty recalling reasons for living) and Beck's cognitive theory (based on hopelessness) (Rudd et al., 2009). Joiner's interpersonal theory has a specific focus on the desire to die and the means to do so, with thwarted belongingness combined with perceived burdensomeness to others particularly risky (van Orden et al., 2010).

The theoretical basis for suicide-related interventions is not strong, with more complex theories needed (Nock, 2012). Developmental theories that incorporate a range of risk and protective factors offer this complexity. For example, Alcántara and Gone (2007) propose a transactional-ecological approach to prevention, encompassing a range of individual and environmental factors within a biopsycho-social framework. Maine's (2006) theory also recognises that, at any point in life, an individual may have accumulated both risk factors for suicide ('suicidal factors') and protective factors (which together constitute resilience). The factors, weighted according to importance, combine to determine risk; if a critical threshold is reached, a 'gate' into suicidality (ideation, plans and attempts) is opened. Interventions to reduce risk and/or increase resilience feed dynamically into the system to return the suicide risk to below the threshold.

Only one study seems to have explicitly set out to examine the combined effect of risk and protective factors for adolescent suicide, in a way that is compatible with these more complex models. Mackin, Perkins, and Furrer's (2012) study of Oregon youth found that protective factors contribute cumulatively, both independently and combined with risk factors, to predict likelihood of having attempted suicide (they buffer against cumulative risk factors). They also found evidence for different weightings: youth with few risk factors were nevertheless relatively likely to have attempted suicide if those factors were emotional ill health or peer harassment. This broad theoretical approach in terms of cumulative risk and resilience offers a framework for considering school-based suicide prevention programs.

Types of school-based suicide prevention programs

Addressing youth suicide is necessarily preventative – there is no coming back from either an intentional, successful attempt, or from a less intentional but nevertheless lethal risky behaviour by a young person who is indifferent to survival. The difficulty for prevention is that suicide is unpredictable, even though we know of many risk and protective factors. For example, depression is a risk factor, but most people with depression do not attempt suicide. One approach is to focus on reducing a small number of highly weighted suicide risk factors, while another is to take a broad approach to try to decrease numbers of known risk factors and/or increase known protective factors to try and shift the odds in favour of survival and wellbeing.

Efforts to address youth suicide often do so through the school system, as a convenient and cost-effective way to reach the broad population of youth (Gould, Klomek, & Batejan, 2009). In public health terminology, school-based efforts may be universal, selective or indicated.

Universal, or primary prevention, programs are the commonest kind. Curriculum-based, they are aimed at whole schools or classes (Miller, Eckert, & Mazza, 2009). Where a health promotion framework is used, they have a positive, resilience-based focus on wellbeing, increasing protective factors by promoting individual skills such as problem-solving. The downside, for suicide prevention, is that the low incidence of suicide attempts and level of generality of the programs may mean that effects for suicide prevention will be weak, and cannot be detected without large sample sizes (Sawyer *et al.*, 2010).

An alternative, but still universal, approach is to focus more specifically on suicide prevention; that is, to work closer to the 'gate' into suicidality. Such programs may address both suicidal factors (for example, by providing information about suicide signs in oneself and others) and protective factors (for example, by encouraging help-seeking). Peer responders are an important focus, given the reluctance of suicidal students to approach adults. This information-giving approach has a chequered history, with information-giving alone having a negative effect on some vulnerable individuals. Also, to reduce the stigma associated with mental illness, one approach was to present suicide as an understandable response to stress, but this 'normalised', and therefore potentially encouraged, suicide (Miller *et al.*, 2009). The alternative is to make it clear that suicidality signals poor mental health that requires addressing. Programs focusing on help-seeking often include components aimed at ensuring that 'gatekeepers', such as teachers, recognise suicide signs and are trained to respond appropriately to approaches for help. One suicide prevention program incorporating steps such as providing students with a list of trained community members improved attitudes and knowledge, and reduced suicide-related stigma (Bean & Baber, 2011).

Targeted, secondary preventative or selective programs are less common. They focus on young people in higher-risk groups, such as Indigenous youth or those with mental health problems (Miller *et al.*, 2009). They may include components aimed at increasing resilience (e.g., promoting help-seeking among victims of bullying) and others aimed at reducing risk (e.g., having policies and procedures for stopping bullying – addressing a contextual risk factor, in line with ecological theories). A more proactive approach is also advocated, in seeking out students at particular risk, through screening, buttressed by evidence that asking explicitly about suicidality does not increase suicide risk or distress (e.g., Gould, Marrocco, *et al.*, 2009). Training teachers to look out actively for signs of student suicidality is less effective than screening for detecting at-risk students (Bean & Baber, 2011; Gould, Marrocco, *et al.*, 2009).

Tertiary, or indicated, programs are aimed at students who have already attempted suicide, or expressed a wish to die, but these are uncommon. The focus is on emergency support (Miller *et al.*, 2009). The aim may be to both reduce immediate suicide risk factors (e.g., by making a written no-suicide contract) and build resilience (e.g., learning to avoid catastrophic thinking through referral for cognitive therapy). Schools need knowledge about suitable community referral agencies (Berman, 2009), though such knowledge alone may be insufficient: the major barrier to gaining professional help for school-identified suicidal youth is the belief of parents and students themselves that the problem is not serious (Gould, Marrocco, *et al.*, 2009). This suggests a need for broad community education that is inclusive of parents; psycho-education can successfully change parental knowledge and attitudes to youth suicide (Maine, Shute, & Martin, 2001). Therapy for young attempters usually takes place in special services outside of school, though schools could provide a venue for multisystemic therapy. Also, liaison between external mental health providers and school counsellors may be needed to support the young person's reintegration into the school community.

Finally, *postvention* refers to actions after a suicide to support the survivors and prevent suicide contagion, to which young people seem particularly vulnerable (Gould, Klomek, & Batejan, 2009). Comprehensive school-based programs may include a spectrum of activities across all these levels, although most are focused on individual rather than contextual factors.

Evidence on school-based suicide prevention programs

Advice on school-based prevention has been given by the World Health Organization (2000), and many school systems have adopted suicide prevention/postvention programs. However, we must now return to Nock's (2012) point that there is a lack of underlying evidence.

Programs began to emerge as a result of increased rates of youth suicide in some countries in the late twentieth century, which ignited an understandable desire among professionals and communities to 'do something' about such a distressing trend. A legal imperative may also have played some part, at least in the United States: although suicide is almost impossible to predict, this has been distinguished from 'forseeability', determined in hindsight (after a suicide) by the legal system, so that school personnel who failed to act appropriately on available evidence about a student's suicidal risk may be open to being sued (Berman, 2009).

One outcome of the growing concern was a so-called 'suicide industry' in Australia and New Zealand, whereby schools engaged outside groups with questionable qualifications to bring programs into schools. Such universal, information-based programs have a very weak evidence base and may have more 'feel-good' than real value (Berman, 2009). In the United States, the parents of a suicided teenager began the *Yellow Ribbon* program, based on promoting help-seeking by suicidal youth or their friends. Widely adopted in the United States, Canada and other countries, the claim on its website in 2009 to have saved 2,500 lives was supported only by anecdotal evidence; a small-scale evaluation study showed no increases in help-seeking from most sources, and an actual decline in help-seeking from parents and friends, with only calls to hotlines increased (Freedenthal, 2010).

Miller *et al.* (2009) could only identify thirteen school-based studies with sufficient detail to include them in their review: ten universal, three selected and none indicated. Consistent methodological weaknesses included a lack of reliable and valid measures. Only three programs were rated highly for methodology, only two had significant effects, and none demonstrated replicability.

One study of which they were critical was nevertheless identified by Nock (2012) as particularly exciting, as it was the first Randomised Control Trial (RCT) to demonstrate a reduction in suicide attempts (Aseltine & DeMartino, 2004). This *SOS* suicide prevention program is action-based (Action, Care, Tell adult) and includes training in suicide awareness and a brief screening. It promotes help-seeking, not just from health professionals, but from school counsellors, teachers and loved ones. Students were randomised within schools to a treatment or a control group (which seems to have been untreated – pragmatism means that this is a common weakness in evaluating school-based programs). Testing only took place after the intervention. There were fewer self-reported suicide attempts in the treated group at three months, as well as more adaptive attitudes to depression and suicide. However, suicidal ideation and help-seeking did not differ between groups, and students were reluctant to approach staff because of confidentiality concerns.

A more recent preliminary study by King, Strunk, & Sorter (2010) in Cincinnati indicates that another promising program is *Surviving the Teens*. It was a short-term 3-month (before and after) study of a program with a specific suicidality focus, such as recognising signs, intending to tell an adult if a friend were suicidal, and managing feelings safely. These all improved, as did having a current suicide plan, attempting suicide or stopping usual activities because of feeling sad and hopeless. Although it is noteworthy for actually demonstrating a reduction in suicide attempts, there was no control group, and no information about the numbers of schools approached and which ones accepted or rejected involvement, so it is uncertain whether any confounding factors might have influenced suicidality, such as seasonality. However, this study has paved the way for more rigorous follow-up studies.

Another recent study, from Australia, is also significant, being one of the few well-designed RCT studies on universal school-based programs utilising a broad risk/protective factor framework. Although suicidality gave some context for the study, the program was aimed at depression (a suicide risk factor) rather than suicidality as such (Sawyer *et al.*, 2010). Under the auspices of the national anti-depression initiative, *beyondblue*, the study was large-scale, multifactorial and considered dynamic relationships between known risk and protective factors. Over three years, it included curriculum features such as training adolescents in coping and problem solving, and considered the school environment and pathways to care within the school and externally; it also included community forums. Unfortunately, although school personnel in the intervention schools rated school climate more positively, there was no evidence of differences between program and control schools in protective factors (such as optimistic thinking and social support) or depressive symptoms. The authors observed that all schools, which were self-selected, may have been on a path to improvement already, washing out any effect of the intervention. Also, this large-scale study highlighted systems issues including the difficulty of servicing large and diverse geographical regions, the long lead time (two years) to bed the program down, and the possibility that fidelity was compromised by differing levels of teacher experience and engagement, despite extensive training and program manualisation. Teacher reporting of fidelity was poor, and students rated the program low for helpfulness and enjoyment. The researchers also queried the readiness of young adolescents to engage in change, and noted that later cohorts may benefit as the program becomes more established.

In sum, while enormous goodwill and effort have been poured into youth suicide prevention programs, results overall have been disappointing, although there are some glimmers of hope.

Meeting the challenges of school-based suicide prevention

Dealing with complexity

School-based prevention efforts throw up many 'big picture' issues. For example, is it best to take an approach that draws on all the available evidence and tries to be fully comprehensive, or to start with some small-scale pilot studies? Should we focus broadly on resilience/mental health or more specifically (and explicitly) on suicidality? Should we take a universal approach that aims to build up resilience and reduce risk factors for the whole school population, or a more targeted one that focuses on those at high risk? What about negative community factors outside the school that threaten to overwhelm prevention efforts, such as community violence and poverty? And what about the practical challenges of bringing together the many organisations and individuals who may have a stake in school-based suicide prevention?

Potentially involved parties may bring a range of perspectives to bear on such issues, with different professionals inhabiting different 'worlds': "Scholars embrace complexity. Policy makers demand simplicity. Scientists suggest that we stop and reflect. Service providers are expected to act" (Shonkoff, 2000, p. 528). For example, when it comes to mental health programs in schools, teachers and researchers may use very different criteria for determining what constitutes a 'good' program (Shute, 2012).

Another possible source of a lack of consensus is attitudes to suicide. Although it seems obvious to many that suicide is a serious problem that needs addressing, community attitudes do vary (e.g., Leane & Shute, 1998). Also, suicide is a rare event and so may not be seen as a priority given other pressures on schools. The lack of success of the *beyondblue* adolescent mental health program evaluated by Sawyer *et al.* (2010) was in part attributed to the possibility that not all teachers and other personnel were fully engaged, and fidelity of implementation was therefore in question. Some teachers are sceptical about school-based mental health programs (e.g., Humphrey, Lendrum, & Wigelsworth, 2010). Teachers also vary in empathy; this can affect their likelihood of intervening to help students subjected to social bullying (Dedousis-Wallace, Shute, Varlow, Murrihy, & Kidman 2013) and, anecdotally, we have noticed in anti-bullying presentations that some teachers respond with eye-rolling at the very mention of youth suicide. It would not be surprising, then, if students do not take seriously lessons about help-seeking from such teachers, or do not seek them out for support. Other teachers may be willing participants, but lack the necessary skills or confidence. While teacher education and skills training are important for suicide prevention programs, it may have to be accepted that a universal approach to teacher involvement may not work.

One way to try to cut through such complexity is through applying ecological systems theory (e.g., Bronfenbrenner & Ceci, 1994). The *Connect* program formally identifies various 'eco-levels', operating at the mesosystem-level to forge links between microsystems such as the family, school and community services. This approach also incorporates the macro-level, in addressing attitudes and ideologies, aiming to reduce the stigma attached to help-seeking for suicide (Bean & Baber, 2011). It also enables the identification of any specific cultural issues. Most programs focus on the individual level, although the *beyondblue* adolescent program did attempt, with some success, to change the school culture. We can ask how effective any individual-based program can be in communities troubled by issues such as cultural displacement, poverty, racism and violence, as experienced by members of some Indigenous communities (Alcántara & Gone, 2007). Approaches beyond the school may be called for in such circumstances, bearing in mind also that the highest-risk young people may be the very ones who are not regular school attenders.

Another approach to 'taming' complexity might be to view youth suicide prevention as a 'wicked problem' (see Beinecke, Chapter 2), where there is no consensus over the nature of the problem or its solution. Roberts (2000) has suggested some possible coping strategies. If power among the parties is not dispersed, strategies can be determined by that power. This authoritative approach, by a small number of experts, is efficient, but has disadvantages: experts may have a narrow view and miss important perspectives, as when a school implements a program that ignores student or teacher perspectives. If power is dispersed and contested, competitive strategies may be used, with parties building power bases to achieve their ends, though a possible outcome is stalemate and gridlock. When power is not contested, collaborative strategies are favoured, under a win–win scenario. Working through processes in these various ways takes a great deal of time and effort, and the situation can collapse into debate and conflict, and harden attitudes. Collaborative skills and leadership are important for working through the issues. Attempts to solve wicked problems are expensive, and can have long-lasting and unintended consequences that may give rise to more wicked problems (Conklin, 2005). One possibility is that when a program is shown to be ineffective, any scepticism of key personnel may be reinforced and create an environment in which it is even harder to attempt future programs.

The real-life 'messiness' of suicide education has been examined in a qualitative study that took a constructivist approach to address the experiences of suicide educators (White, Morris, & Hinbest, 2012). One reflected:

> In the studies I read, why did it always seem as though suicide prevention education was nothing more than a straightforward technical task of delivering a product? . . . Why was so much of the published literature . . . focused on research design, methodology, rigour, credibility and evidence? Why didn't I recognize myself and my experience in these published accounts?
>
> (p. 340)

White and colleagues note the concern with 'fidelity' and the difficulty of achieving this, and the contrasting approach of being responsive to students 'in the moment'. They provide the example that a particular program had a component about 'blame', aimed at reassuring students that if they tried to help a suicidal person who later suicided, that was the person's choice, and not the helper's fault; the educator was nonplussed when a student raised the point that it was not that simple, that one would inevitably experience self-blame. This called for deeper discussion about matters of autonomy and collective responsibility, but 'fidelity' demanded pushing the 'not to blame' line. White and colleagues suggested that the tension between these two approaches is "endemic to the programme delivery setting" (2012, p. 346), and that reflection on this can offer new insights into local sense-making and realities.

Suggestions for the future

Based on this review, the following considerations may be helpful for future work on suicide prevention through schools.

1. A cumulative suicide risk and protective factors framework captures the complexity of youth suicide. Both risk and protective factors offer possibilities for prevention and intervention.

2. An explicitly ecological approach encourages an identification of relevant microsystems, their interrelationships (the mesosystem) and the macrosystem within which prevention efforts occur.
3. Devising, implementing and evaluating schools-based prevention programs involve diverse parties with various perspectives. Ecological systems theory and the notion of wicked problems offer conceptual frameworks for understanding these processes.
4. A public health approach can help decision-making about the levels of intervention to be incorporated into a program.
5. Small-scale piloting may avoid larger-scale disasters that impede future efforts.
6. Evaluation should be built into the program.
7. Suicide-focused programs show more promise than generic programs.
8. The tension between generic mental health programs and a specific focus on suicide may perhaps be addressed by including, within broad-based programs, a suicide module that is nevertheless integrated with generic aspects (e.g., help-seeking).
9. A view of suicide as a mental health issue is preferable to a view that it is a normal response to stressors.
10. A school ethos that promotes partnerships with families and outside agencies offers a basis for community education about suicide prevention.
11. Screening for suicidality is more effective than identification by gatekeepers.
12. Education of teachers, students and others as gatekeepers is nevertheless important.
13. Gatekeeper education should include provision of information about what other parties, such as mental health providers and police, might do in response to suicide.
14. Not all teachers are suited for participation in suicide prevention programs.
15. Students should be provided with a list of community members trained to help.
16. Referral paths need to be identified.
17. Support for families in follow-up of referred students is needed.
18. Programs need to incorporate a blend of fidelity and adaptation.
19. Qualitative research may offer helpful perspectives on local conditions and program adaptation.

Conclusions

While schools have been identified as suitable places for addressing youth suicide prevention, there are considerable challenges in designing, implementing and evaluating programs. Helpful approaches that acknowledge the complexity of both suicidality and preventative efforts include cumulative risk and resilience models, a public health approach, ecological theories and the notion of wicked problems. While theory and research to date offer no ideal formula for school-based prevention programs, there are some promising leads. Although most programs take an individualistic approach to prevention, an ecological approach enables consideration of a broad range of systems within which individuals develop their risk of suicide and within which preventative efforts may occur.

References

Alcántara, C., & Gone, J. P. (2007). Reviewing suicide in Native American communities: Situating risk and protective factors within a transactional-ecological framework. *Death Studies*, *31*, 457–477.

Apter, A., Bursztein, C., Bertolote, J. M., Fleischmann, A., & Wasserman, D. (2009). Suicide on all the continents in the young. Ch. 80 in Wasserman, D., & Wasserman, C. (Eds). *Oxford textbook of suicidology and suicide prevention: A global perspective*. Oxford: OUP, pp. 621–628.

Aseltine, R. H., & DeMartino, R. (2004). An outcome evaluation of the SOS suicide prevention program. *American Journal of Public Health*, *94*(3), 446–451.

Bean, G., & Baber, K. M. (2011). Connect: An effective community-based youth suicide prevention program. *Suicide and Life-Threatening Behavior*, *41*(1), 87–97.

Berman, A. L. (2009). School-based suicide prevention: Research advances and practice implications. *School Psychology Review*, *38*(2), 233–238.

Bronfenbrenner, U., & Ceci, S. J. (1994). Nature-nurture reconceptualized in developmental perspective: A bioecological model. *Psychological Review*, *101*, 568–586.

Conklin, J. (2005). Wicked problems and social complexity. Ch. 1 in J. Conklin, *Dialogue mapping: Building shared understanding of wicked problems*. Chichester: Wiley, pp. 2–20.

Dedousis-Wallace, A., Shute, R., Varlow, M., Murrihy, R., & Kidman, A. (2013). Predictors of teacher intervention in indirect bullying at school and outcome of a professional development presentation for teachers. *Educational Psychology*. Accessed 27.11.2015 at www.tandfonline.com/action/showCitFormats?doi=10.1080/01443410.2013.785385

Freedenthal, S. (2010). Adolescent help-seeking and the Yellow Ribbon Suicide Prevention Program: An evaluation. *Suicide and Life-Threatening Behavior*, *40*(6), 628–639.

Gould, M. S., Klomek, A. B., & Batejan, K. (2009). The role of schools, colleges and universities in suicide prevention. Ch. 73 In Wasserman, D., & Wasserman, C. (Eds), *Oxford textbook of suicidology and suicide prevention: A global perspective*. Oxford: OUP, pp. 551–560.

Gould, M., Marrocco, F. A., Hoagwood, K., Kleinman, M., Amakawa, L., & Altschuler, E., (2009). Service use by at-risk youths after school-based suicide screening. *Journal of the American Academy of Child and Adolescent Psychiatry*, *48*(12), 1193–1201.

Humphrey, N., Lendrum, A., & Wigelsworth, M. (2010). *Social and emotional aspects of learning (SEAL) programme in secondary schools: National evaluation*. Manchester: Department for Education.

King, K. A., Strunk, C. M., & Sorter, M. T. (2010). Preliminary effectiveness of Surviving the Teens Suicide Prevention and Depression Awareness Program on adolescents' suicidality and self-efficacy in performing help-seeking behaviors. *Journal of School Health*, *81*(9), 581–590.

Leane, W., & Shute, R. (1998). Youth suicide: The knowledge and attitudes of Australian teachers and clergy. *Suicide and Life-Threatening Behavior*, *28*(2), 165–173.

Mackin, J., Perkins, T., & Furrer, C. (2012). The power of protection: A population-based comparison of Native and Non-Native suicide attempters. *American Indian and Alaska Native Mental Health Research*, *19*(2), 20–54.

Maine, S. (2006). Parental support for youth: A parenting programme for youth suicide prevention. Unpublished PhD thesis, Flinders University, South Australia.

Maine, S., Shute, R., & Martin, G. (2001). Educating parents about youth suicide: Knowledge, response to suicidal statements, attitudes and intention to help. *Suicide and Life-Threatening Behavior, 31*(3), 320–332.

Mäkinen, I. H. (2009). Social theories of suicide. Ch. 23 in Wasserman, D., & Wasserman, C. (Eds). *Oxford textbook of suicidology and suicide prevention: A global perspective.* Oxford: OUP, pp. 139–147.

Miller, D. N., Eckert, T. L., & Mazza, J. J. (2009). Suicide prevention programs in the schools: A review and public health perspective. *School Psychology Review, 38*(2), 168–188.

Nock, M. K. (2012). Future directions for the study of suicide and self-injury. *Journal of Clinical Child and Adolescent Psychology, 41*(2), 255–259.

Roberts, N. (2000).Wicked problems and network approaches to resolution. *International Public Management Review Electronic Journal 1*(1), at www.ipmr.net

Rudd, M. D., Trotter, D. R. M., & Williams, B. (2009). Psychological theories of suicidal behaviour. Ch. 25 in Wasserman, D. & Wasserman, C. (Eds), *Oxford textbook of suicidology and suicide prevention: A global perspective.* Oxford: OUP, pp. 159–164.

Sawyer, M. G., Pfeiffer, S., Spence, S. H., Bond, L., Graetz, B., Kay, D., Patton, G., & Sheffield, J. (2010). School-based prevention of depression: A randomised controlled study of the *beyondblue* schools research initiative. *The Journal of Child Psychology and Psychiatry, 51*(2), 199–209.

Shonkoff, J. P. (2000). Science, policy, and practice: Three cultures in search of a shared mission. *Child Development, 71,* 181–187.

Shute, R. H. (2012). Promoting mental health through schools: Is this field of development an evidence-based practice? *The Psychologist, 25*(10), 752–755.

van Orden, K. A., Witte, T. K., Cukrowicz, K. C., Braithwaite, S. R., Selby, E. A., & Joiner, T. E. (2010). The interpersonal theory of suicide. *Psychological Review, 117*(2), 575–600.

White, J., Morris, J., & Hinbest, J. (2012). Collaborative knowledge-making in the everyday practice of youth suicide prevention education. *International Journal of Qualitative Studies in Education, 25*(3), 339–355.

World Health Organization (2000). *Preventing suicide: A resource for teachers and other school staff.* Geneva: WHO.

World Health Organization (2014). *Preventing suicide: A global imperative. Executive summary.* Geneva: WHO. Accessed 13.10.2014 at www.who.int/mental_health/suicide-prevention/exe_summary_english.pdf?ua=1

14

PREVENTION PROGRAMS FOR DEPRESSION AMONG CHILDREN AND ADOLESCENTS IN JAPAN

Challenges and opportunities

Shin-ichi Ishikawa, Satoko Sasagawa, Junwen Chen and Cecilia A. Essau

This chapter discusses key issues and challenges in implementing prevention programs for depression in Japanese educational settings. The implementation of school-wide mental health programs is still embryonic in Japan. Simply translating evidence-based interventions developed and evaluated in western countries poses numerous challenges due to differences in education systems, mental health services and cultural values. We present the way in which three CBT programs for the prevention of depression in Japanese schools were implemented, and discuss how the challenges in their adaptation and implementation were addressed. A framework for the future implementation and dissemination of evidence-based programs for depression in children and adolescents, and how this framework may be applied in different cultures, is explored.

The challenge

As in many western societies, depression is one of the commonest mental health problems among Japanese children and adolescents (Ishikawa, Togasaki, Sato, & Sato, 2006), stressing the need for evidence-based programs to prevent and treat this debilitating condition. For evidence-based programs to have a wide reach and impact, schools offer an excellent venue for their delivery, especially in Japan because all children are enrolled in school (The World Bank, 2014). However, only a small percentage of Japanese schools implements universal mental health interventions, and this may be attributed to three factors: 1) lack of mental health literacy among school officials and wider society; 2) limited understanding of evidence-based treatment; and 3) transportability of western-made prevention programs to the Japanese 'context'. This chapter presents the way in which we address each of these issues when implementing three school-based depression prevention programs in children.

Background

In Japan, school officials have been repeatedly accused of making inopportune decisions and taking actions only in hindsight. An example was an incident in Shiga prefecture in which a middle school student bullied by his peers suicided. Although he and his friends had reported the bullying to their teacher and school personnel, no concrete action was taken. It was only after this tragic incident that the government introduced a bullying prevention law, which was quickly deliberated in the Diet and passed in 2013. The law mandated each school to report any cases of severe bullying to the local government official and/or the Japanese Minister of Education. *A posteriori* action that follows such a serious incident is common practice in Japan. Development of *a priori* interventions, that is, psychosocial prevention programs for mental health promotion, however, is less common.

Depression among children and adolescents in Japan

Between 4.2 percent and 8.8 percent of children and adolescents in Japan are estimated to have depressive disorders (Denda, 2008; Sato, Shimotsu, & Ishikawa, 2008). The occurrence of sub-clinical depression among adolescents in middle school is much higher, at 22.8 percent (Denda *et al.*, 2004). Among elementary school children aged 10 to 12 years, 11.6 percent show high levels of depressive symptoms (Sato *et al.*, 2006). Rates of suicide attempts are also high, ranging from 18.8 percent to 31.3 percent among currently depressed, and from 1.9 percent to 2.6 percent among non-depressed adolescents. Depression co-occurs frequently with other disorders such as anxiety, somatoform and substance use disorders (Essau, Lewinsohn, Seeley, & Sasagawa, 2010). It also tends to act as a risk factor for the development of depression and/or other mental disorders in adulthood (Essau *et al.*, 2010).

Studies conducted in western countries have consistently reported that depression in young people is associated with impairment in various life domains (Essau *et al.*, 2010). This impairment is long-lasting in that formerly depressed adolescents have been found to be less likely to have completed college, more likely to have been unemployed, to have low life satisfaction and self-esteem, poor physical health, and to require high levels of mental health treatment (Lewinsohn, Rohde, Seeley, Klein, & Gotlib, 2003). Left untreated, depression tends to have a chronic course with a low remission rate (Essau *et al.*, 2010; Harrington, Fudge, Rutter, Pickles, & Hill, 1990). Approximately 40 percent of adolescents who have recovered from a depressive episode relapse into a second depressive episode after an interval of one year (Lewinsohn, Rohde, & Seeley, 1994); longer lasting depressive episodes were found to be associated with an early onset of depression (i.e., before age 15) and the presence of suicidal ideation.

Although depression is associated with a high level of impairment, the percentages of depressed young people who receive mental health services are low. For example, in a study by Essau (2005), only 23 percent of adolescents with depression received mental health services. That study was conducted in Germany where, at the time, the German health care system was not based on a gatekeeper system where patients have the right to select any health professional for treatment; the main predictor of the use of mental health services was a history of attempted suicide. In a US study (Lewinsohn, Rohde, & Seeley, 1998), predictors of mental health service usage were found to be the presence of comorbid mental disorders, a history of suicide attempts, academic problems, having a non-intact family, female gender, severity of depression, and the number of previous depressive episodes.

These findings suggest that prevention of mental health problems among children and adolescents is an urgent and critical issue in modern Japan. In this chapter, we review the current trends in child and adolescent mental health and discuss challenges in implementing prevention programs in Japanese educational settings.

Barriers to the implementation of prevention programs

Despite the high rates of depression, its negative consequences (e.g., academic underachievement, social isolation) and frequent comorbidity with other mental disorders, little attention has been devoted to developing prevention programs for these mental health problems (Ishikawa *et al.*, 2006); other problems like bullying and school refusal have attracted more public attention than mental health issues per se. Nevertheless, 'anxiety and emotional problems' (e.g., Ministry of Education, Culture, Sports, Science and Technology, 2013) and 'feeling of worthlessness' have been reported to be amongst the most common maintenance factors for school refusal behaviors. Furthermore, a Japanese form of social withdrawal (*hikikomori*) is often associated with difficulty in school and school truancy (Teo, 2010). These findings suggest that a substantial proportion of these students may benefit from a universal intervention program targeting internalizing disorders.

There are several factors that may have contributed to the difficulty in implementing prevention programs in Japan. First, the level of mental health literacy is low and stigmatizing attitudes toward mental health problems are stronger than in other countries such as Taiwan or Australia (Griffiths *et al.*, 2006), which could be due to a lack of national campaigns to tackle stigma, and to society's valuing of conformity. More importantly, adults have difficulty in accepting the fact that children and adolescents can be depressed. The latter is related to the widely held perception that childhood is associated with 'cheeriness' and 'naivety', or is 'worry-free'. Furthermore, the most commonly reported depressive symptoms by Japanese adolescents are insomnia, weight loss, and psychomotor agitation or retardation, rather than depressed mood (Sato *et al.*, 2008). Since these symptoms are not typical manifestations of depression, teachers and parents may overlook the presence of depression in young people. Thus, in order for adults to be more accepting of psychosocial intervention programs in the school setting, there is a need to disseminate information about child and adolescent mental health problems, their consequences, and their prevention and treatment.

A second barrier is that evidence-based intervention is not part of Japanese school counseling practices. School counseling was introduced into Japanese elementary and middle schools in 1995 and institutionalized as a nation-wide project in 2001 (Ministry of Education, Culture, Sports, Science and Technology, 2010). Clinical psychologists (or psychiatrists and university faculty in some cases) are employed as school counselors. Clinical psychology training is provided by accredited institutions which have, historically, placed considerable emphasis on psychoanalysis and other non-empirically supported interventions. Consequently, many clinical psychologists are unaware or even resentful of the notion of evidence-based practice. Educational personnel are more accepting of evidence-based interventions because they can see improvements in children's behavior; however, it is difficult for them to discern whether their school counselor possesses appropriate skills and training to deliver mental health interventions. Consequently, some school officials are skeptical of the school counseling system, and propose that a wider range of professionals should participate in promoting child mental health (Metropolitan Assembly, 2012). Clearly, the standard of mental health services provided by school counselors needs to improve and schools need to invest in evidence-based mental health programs.

The demand for training in evidence-based intervention is high. According to the Japanese Society of Certified Clinical Psychologists (2009), approximately 72.8 percent of clinical psychologists are seeking to learn empirically supported intervention methods such as behavioral or cognitive-behavioral therapies. However, training opportunities are limited, and numerous graduate schools teaching clinical psychology do not provide a course in CBT. Thus, in order to promote evidence-based practice in schools, opportunities to be trained in evidence-based treatment need to be increased.

Third, due to differences in cultural values, empirically-supported programs, which are mostly developed in western countries, need to be adapted for the Japanese context. However, some aspects of CBT are difficult to directly translate to fit the Japanese cultural context due to differences in the cognitive framework and social norms. For example, the dominance of collectivist values in Japanese culture means that proactive behavior, which is socially desirable in many western countries, may be perceived differently in Japan. Rather, the ability to inhibit one's impulsive responses, and to reflect on how one might act in a way that would benefit both the individual and the group, is highly regarded as a way to enhance subjective adaptation (Hess, Kashiwagi, Azuma, Price, & Dickson, 1980). Indeed, children who report high internalizing symptoms are likely to be perceived as obedient and/or compliant by their teachers (Ollendick & Ishikawa, 2013).

Furthermore, in a collectivist culture such as in Japan, the relationship among the in-group is seen as one in which there is a willingness and ability to think about and feel what others are feeling and thinking, to absorb this information without being told, and to help others satisfy their wishes and realize their goals (Markus & Kitayama, 1991). Another of collectivism's qualities that is associated with Japanese culture is related to the concept of *amae* (dependence) (Doi, 1973).

Some authors have argued that it is part of Japanese socialization to promote *amae* in children (Azuma, 1986). Specifically, when a child is born, the mother remains close to the child to ensure that the child feels secure, and to minimize the boundary between the mother and the child; this closeness also ensures that the child's needs are met. This type of socialization creates the bond of *amae*, in which children's emotional and existential needs are satisfied by their mothers' indulgent devotion.

Moreover, the Japanese education system has a unique culture of its own, which needs to be considered when implementing prevention programs. In particular, Japanese schools tend to emphasize educational equality and avoid giving special treatment to a specific child or class due to stigmatization. This can prove problematic when implementing selective or indicated prevention programs. Thus, the cultural adaptation of empirically supported programs needs to be considered when implementating evidence-based programs in Japanese schools.

Addressing the challenge

In light of the above barriers, our research team (Ishikawa, Iwanaga, Yamashita, Sato, & Sato, 2010; Ishikawa, Togasaki, Sato, & Sato, 2009; Sato *et al.*, 2009) has examined the efficacy of the Japanese adaptation of three universal depression prevention programs. The first program was the *Phoenix Time* program, which has been developed for 5th and 6th graders. This program is CBT-based and consists of psychoeducation, social skills training, and cognitive restructuring. In our study, 310 children (aged 10–12 years) were assigned to either the CBT group (n=150) or to no-treatment control condition (n=160). Results indicated that CBT was superior to the control condition in reducing children's depressive symptoms and cognitive dysfunction, and in increasing their social skills and school functioning (Sato *et al.*, 2009).

The second program, the *Smile* program, focuses on class-wide group social skills training, which includes introduction and listening skills, giving positive messages, asking for a favor, and declining an offer. Its efficacy was examined in 3rd grade children who were assigned to the *Smile* group ($n = 114$) and the wait-list control group ($n = 75$) (Ishikawa *et al.*, 2010). Children who participated in the *Smile* group showed significant improvement in their social skills and a reduction in depressive symptoms at post-intervention compared to children in the wait-list control group. A subsequent study supported the effectiveness of the *Smile* program in reducing children's depression, and the positive effect was maintained three years later (Sato, Ishikawa, *et al.*, 2013).

The third program, *Challenge for the Mind*, consists of eight sessions and includes multiple components such as social support seeking, social skills training, relaxation, cognitive restructuring, and behavioral activation. In a pilot study that involved students in 8th grade, significant improvements in social skills and social support were obtained. Depressive symptoms and friendship stress also decreased among students in the prevention group, whereas the depressive symptoms of those in the control group ($n = 22$) persisted (Ishikawa *et al.*, 2009).

In addressing the challenges presented in the former section, similar adjustments were made to all the three programs. To overcome the lack of awareness regarding mental health problems among school officials, the three programs were introduced during workshops and after a preliminary survey. In the Japanese educational system, various workshops (covering numerous topics such as how to teach specific subjects such as science, and how to manage the class) are held during the summer break. During a series of workshops that we delivered to school officials, we presented the rationale for a school-based depression prevention program and current knowledge on youth mental health.

Following the workshops, we administered a preliminary survey in schools that were interested in launching one of the three prevention programs. The purpose of the survey was to estimate the prevalence of depression and to enhance school officials' and teachers' understanding of mental health issues among children and adolescents in their school. At the end of the school semester, we discussed with the teachers the feasibility of implementing the depression prevention program in their schools. These activities helped teachers to improve their skills in identifying students with internalizing problems.

To overcome the second barrier, that is, the dissemination of evidence-based psychology, a team of professionals and graduate students with experience in CBT programs trained the classroom teachers to implement the CBT. Such training works well in Japan because teachers have an opportunity to observe other teachers' classes to improve their teaching skills. Such an activity is called a 'demonstration lesson', where the teacher who is in charge of the demonstration develops a 'teaching plan' that outlines the content of the class. Based on this teaching plan, the teachers who observe the class can share the general outline of the lesson from the beginning to the end. The demonstrator and observers participate in an after-meeting to discuss the achievements and problems of the class. We adapted this system for the training and supervision of our program by preparing a teaching plan for the depression prevention program. The pilot version was refined based on the discussion in the pre-meeting; the first version was further revised to include the information that was discussed at the post-meeting with the research team and teachers. This effort ensured that teachers could learn to effectively deliver CBT-based treatment programs independently of our research team and, more importantly, beyond the lifetime of our research project.

Allocating classroom teachers as the providers of mental health education has numerous advantages. All Japanese teachers undergo mandatory training in school guidance or educational counseling, which offer an excellent opportunity to provide them with the basic skills to deliver class-based prevention programs. Teachers normally do not possess a specific attitude or pre-judgment towards evidence-based practice, which makes it easier for them to be trained in delivering evidence-based intervention such as CBT skills. Classroom teachers also spend most of their time with their students and work full time for years, whereas school counselors usually work part time on a single-year basis. These characteristics make the teacher an ideal person to implement the program over a longer time span.

Concerning the third barrier, the cultural adaptation of the CBT program, all three programs that we adapted to the Japanese setting were delivered in the form of universal prevention to avoid labeling and stigmatization, and to reduce the discomfort that teachers and parents may have when a specific child is targeted. The 90–120 minute sessions common in western programs were shortened to fit the typical Japanese class hours, that is, 45 minutes in elementary school and 50 minutes in middle school. Social skills training and peer relationships were given a strong focus in each of the programs to accommodate to the Japanese culture, which emphasizes within-group harmony and positive development. Japanese schools are becoming highly sensitive to students' relationships following the introduction of the bullying prevention law. Therefore, school officials are more accepting of a friendship-building program than a program to decrease the incidence rate of depression per se. These modifications are compatible with studies that demonstrated the importance of the socio-contextual aspects of depression (Herman, Reinke, Parkin, Traylor, & Agarwal, 2009) and the dual approach that proposes the importance of addressing individual factors (e.g., building children's cognitive-behavioral skills) and environmental protective factors (e.g., peer support and positive classroom environments) in universal depression preventive interventions (Spence, 2008). The dual approach can provide environmental support to peers and teachers, which in turn creates a preventive environment for all students, whether they are currently depressed or at risk of experiencing depression.

The CBT workbook was adapted by including *anime*, cartoon artwork that is familiar to Japanese children and adolescents (Figures 14.1 and 14.2). This material was part of the *Phoenix Time* program, which is created as a detective story (Sato, Sato, *et al.*, 2013). Children are encouraged to play the role of a detective and learn the different components of CBT. Japanese children are familiar with the TV game culture, and role-playing a character is an enjoyable activity. The dog in Figure 14.1 (original: anime) that acts as a general manager of a detective firm introduces secret gadgets which are metaphors for each cognitive behavioral skill. Figure 14.1 shows a 'feeling finder', which is used to search and measure one's feelings. The last page of each session (Figure 14.2) gives the general manager's comments on the detective level (e.g., students get to 'freshman level' at lesson 3). As lessons progress, they receive a higher rank such as 'independent', 'expert' and 'master level'.

Children's developmental levels were also considered. Figures 14.3 and 14.4 were taken from the *Challenge for the Mind program*, which targeted adolescents in middle school. In the Japanese educational system, there is a substantial difference between elementary and middle schools in terms of what is expected of the students. For instance, school uniforms (Figure 14.4), structured club activities, and rigorous school rules are first introduced in middle school. Prevention programs should be adapted to the children's age and school climate in order for the school to be accepting of these programs.

How does Misaki feel?
Your first mission is to identify her feeling!
I will give you this secret detective gadget...

Secret Gadget
No.01

Feeling Finder

With this gadget, you can identify your friends' feelings as well as your own.

The details are provided in the next page...

FIGURE 14.1 Feeling finder page from *Phoenix Time* program
Courtesy of NIPPON HYORON SHA, LTD.

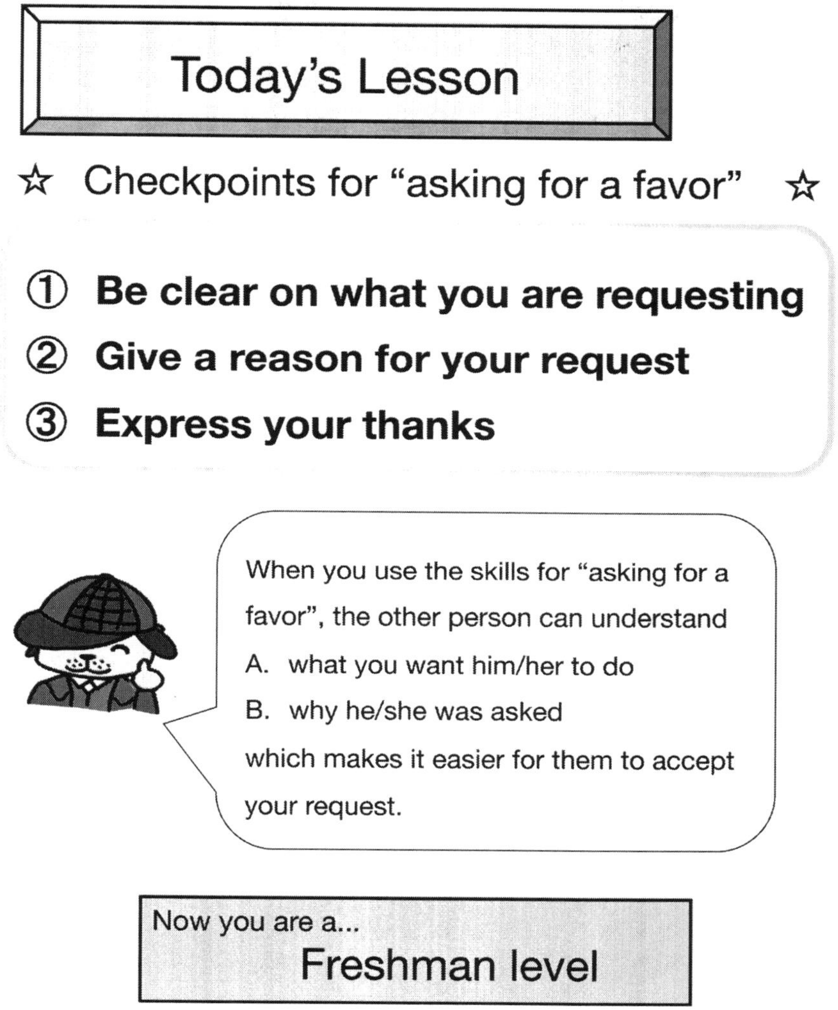

Today's Lesson

☆ Checkpoints for "asking for a favor" ☆

① **Be clear on what you are requesting**

② **Give a reason for your request**

③ **Express your thanks**

When you use the skills for "asking for a favor", the other person can understand

A. what you want him/her to do

B. why he/she was asked

which makes it easier for them to accept your request.

Now you are a...
Freshman level

FIGURE 14.2 Last page from a *Phoenix Time* lesson
Courtesy of NIPPON HYORON SHA, LTD.

| Homework |

Examining the relationship between daily pleasant activities and your feelings

Record the number of times you experience happy things and pleasant activities each day. Next, rate your feelings on a scale of -5 to +5. Higher scores represent good feelings, lower scores show bad feelings, and 0 stands for regular feeling.

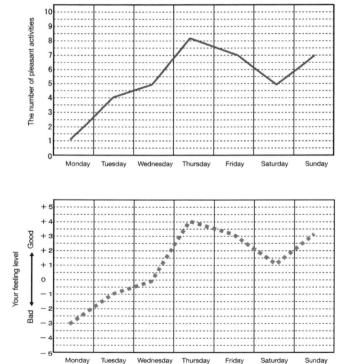

FIGURE 14.3 A homework page from *Challenge for the Mind* (middle school program) Courtesy of NIPPON HYORON SHA, LTD.

How did you feel when you practiced the skills of "declining an offer"? Summarize what you noticed below.

How did you feel when your partner turned down your request in the role-play? Summarize what you noticed below.

If you decline an offer, would you be disliked?....**NOT AT ALL!**

You may worry that you would be rejected by your friends if you turn down their request. Let's recall the role-play session when you were the one who was turned down. When other people used appropriate skills of declining an offer, you didn't feel bad about them.

If you can say no with appropriate skills of declining an offer, the other person, like you, would not feel bad.

OK! Next time!

I'm so sorry. I have to look after my sister today. Would you call on me another time?

FIGURE 14.4 A page from *Challenge for the Mind* showing characters in school uniform
Courtesy of NIPPON HYORON SHA, LTD.

Conclusion

Despite the presence of factors that hinder the implementation of prevention programs in Japan, our studies suggest that intervention procedures developed in western societies can be adapted to fit the needs of the Japanese culture and school environment. Four points emerge as the key to success: (1) the concise understanding and translation of the basic theoretical background, (2) the development of a context-sensitive program, (3) adjustment to fit the needs of a particular group or environment, and (4) dissemination efforts in maintaining the program. Changes in the structure of the CBT program are feasible insofar as the material does not lose its authenticity; word-for-word translation often fails to capture the essentials of the intervention, and grasping the objective of each component is much more important. The material needs to stimulate interest by using visual cues and examples that are familiar in the particular cultural context, so the participants can relate to and adapt what they have learned to their own situations. Specific components of the intervention program should accommodate to the needs derived from social norms to increase the possibility of positive reinforcement. In order to make this possible, detailed adjustment based on feedback from professionals as well as adults who know the children well is invaluable. Finally, sustainability of the program is crucial in the dissemination process, and the focus should be on both the evidence-based program and the educational system (i.e., the school).

References

Azuma, H. (1986). Why study child development in Japan? In H. Stevenson, H. Azuma, & K. Hakuta (Eds.), *Child development and education in Japan*. New York: W. H. Freeman, pp. 3–12.

Denda, K. (2008). Mood disorders in children and adolescents: Clinical features, modern views and recent problems. *Japanese Journal of Child and Adolescent Psychiatry, 49,* 89–100.

Denda, K., Kako, Y., Sasaki, Y., Ito, K., Kitagawa, N., & Koyama, T. (2004). Depressive symptoms in a school sample of children and adolescents: Using the Birleson Depression Self-Rating Scale for Children [DSRS-C]. *Japanese Journal of Child and Adolescent Psychiatry, 45,* 424–436.

Doi, T. (1973). *The anatomy of dependence.* Tokyo: Kodansha International.

Essau, C. A. (2005). Use of mental health services among adolescents with anxiety and depressive disorders. *Depression and Anxiety, 22,* 130–137.

Essau, C. A., Lewinsohn, P. M., Seeley, J. R., & Sasagawa, S. (2010). Gender differences in the developmental course of depression. *Journal of Affective Disorders, 127,* 185–190.

Griffiths, K. M., Nakane, Y., Christensen, H., Yoshioka, K., Jorm, A. F., & Nakane, H. (2006). Stigma in response to mental disorders: A comparison of Australia and Japan. *BMC Psychiatry, 6,* 21.

Harrington, R., Fudge, H., Rutter, M., Pickles, A., & Hill, J. (1990). Adult outcomes of childhood and adolescent depression. *Archives of General Psychiatry, 47*(5), 465–473.

Herman, K. C., Reinke, W. M., Parkin, J., Traylor, K. B., & Agarwal, G. (2009). Childhood Depression: Rethinking the role of the school. *Psychology in the School, 45*(5), 433–443.

Hess, R. D., Kashiwagi, K., Azuma, H., Price, G. G., & Dickson, W. P. (1980). Maternal expectations for mastery of developmental tasks in Japan and the United States. *International Journal of Psychology, 15,* 259–271.

Ishikawa, S., Iwanaga, M., Yamashita, B., Sato, H., & Sato, S. (2010). Long-term effects of social skills training on depressive symptoms in children. *Japanese Journal of Educational Psychology, 58,* 372–384.

Ishikawa, S., Togasaki, Y., Sato, S., & Sato, Y. (2006). Prevention programs for depression in children and adolescents: A review. *Japanese Journal of Educational Psychology, 54,* 572–584.

Ishikawa, S., Togasaki, Y., Sato, S., & Sato, Y. (2009). Development of school-based prevention programs for depression in junior high school students: A preliminary trial. *Japanese Journal of Behavior Medicine, 15,* 69–79.

Japanese Society of Certified Clinical Psychologists (2009). *Investigation of trend and consciousness of clinical psychologists.* Vol. 5. Tokyo: Japanese Society of Certified Clinical Psychologists.

Lewinsohn, P. M., Rohde, P., & Seeley, J. R. (1994). Psychosocial risk factors for future adolescent suicide attempt. *Journal of Consulting and Clinical Psychology, 62,* 297–305.

Lewinsohn, P. M., Rohde, P., & Seeley, J. R. (1998). Treatment of adolescent depression: Frequency of services and impact on functioning in young adulthood. *Depression and Anxiety, 7,* 47–52.

Lewinsohn, P. M., Rohde, P., Seeley, J. R., Klein, D. N., & Gotlib, I. H. (2003). Psychosocial functioning of young adults who have experienced and recovered from major depressive disorder during adolescence. *Journal of Abnormal Psychology, 12,* 353–363.

Markus, H. R. & Kitayama, S. (1991). Culture and the self: Implications for cognition, emotion, and motivation. *Psychological Review, 98,* 224–253.

Metropolitan Assembly (2012, June, 4th) Committee on education shorthand notes, Vol. 8. [Online report]. Retrieved 24.11.2015 from www.gikai.metro.tokyo.jp/record/bunkyo/d3030263.html

Ministry of Education, Culture, Sports, Science and Technology (2010, January, 12th). Enhancement of school guidance for children and adolescents. Retrieved 24.11.2015 from www.mext.go.jp/a_menu/shotou/seitoshidou/kyouiku/houkoku/07082308.htm

Ministry of Education, Culture, Sports, Science and Technology (2013, December, 10th). The Survey of behavioral problems of students (school nonattendance in elementary and junior high school) in 2013 [Online report]. Retrieved 24.11.2015 from www.mext.go.jp/b_menu/houdou/25/12/1341728.htm

Ollendick, T.H., & Ishikawa, S. (2013). Interpersonal and social factors in childhood anxiety disorders. In C. A. Essau & T. H. Ollendick (Eds.), *Treatment of Childhood and Adolescent Anxiety Disorders.* London: Wiley-Blackwell, pp. 117–139.

Sato, H., Imajyo, T., Togasaki, Y., Ishikawa, S., Sato, Y., & Sato S. (2009). School-based cognitive behavioral intervention for depressive symptoms in children. *Japanese Journal of Educational Psychology, 57,* 111–123.

Sato, H., Nagasaku, M., Kamimura, K., Ishikawa, M., Honda, M., Matsuda, Y., Arai, K., Ishikawa, S., & Sakano, Y. (2006). A community-based investigation of depressive symptoms in children. *Japanese Journal of Child and Adolescent Psychiatry, 47,* 57–68.

Sato, H., Shimotsu, S., & Ishikawa, S. (2008). Prevalence rate of depressive disorders in a community sample of adolescents in Japan. *Clinical Psychiatry, 50,* 439–448.

Sato, S., Ishikawa, S., Togasaki, Y., Ogata, A., & Sato, Y. (2013). Long-term effects of a universal prevention program for depression in children: A 3-year follow-up study. *Child and Adolescent Mental Health, 18,* 103–108.

Sato, S., Sato, Y., Ishikawa, S., Sato, H., Togasaki, Y., & Ogata, A. (2013). *Depression prevention program for elementary school children.* Tokyo: Nihon-hyoron-sha. (in Japanese).

Spence, S. H. (2008). Integrating individual and whole-school change approaches in the prevention of depression in adolescents. In J. R. Z. Abela & B. L. Hankin (Eds.), *Handbook of depression in children and adolescents*. New York: Guilford Press, pp. 333–353.

Teo, A. R. (2010). A new form of social withdrawal in Japan: A review of hikikomori. *International Journal of Social Psychiatry, 56,* 178–185.

The World Bank (2014). *Risk and opportunity: Managing risk for development.* Washington, DC: World Bank.

SECTION 6

Reflections

15

MONITORING SCHOOL CLIMATE AND SOCIAL EMOTIONAL LEARNING

Lessons from Israel and California

Ron Avi Astor, Gordon Capp, Hadass Moore and Rami Benbenishty

We present a framework based on the foundation that social emotional learning (SEL) and mental health are imperative components of schools' missions. Efforts to understand problems and intervene should be based on a contextual understanding of student experiences and be rooted in data. Systems for monitoring data from multiple ecological levels need to be in place, and information shared with all stakeholders. This monitoring framework suggests that providing local, regional and national data will allow schools and districts to make decisions regarding the adaptation, development, implementation and evaluation of interventions. We draw on our research to provide examples of how monitoring can impact the experiences of students, families, teachers, administrators, schools, and districts.

The challenges addressed in the chapters of this book represent contextual gaps in theory and practice with the goal of promoting the social and emotional wellbeing of students in schools. Through the present authors' research projects in the United States, Israel and Chile over the past 30 years, and within the research literature, we have come across scholars, policymakers and practitioners who are deeply concerned about these issues. Our large-scale monitoring work has provided alternative research perspectives, assumptions and methodologies pertaining to many of the topics discussed in this book (e.g. Astor, Benbenishty, Wong, & Jacobson, 2014). The conclusions from our research projects will be the main source of our suggestions for future research, theoretical development and intervention. One project is an ongoing series of large-scale studies that utilize nested local-regional-national surveillance data representing all 3,000 Israeli schools over the past 20 years (Benbenishty & Astor, 2012a). In Chile we are collaborating with researchers and educators using a monitoring methodology framework for the entire city of Valparaiso.

In the United States we will draw on findings from a seven-year research intervention that focuses on how public civilian schools can support students who have had family members serving in the military, especially during the past 13 years of war in Afghanistan and Iraq (Astor & Benbenishty, 2014; Benbenishty, 2014). According to the Military Child Educational Coalition, there are up to four million children of active military members and post-9/11 veterans in public schools who have had parents serve in Iraq or Afghanistan (Military Child Education Coalition, 2012).

In our project in California we are working with the California Department of Education and WestEd (Benbenishty, Esqueda, & Couture, 2012; WestEd, 2015) examining longitudinal databases and monitoring structures of schools that represent close to 10,000 schools statewide. Additionally, we have developed a regional monitoring system (encompassing eight districts, 140 schools and more than 100,000 students). This system used surveys, interviews and observations with multiple constituents (e.g., students, staff, parents, interns, field instructors) to monitor each school and district over time. Hence, all our monitoring projects begin 'at scale' ecologically. Each school is examined within its community context, each community context within a district or regional context, and every region within a larger state or country context. Thus, although we have many schools and communities, we can begin to understand them individually, comparatively, and as a whole within each of the layered ecological contexts. The data collected have ecological relevance to specific physical locations, schools within a district, and larger specific particular geographical regions. Our work includes the scope of impact that interventions or policies have on those regions, and an examination of sustainability of practices over time.

Starting at scale: ecologically reliable, valid, and layered data

By definition, our theoretical model acknowledges and takes into account the normative potential for unique qualities in each individual school within each district setting, including the variations within and between settings on an array of variables, even with schools in the same communities with similar risk or resilience factors. This means that our theoretical model starts ecologically 'at scale', focusing first on creating a monitoring system for each individual school and district or region that uses layers of granular data from specific geographical locations that are nested physically, socially, organizationally, and ecologically (Benbenishty & Astor, 2007). The data can be used collectively across each district or region, but also by each school individually within the region.

Our monitoring model is built on strong ecological validity and reliability. It begins with the particular geographical context of the school, school district, and larger region, as they currently exist and change over time. All schools, neighborhoods, services, communities, staff members, parents, and students in the school, region, or nation could be included in our conceptualization of a data monitoring system, data usage, interventions, and research designs. We assume that the interventions in different regions and settings are likely to have both similarities and differences depending on the contextual needs, resources, and views of each social-ecological setting.

Our key principle proposes that the integration of an ecological perspective should be applied throughout all the different phases of intervention, from data collection to decision making, rather than in the implementation phase alone.

Most evidence-based program (EBP) intervention studies begin with a psychologically or skill-based theoretically driven program, or a set of empirically driven principles. With many EBPs, the contextualization process begins only after a practice or procedure is designated as an EBP, often through a randomized control trial (RCT) research design (Leadbeater and Gladstone, this volume). The ecological application, implementation, and scaling-up process begins only after a generic EBP is introduced into a variety of new diverse and complex contexts (Lendrum *et al.*, this volume). This may be a source of many of the problems described in this book and in the implementation science literature, such as difficulties in scaling up interventions and in sustaining programs over time.

Components of the multi-level monitoring method

Accurate and timely local data over time

We believe that every teacher, principal, parent, superintendent, support staff member, and student needs to have ongoing, timely, accurate, scientifically reliable and valid data on students' social and emotional needs, and that the data need to represent multiple ecological layers. This means that the measures and data need to be reliable and valid for each of these ecologically nested layers (Benbenishty & Astor, 2007). With rapid advances in technology, the growth of existing universal administrative academic and social indicator systems, and sophistication in web applications and computer software, large-scale data collection, data structures, and census-like feedback systems have become feasible and are relatively inexpensive to maintain.

With these types of data designs, scientists can examine complex and sophisticated questions that were not possible to address in earlier decades (Lendrum *et al.*, this volume). In fact, most current centralized state and national academic accountability systems fit the parameters of monitoring described so far in this chapter. Our research team worked with the Israel Ministry of Education and the California Department of Education to include SEL measures in existing monitoring systems (Benbenishty, 2014; Benbenishty & Astor, 2012b). Slightly altering or adding questions to existing administrative academic accountability systems is a fairly inexpensive way to create a SEL monitoring system.

Natural variation between and within schools

We believe there are scientific reasons why this monitoring system is essential as an infrastructure tool for sustained 'at scale' SEL in schools. Wide variation in SEL and academic outcomes between schools is one major reason. There are meaningful variations between schools on students' social-emotional and behavioral outcomes – even in schools within the same socioeconomic communities, and even in the same schools over time (Astor, Benbenishty, & Estrada, 2009). To be effective, monitoring systems need to be mandatory and include all schools within a select region. Given all the systemic variability within and between schools, the totality of schools in a given region or state is needed in order to accurately compare progress in any single school within each larger ecological context over time. This becomes scientifically essential if schools judge their progress by comparing outcomes over time with other schools in a district, region, and state or nationally. Having the totality of schools in a geographic region also captures successful practices in schools that have made the greatest progress as well as identifying those that have not made progress.

Over time, demographic shifts may account for portions of local, regional, and national variability. Even with moderate levels of turnover and culturally normative shifts in attitudes and behaviors, the same schools can show different social and emotional issues over time. The predictable staff turnover and staff burnout that we observed is missing in most theoretical and intervention strategies. Personnel shifts necessitate frequent retraining on each EBP (Askell-Williams & Murray-Harvey, this volume). Changing population dynamics also require ongoing evaluation to identify the needs of various school communities. Even with strong university partnerships and federal or foundation grants, we observed that shortly after external funding ceased, very few schools still used the programs in any way that resembled the original implementation (Esqueda, Astor, & De Pedro, 2012). Sometimes programs disappeared altogether (Esqueda *et al.*, 2012). The needs of settings across time, and the role of external vs. internal funding strategies, especially for ongoing training, are not widely addressed by the research or EBP literature (Astor, Wong, & Benbenishty, 2014).

Variability in types of problems across time

We believe monitoring systems could cover a wide array of social, emotional, and mental health topics that occur on school grounds or impact schooling. A regional school monitoring system can create an aggregated portrait of relevant issues present in each class, school, school district, county or country.

The same valid school site data can be used and aggregated to build awareness, mobilize internal and community resources, develop intervention or policy plans, evaluate the effectiveness of efforts at various organizational levels, and alter plans if needed. Having layered, multiple-perspective data within each school and across regions needs to be meaningful to each organizational structure within nested ecological contexts (e.g., the principal, school staff, the district superintendent, and state education department). If designed in an ecologically sound and nested way, the structure of a data system can compare across settings longitudinally (same settings or regions over time), horizontally (across settings in the same region or between multiple regions), and vertically (e.g., between a school, its district, its county, and larger regulatory entities). This type of design and structure can become a central tool organizing the allocation of physical, social, and knowledge resources in a particular region or country. This type of data system can also help inform university training programs and internships for SEL-associated professionals, and provide scientific data about causal and structural relationships between variables in schools. The data could answer both theoretical and policy questions about the nature of behaviors and issues amongst populations and regions, and the success of policies and interventions.

Local decision making and empowerment

There are practical and democratic advantages to this type of nested, regional monitoring system as well. From a practical perspective, large-scale and accurate SEL monitoring data allow educators, parents, and students to easily compare their collective progress on specific issues over time, compared to other groups of students, classes, or schools in their district or across the country and make decisions based on empirical data. From a democratic perspective, the data essentially represent the collective voices of those in the schools, and the disparate groups' potential solutions. When data are shared at a local level, monitoring designs can also allow distinct populations within a school to see the extent of variation within each school, district or regional setting. This could indicate areas of agreement and coalition building, deep disagreements, or allude to levels of awareness between groups in shared settings.

Sharing data could facilitate decision-making processes by bringing a level of scientific accuracy and by using comprehensive data to triage which problems to address. From an intervention perspective, it could empower groups to work more effectively with each other by seeing the totality of views and solutions, not only within each school, but also between and across schools on a large geographical scale. A multiple-perspective regional monitoring system could facilitate communication between groups since the data are collected regularly and multiple perspectives could be contrasted and used to address problems or intervention progress (Benbenishty, Astor, & Estrada, 2008).

Local and regional data-driven interventions

We continually observe that EBPs are adopted based on the popularity of programs, word of mouth, marketing campaigns, or media coverage of problems rather than on empirically based, local and reliable data outlining the needs within each school. The 'one-size-fits-all' approach across large regions commonly fails because it does not address the naturally occurring variation between needs within schools. Given that many EBPs are proprietary, distributed at a cost by organizations outside school districts, choosing widely which problems to work on and what programs are most relevant for the local context becomes even more important. Monitoring systems can provide the empirical foundation for making such choices.

Primary role of administrators and principals

We observed that almost exclusively, ministry-level administrators, regional supervisors, district administrators, and school principals were the key orchestrators, translators of mission, initiators for change, and sustainers of successful SEL programs in the schools (De Pedro *et al.*, 2014). Yet, it is not clear why these central organizational leaders are not included more prominently in the initial conceptualization of intervention models. In fact, in one of our monitoring studies, we concluded that it was the principal's and administrative staff's organizational skill, initiative, and vision that could account for stellar school safety interventions (Astor, Benbenishty, & Estrada, 2009). Their views and choices surrounding the interventions played a central role in our theoretical monitoring model. Administrator attitudes and understanding surrounding the usage of the local data monitoring system often hinges on their convictions around the validity and meaning of the data for their regions' SEL mission.

Ground-up innovations

We have noticed that most regional educational governments provide limited choices for EBPs, while allowing for relatively minor adaptation and narrow implementation parameters. Almost all the foregoing chapters suggest EBPs that were generated outside the school. In our work we continually encounter remarkable schools that address our outcomes of interest without using EBPs (Benbenishty & Astor, 2012b). Most have created ground-up solutions generated by the principal or staff members of the school. The current theoretical intervention paradigms do not allow exceptional schools a scientifically valid method to share their philosophies, organizational/training insights, and successes. These organic, school-generated processes have much to offer other schools and communities struggling with similar issues. Theory, intervention science, implementation science, and policy are impacted by the loss of lessons learned from schools that have created outstanding SEL environments (Barnes *et al.*, this volume). These types of schools may provide empirical clues on how to create more sustainable models of education that integrate SEL with academics. A comprehensive monitoring system provides a potential alternative way to capture the practices of these remarkable examples where SEL is organically part of the schools' way of being (Astor *et al.*, 2009).

Increasing capacity, resources for SEL

We have used monitoring systems to go beyond selecting and implementing EBPs. For example, through our systematic monitoring of resources and needs, we often found that some schools lacked expertise or professional capacity; some school districts did not have psychologists, counselors, or social workers to help coordinate or deal with mental health issues. Based on the data provided by the monitoring approach, we worked with districts to hire professionals trained in SEL. Some already had mental health professionals, but they were trained in more-targeted interventions and lacked training to run prevention, school climate, school safety, or district-wide SEL programs.

Moreover, some schools are isolated and not aware of local or national SEL resources and potential collaborations (e.g., partnering with local non-governmental organizations or local military resources). Some school districts are not aware of external funding available to help them address problems (Benbenishty, 2013). Over a four-year period, the monitoring system in California provided data that led to increased funding, with tens of millions of dollars coming to the districts through grants, federal funding programs, and local resources – even during an economic downturn.

In Israel, monitoring data allowed a dramatic increase in the number of human-resource hours. Most of the approximately 8,000 psychological support staff members are now dealing programmatically with SEL issues in schools, based on school-specific data. In many of these contexts, EBPs may not have helped without appropriate supports for implementation, and without addressing a school's lack of capacity to address an issue. Sometimes problem areas improved by addressing contextual capacity and resource issues (Astor, Benbenishty, Wong, & Jacobson, 2014). Hence, the monitoring approach assumes that problems can be addressed by using school site data, while capturing the potential for capacity building in regard to internal resources, procedures, training, funding and collaboration with other services.

Using data for constructive purposes

We have observed that when authorities use data solely to punish schools or professionals, the use of these systems is greatly degraded and in some cases is eventually eliminated. Currently, in the United States and other countries, there is a massive social and political backlash over the draconian academic indicator systems that punish low-performing schools.

Hence, we have focused on using local data for constructive purposes. We use information for training, growth, finding best practices, highlighting promising procedures developed by schools, and matchmaking principals from different settings so they can learn from each other. As scientists and practitioners, it is critical to promote positive and constructive ways to use data locally, regionally, and nationally. This means working with policymakers, the media, and the public to honor positive uses and interpretations of local and regional data (Astor, 2011).

Applications of the monitoring system

Using monitoring to alter the school's role in SEL

The monitoring system has a primary goal of raising the awareness of school staff members about issues that they may not consider to be their main responsibility. By making educators and the community aware of SEL issues, the school ecological system can begin to address the existing problems. However, the monitoring system can also be used to change regional and national norms surrounding the purpose and mission of the school. In this sense, monitoring is an intervention aimed at norms surrounding the SEL role of schools.

Including these SEL measures also makes schools' explicit SEL mission visible in national and global research agendas. There is a long societal history of diverse public views surrounding the mission of schools. One of the greatest cited obstacles for the implementation, sustenance, and integration of SEL programs in schools is a lack of clarity that SEL is central to the mission and purpose of schools. Having an integrated and mandated monitoring system sends a clear message to schools and society that SEL is also important for accountability, monitoring, and research designs. In fact, from our experiences, including SEL measures in long-term accountability systems is the most efficient way to increase sustainability and awareness. It also provides a platform where all members of society see that SEL issues are also part of the school's mission.

In several cases we were able to slightly alter existing accountability monitoring systems to help increase awareness. Up until 2005, Israel, like most other countries, collected mainly academically oriented data from each school. Through our work with the ministry, the revised monitoring systems also included questions for students and staff surrounding school climate, teacher/child relationships, school safety, and social-emotional issues into the existing state monitoring system (Benbenishty & Astor, 2005). Schools now automatically receive feedback on academic and SEL outcomes on a regular basis (Israel Ministry of Education, 2014).

From 1999 to the present, Israeli data show that school victimization has markedly decreased in areas where principals, teachers, and support service staff members have joined forces to tackle the problem (MITZAV – Israel's Measurements of Efficiency and Growth in Schools, 2013). The inclusion of SEL and climate measures has created national norms and standards around climate, social and emotional wellbeing, school safety and resources for special populations or schools in need (Benbenishty, Khoury-Kassabri, & Astor, 2007).

In California, the monitoring system is not integrated with the academic system, nor is it mandatory for schools unless they want to be eligible for specific state or federal grants. We focused on a relatively invisible group of students with active military or post-9/11 veteran parents. Working with the California Department of Education and WestEd, which administers the California Healthy Kids Survey (CHKS), our research team developed a military survey module and a military identifier for the core CHKS survey (Gilreath, Estrada, Pineda, Benbenishty, &

Astor, 2014). We were able to provide each school in our project and the whole state with detailed data on the SEL needs and strengths of military and non-military children. Many of the approximately 10,000 schools across the state had no idea that they had military or veterans' children in their classes (Benbenishty, 2014). Many did not know they could apply for grants or supports for this group. By including these issues in the monitoring system, schools across the state and nation can identify needs and strengths of this group of students.

Using monitoring to increase personnel capacity

Training mental health professionals, educational leaders, and school staff members to be aware of EBPs and how to address SEL in schools is a central issue. Most training related to SEL and EBPs occurs after completing college-based education post-graduation, either voluntarily or during in-service programming. Often, university researchers create or evaluate EBPs, but ironically these programs or methods are not commonly used in university pre-service programs, nor is student acquisition and application of skills measured.

In our California monitoring project we used school data to first identify the needs of each school (De Pedro, Esqueda, Cederbaum, & Astor, 2014). Our monitoring clearly suggested that staff members felt that they needed training in specific SEL areas including bullying, weapons on campus, substance use, mental health, wellbeing, and suicidal behavior (De Pedro, Esqueda, *et al.*, 2014). However, the mapping of skills and services at each school district showed that districts lacked mental health professionals. Most of the districts in the Consortium did not have anyone trained in SEL or mental health (Cederbaum *et al.*, 2014).

Our monitoring revealed, therefore, that an EBP may not have helped the schools since they lacked the professionals to run the program. This prompted a joint effort to increase the number of SEL professionals in those locations to help build capacity for SEL intervention in the district. Since many of these schools were dealing with children who had family members serving in the military, the unique mental health needs of these families were of great concern.

Aside from strategizing ways to hire full-time school and district employees, members of the project forged connections with three large local universities (San Diego State University, University of California, San Diego, and the University of Southern California) to build capacity-creating graduate-level internship programs within each of the districts that did not have SEL interns prior to this project (Esqueda *et al.*, 2014). We aimed to train large cohorts of local school-based professionals, including teachers and other support staff, at both pre-service level (during their university academic and field training) and in-service, through training workshops, so skills could be sustained. Over a four-year period, approximately 170 graduate interns in social work, psychology, and counseling were placed and supervised two to three days a week in these schools (Benbenishty, 2014). This provided approximately 85,000 internship hours in schools that had no SEL services prior to these placements. To help guide their efforts, interns, their field instructors, and their school principals were given the risk and resiliency data for their particular school that came from the monitoring system (Cederbaum *et al.*, 2014).

Seminars, speakers, coursework, and other training opportunities on EBPs directly associated with risk factors in the schools were presented weekly both at the university and school sites to increase the skills of the students and school staff members (Benbenishty, 2014). Short videos of model grassroots interventions identified through the monitoring system, research reports documenting their effectiveness, and newsletters highlighting the professional contacts in those schools were provided (Astor, Wong, & Benbenishty, 2014).

Eventually, four guidebooks based on these data were created for teachers, principals, parents, and mental health professionals and then disseminated among them (e.g. Astor *et al.*, 2012). These books were integrated into social work courses focusing on school-based services and assignments at the university level. The creation and integration of these guidebooks also illustrates the importance of using data as they become available, rather than waiting long periods of time for data analysis, to inform decisions and practices. As far as we know, the monitoring system was one of the first empirical examples of using data to see if our professionals being trained at the university are actually learning those skills at the pre-service level and assessing their ability to use them appropriately in their settings. These and other local school districts eventually hired many of the trained graduate students precisely due to those EBP methods and skills (Garcia, De Pedro, Astor, Lester, & Benbenishty, in press).

Similarly, the monitoring data were used to identify academic areas where students lacked support. A partnership with a large local university enabled the schools to have over 500 undergraduate students as academic tutors and mentors for students or groups (Astor, Wong, & Benbenishty, 2014). This was particularly important for the military-connected students who had attended many schools and experienced parental deployment, often to war zones. The university trained tutors and mentors in military family culture, methods to increase pride and belongingness, and to help fill gaps in academic knowledge due to frequent moves. Some of the undergraduate students majored in the sciences, but others were in the arts and were able to provide needed support in music, drama, and visual arts (Benbenishty, 2014). These students provided approximately another 20,000 hours a year of academic, social, and emotional support to students and schools that had no prior services (Partners at Learning, 2015).

In many parts of the world (e.g., United States, Israel) university internship programs are sustainable because they are free or provided at minimal costs to schools and continue beyond the end of the project. Furthermore, the material integrated into the university courses and placements is ongoing and educates new professionals at the pre-service levels to deal with these issues. Universities rarely empirically examine how well their students learn EBPs or skills in the field (Astor, Wong, & Benbenishty, 2014). In the present project, the monitoring systems helped accomplish some of these capacity-building goals at scale.

Conclusion

In this chapter we refer to gaps in practice and theory raised in this book. We propose a method of addressing some of these gaps by instituting a scientifically valid and reliable monitoring system that includes each local school, region, and state and measures progress on a wide array of SEL behaviors and supports over time. These monitoring infrastructures and methods could also create databases that increase our scientific knowledge of SEL issues in schools. Futhermore, the system could help identify needs, as well as resources to address them.

References

Astor, R. A. (2011 *Commentary*). Making sure children from military families are not left behind. *Huffington Post*. Retrieved 24.11.2015 from www.huffingtonpost.com/ron-avi-astor/making-sure-children-in-m_b_849055.html

Astor R. A., & Benbenishty, R. (2014). Supporting military-connected students: The role of school social work. *Children and Schools, 36*(1), 5–7.

Astor, R. A., Benbenishty, R., & Estrada, J. (2009). School violence and theoretically atypical schools: The principal's centrality in orchestrating safe schools. *American Educational Research Journal, 46*(2), 423–461.

Astor, R. A., Benbenishty, R., Wong, M., & Jacobson, L. (2014). Building Capacity in Military-Connected Schools: Annual Report Year 4, Los Angeles, CA: USC School of Social Work. Building Capacity_2013–2014 Annual Report 4

Astor, R. A., Jacobson, L., Benbenishty, R., Atuel, H., Gilreath, T., Wong, M., De Pedro, K. M., Esqueda, M. C., & Estrada, J. N. (2012). *A school administrator's guide to creating supportive schools for military students*. New York: Columbia University, Teachers College Press.

Astor, R. A., Wong, M., & Benbenishty, R. (2014). Building Capacity in Military-Connected Schools Consortium Final Technical Evaluation Report.

Benbenishty, R. (2013). Building Capacity in Military Connected Schools Consortium: Technical Evaluation Report: Year 3, 2013. Los Angeles, CA: USC School of Social Work.

Benbenishty, R. (2014). Building Capacity in Military Schools: Final Technical Evaluation Report. Los Angeles, CA: USC School of Social Work.

Benbenishty, R., & Astor, R. A. (2005). *School violence in context: Culture, neighborhood, family, school, and gender*. New York: Oxford University Press.

Benbenishty, R., & Astor, R. A. (2007). Monitoring indicators of children's victimization in school: Linking national-, regional-, and site-level indicators. *Social Indicators Research, 84*(3), 333–348.

Benbenishty, R., & Astor, R. A. (2012a). Monitoring school violence in Israel, National studies and beyond: Implications for theory, practice, and policy. In S. R. Jimerson, A. B. Nickerson, M. J. Mayer, & M. J. Furlong (Eds). *Handbook of school violence and school safety: International research and practice*. Second Edition. New York: Routledge, pp. 191–202.

Benbenishty, R., & Astor, R. A. (2012b). Making the case for an international perspective on school violence: Implications for theory, research, policy, and assessment. In S. R. Jimerson, A.B. Nickerson, M.J. Mayer, & M. J. Furlong (Eds). *Handbook of school violence and school safety: International research and practice, Second Edition*. New York: Routledge, pp. 15–26.

184 Ron Avi Astor *et al.*

Benbenishty, R., Astor, R. A., & Estrada, J. N. (2008). School violence assessment: A conceptual framework, instruments and methods. *Children & Schools, 30*(2), 71–81.

Benbenishty, R., Esqueda, M., & Couture, J. (2012). Building capacity in Military Connected Schools Consortium: Technical Evaluation Report: Year 2, 2012. Los Angeles, CA: USC School of Social Work.

Benbenishty, R., Khoury-Kassabri, M., & Astor, R. A. (2007). Findings from the National School Violence Study – 2005. *Mifgash L'Avoda Chinoochit Sozialit, 23*, 15–23 [Hebrew].

Cederbaum, J. A., Malchi, K., Esqueda, M. C., Benbenishty, R., Atuel, H. R., & Astor, R. A. (2014). Student-instructor assessments: Examining the skills and competencies of social work students placed in military-connected schools. *Children and Schools, 36*(1), 51–59.

De Pedro, K. T., Atuel, H., Malchi, K., Esqueda, M. C., Benbenishty, R., & Astor, R. A. (2014). Responding to the needs of military students and military-connected schools: The perceptions and actions of school administrators. *Children and Schools, 36*(1), e18–e25.

De Pedro, K. T., Esqueda, M. C., Cederbaum, J. A., & Astor, R. A. (2014, November). District, school, and community stakeholder perspectives on the experiences of military-connected students. *Teachers' College Record, 116.*

Esqueda, M. C., Astor, R. A., & De Pedro, K. M. T. (2012). A call to duty: Educational policy and school reform addressing the needs of children from military families. *Educational Researcher, 41*(2), 65–70.

Esqueda, M. C., Cederbaum, J. A., Malchi, K., Pineda, D., Benbenishty, R., & Astor, R. (2014). The military social work fieldwork placement: An analysis of the time and activities graduate student interns provide military-connected schools. *Children and Schools, 36*(1), 41–50.

Garcia, E., De Pedro, K., Astor, R. A., Lester, P., & Benbenishty, R. (in press). Evaluating the impact of training social work interns in FOCUS skill-building groups on school climate. *Journal of Social Work Education.*

Gilreath, T. D., Estrada, J. N., Pineda, D., Benbenishty, R., & Astor, R. (2014). Development and use of the California Healthy Kids Survey Military Module to support students in military-connected schools. *Children and Schools, 36*(1), 23–29.

Israel Ministry of Education (RAMA) (2014). Monitoring levels of violence according to students' reports 2012, 2013, 2014. Retrieved 27.11.15 from http://buildingcapacity archive.usc.edu/individual_presentations/Nitur_Alimut_Report_2014%20(1).pdf

Military Child Education Coalition (2012). A Policy leaders' guide to military children. Retrieved 24.11.2015 from www.militarychild.org/public/upload/files/LegislativeGuide 2012.pdf

MITZAV (Israel's Measurements of Efficiency and Growth in Schools), (2013) Climate and Pedagogic Environment report. Retrieved 27.11.15 from http://buildingcapacityarchive. usc.edu/individual_presentations/Aklim_Report_2013_full.pdf

Partners at Learning (2015). Retrieved 24.11.2015 from http://palprogram.ucsd.edu/

WestEd (2015). California health kids survey. Retrieved 24.11.2015 from http://chks.wested. org/administer/download

16

MENTAL HEALTH AND WELLBEING THROUGH SCHOOLS

Thinking big, acting wisely

Rosalyn H. Shute and Phillip T. Slee

Here, we discuss a number of themes emerging from the foregoing chapters, including: adopting a systems framework; hard-to-tame problems; leadership and boundary spanners; models of organisational change; and teacher buy-in to programs. Some additional themes that we consider worthy of greater attention include the voices of young people, gender, and green schooling. We conclude that 'thinking big' is not antagonistic to 'acting small', if our interventions are wise.

Schools in many countries have a long history of supporting students' physical health (Srabstein, 2011), but many challenges face the more recent efforts to introduce mental health and wellbeing initiatives. Yet, as both Brian Graetz (Chapter 1) and Richard Beinecke (Chapter 2) point out, schools cannot opt out and, as a minimum, must 'firefight' problems with whatever resources are to hand. More proactive, preventative approaches shown to be efficacious in small-scale, highly controlled conditions often defy efforts to be taken to scale, and matters of implementation, diffusion and sustainability are keenly discussed in the foregoing chapters. Here, we reflect and expand on some of the issues raised, and draw attention to several important matters that are largely missing from current discourse.

Adopting a systems framework

Many of the present authors use 'systems thinking' for understanding mental health and wellbeing initiatives in schools. Bronfenbrenner's work has been particularly influential in this regard, with his initial 'ecological systems theory' in the 1970s later modified to become even more holistic, explicitly including biology and further emphasising the 'chronosystem' – the dimension of time (e.g., Bronfenbrenner & Morris, 1998). In keeping with a systemic approach, many of the current authors view school-based initiatives as existing within a complex web of individuals, contexts (including culture, policy settings and organisations) and their interactions. These interactions now encompass virtual communication channels, the significance of which we are still coming to terms with (Barnes *et al.*, Chapter 10; Brighi *et al.*, Chapter 8; Richards & Hughes, Chapter 9). A systems perspective is consonant with a public health approach (World Health Organization, 2000) and has some commonality with the worldviews of many communities around the world, such as Canadian Indigenous people, who see mental health as holistic and based on interdependence and healing (Stewart, 2008). Similarly, in Australia:

> [T]he Aboriginal concept of health is holistic, encompassing mental health and physical, cultural and spiritual health. This holistic concept does not just refer to the whole body but is in fact steeped in harmonised inter relations which constitute cultural well being. These inter relating factors can be categorised largely into spiritual, environmental, ideological, political, social, economic, mental and physical.
>
> (Swan & Raphael, 1995, p. 19)

Such views are at odds with mental health systems geared towards curing individual psychopathology. This narrower approach is illustrated by advertisements for the 16th International Mental Health Conference (2015), concerned with "the broad spectrum of mental disorders including Anxiety, Depression, Post-Traumatic Stress Disorders, Bipolar, Dementia and Suicide". This suggests a greater focus on mental *ill* health than mental health and, notably, educators are not among those invited to that particular conference table.

The primacy afforded to individual psychopathology creates dilemmas for practitioners who think systemically (Shute & Slee, 2015, p. 45), as well as for those undertaking mental health initiatives in non-western communities: Salwa Massad and Umaiyeh Khammash (Chapter 4), point out that an imported medicalised view of trauma and distress in Palestine sidelines efforts to recognise and promote children's resilience, while western-developed cognitive behavioural methods may not be suited to Japan's collectivist culture (Ishikawa *et al.*, Chapter 14).

An important aspect of systems theories is their trandisciplinary nature (Shute & Slee, 2015, p. 176) and, as shown repeatedly in this book, creating and sustaining effective programs in schools calls for collaboration between those from a range of backgrounds, including policy makers, practitioners and researchers. Yet these groups have different worldviews (Shonkoff, 2000). How can those working in different organisations, with different professional (or lay) backgrounds, beliefs and imperatives, possibly hope to 'get on the same page'?

Embracing complexity: hard-to-tame problems

We are helped here by Beinecke's discussion of 'wicked problems' (Chapter 2). This idea, well-established in the literature on organisational change, has been applied to addressing complex problems such as environmental issues (van Bueren, Klijn,

& Koppenjan, 2003). The terminology is rather unfortunate. Although authors are always at pains to explain that no moral judgement is intended, we have found that some concerned with mental health object to the term: when working with students with problems, the last thing they want to do is use the word 'wicked', even if it does apply to the problem and not the individuals concerned! We shall therefore call them 'hard-to-tame' problems. Regardless of terminology, the concept is valuable in providing a framework for understanding what we experience on the ground: that various parties involved (or potentially involved) in mental health interventions in schools often do not agree on the nature of the problem, let alone its solution or level of priority. Beinecke suggests that such situations call for systemic and flexible thinking and appropriate leadership.

Within a systemic approach, Heifetz's (e.g., Heifetz, Linsky, & Grashow, 2009) metaphor is apt: it is important to withdraw occasionally from the whirl and complexity of the dance to achieve an overview from the balcony. What policy settings, at various levels, influence what we may, or must, do? How will the retirement of the supportive school principal affect the program? What are the teachers' priorities for their professional development? Successful implementation depends on purposively managing complexity and change on an ongoing basis, and this takes adaptive leadership – transactional and transformative (Beinecke, Chapter 2).

Adaptative leadership and boundary spanners

To elaborate a little, transactional leadership encompasses important managerial skills such as efficiency and goal-setting. By contrast, transformative leadership is inspirational and focuses on factors such as interpersonal relationships and fostering autonomy, teamwork, creativity, empowerment and ongoing learning (Beinecke, 2009). These are the skills needed for enthusing and energising a range of possibly sceptical stakeholders contemplating the introduction of new approaches to mental health in schools.

Who are these adaptive leaders, and how do they develop their wide-ranging skills? Although some are more naturally talented than others, leadership skills can be developed by training. Not everyone has every skill, and assembling a team with complementary skills can itself be transformative (see Beinecke, 2009, and International Initiative for Mental Health Leadership website). Although those higher in organisations tend to use transformative skills more often, their use is not confined to the upper echelons (Beinecke, 2009), and various contributors to this book refer to the importance of program advocacy by champions or mentors, whether enthusiastic teachers, prominent community members or students themselves.

Leadership is not synonymous with one's job description, therefore, although those with more organisational power do at least need to provide a supportive framework. Amy Barnes and her colleagues, for example (Chapter 10), conclude that enhancing teacher capacity to address cyberbullying is not sufficient – there must be organisational and leadership support. Commensurate with this aim, one of the present authors (PS) has recently delivered a co-authored report on cyberbullying, sexting and the law to the South Australian Minister for Education; it discusses how the hard-to-tame issue of sexting could be addressed at an organisational level (Spears, Slee, & Huntley, 2015). Bonnie Leadbeater and Emilie Gladstone (Chapter 3) draw attention to a further matter: the importance of a flat organisational structure, whereby investment in a program becomes so widespread that it does not collapse when one strong leader moves on.

An important aspect of transformative leadership is the ability to cross boundaries (Beinecke, 2009), and there needs to be agreement about the roles, relationships and responsibilities of various agencies (Graetz, Chapter 1). Shute (2012) views social-emotional education as a 'borderland' enterprise between research psychologists and teachers, while the need for greater collaboration between schools and mental health services is seen as a policy priority by Vostanis *et al.* (2011). These researchers have observed a greater emphasis in the UK on educating teachers about mental health than in educating clinicians about education; they identify a need for dual appointments or personnel with a dedicated role in boundary-crossing, giving the example of UK school nurses forming linkages between schools and child and adolescent mental health services. Jane Jarvis and Julie McMillan (Chapter 11) highlight an impressive US project where schools systems, researchers and practitioners work in a unified way, with a common language, to meet the mental health needs of all students, including those with disabilities. Beinecke (2009) notes leaders' roles in highlighting shared values among different stakeholders. Also helpful is Shute's (1997) social psychological analysis of multidisciplinary teamwork in child health, and Hughes' (2011) work on collaboration across professional boundaries.

A final caution is that some of the work on adaptive leadership has been critiqued as privileging "charismatic personas, masculinity and Western culture", and as needing to take its own advice on embracing ambiguity and exploring complexity (Baylor, 2011). A postmodern reflection on educational leadership, as relationship-focused and flexible, can be found in Bell and Palmer (2015).

Models of organisational change

Graetz (Chapter 1) identifies the need for better models to guide practice, and Fixsen's work on organisational change has been influential (Fixsen, Naoom, Blase, Friedman, & Wallace, 2005; Leadbeater & Gladstone, Chapter 3; Lendrum *et al.*, Chapter 5). Thinking about organisational change may be further advanced by considering Weiner's (2009) work. Finding that the literature on 'readiness for organisational change' lacked a strong evidence base, he developed a theory to guide future research. It brings together the approaches in the literature based on either organisational structure or on individual psychology, to conceptualise readiness within an organisation as a shared psychological state that includes members' commitment to change and a shared belief in their capacity to do so. Readiness is determined by the value placed on the proposed change, and the evaluation of task demands, resources and situational factors. When these are highly rated, then initiation, effort, persistence and cooperation are expected, resulting in more effective implementation.

Hargreaves and Goodson (2006) point out that theories of educational policy change ignore the history of schools and teachers that may stretch back decades and determine responses to new initiatives. Such short-termism is also a major impediment to action on mental health and wellbeing (Scheftlein, 2012). Hard-to-tame problems require time (Wotherspoon *et al.*, Chapter 12) and, in fact, a final state is never reached (Beinecke, Chapter 2). Sawyer *et al.* (2010) found that it took two full years to bed down a new mental health program into schools, while Leadbeater and Gladstone (Chapter 3) mention the importance of refreshing programs in order to avoid 'cruising'. Sustainability, therefore, does not mean continuing to do the same, but remaining adaptable. Ron Avi Astor and colleagues (Chapter 15) emphasise the value of regular, system-wide data collection on social-emotional functioning in order to monitor change on an ongoing basis. It seems, then, that there would be benefit from paying closer attention to Bronfenbrenner's 'chronosystem'.

Lifting the barriers to teacher 'buy-in'

Teachers can be excellent providers of mental health education (Durlak *et al.*, 2011; Ishikawa *et al.*, Chapter 14; Slee *et al.*, 2009). Without their commitment and expertise, mental health and wellbeing initiatives in schools are not possible. However, teachers are often identified as 'resistant'. To draw a parallel with clinical psychology, client 'resistance to change' has been given much attention. Yet, in multisystemic therapy, therapists cannot use this as a reason for a lack of client change; they must keep re-analysing a broad range of individual, interpersonal and contextual issues, until they find ways to break through and use systemic strengths as 'levers for change' (Henggeler, Schoenwald, Borduin, Rowland, & Cunningham, 1998). Similarly, a systems perspective on implementation encourages us to take account of teachers' perspectives on mental health interventions in terms of strengths and barriers (Reinke, Stormont, Herman, Puri, & Goelet, 2011).

"You'll be gone in a week, ya f. . .in' pedo" (Dalton, 2014, p. 11). This is how a Year 9 boy greeted an experienced teacher on her second day at a Queensland regional school (threatening to get her sacked through a false accusation of paedophilia). Over the previous five years, teachers in that Australian state had received over $10 million in workplace claims for psychological damage sustained in schools (ibid). There are areas in schools where teachers feel particularly open to intimidation and confrontation, to the detriment of their own wellbeing (Wyra, Lawson, & Askell-Williams, 2011). Yet teachers' own mental health is a lower priority for principals than student mental health, especially bullying and harassment, impulsive behaviour and anger management (Intercamhs, 2009). Apart from indirect bullying, these are highly visible problems that are most likely to impact upon behaviour management and teacher stress. Linking mental health initiatives explicitly to addressing these issues and potentially reducing teacher stress may give a three-way win for teachers, students and principals. Nevertheless, students who are invisibly suffering internalising problems must not be overlooked. In Japan, for example, these students are perceived by teachers as obedient and compliant (Ishikawa *et al.*, Chapter 14). A universal program that includes such students is the preferred Japanese solution, though elsewhere screening for indicated intervention is an (admittedly controversial) option.

Teachers internationally face curriculum overload and a concomitant lack of time for new initiatives. Examples given by the National Council for Curriculum Assessment, Ireland (2010, p. 8) include: teachers in England identifying "unrelenting, piecemeal reform" over many years; teachers in Ireland feeling overwhelmed by the pace of change; Australian principals blaming the breadth of changes imposed by governments for the overcrowded curriculum; and Philippine students' achievement being hampered by frequent policy changes. Hargreaves and Goodson's (2006) analysis of cohorts of US and Canadian teachers over decades, and their differing experiences of their educational 'mission' and policy changes, casts further light on why teachers may have conflicting attitudes to the introduction of new programs; leaders need to explore and take account of this history rather than labelling more-experienced teachers, for example, as resistant fuddy-duddies. This is perhaps an area where values-based change might be considered to good effect by identifying common ground. For example, a shared interest in improving academic learning may provide a basis for taking on board the growing evidence that social-emotional learning is intimately connected to academic progress (Dix, Slee, Lawson, & Keeves, 2011; Durlak *et al.*, 2011). Page and Clark (2015) have called for such 'affect knowledge' to be incorporated into pre-service and in-service teacher education. Pedagogy itself has an impact on students' wellbeing (Grandin, 2011; Jarvis, 2011) and any discussion of pedagogy is, *ipso facto*, a discussion of wellbeing (Jarvis, 2011).

In practical terms, too, reducing the burden imposed by mental health programs is crucial. Teachers will more easily be able to accommodate programs that are not over-prescriptive; therefore a balance between fidelity and adaptation, within a quality-based framework, needs careful consideration (Lendrum *et al.*, Chapter 5; Slee *et al.*, 2009). Several chapters mention the importance of identifying core components of programs that can be linked with other programs in the school. In the case of professional development, too, Helen Askell-Williams and Rosalind Murray-Harvey (Chapter 7) found efforts were made at some Australian early childhood sites to create coherence between *KidsMatter* and other mandated programs.

Being stressed and time-poor are not the only reasons teachers may fail to embrace mental health initiatives. Some see this as 'not their area' (Askell-Williams & Murray-Harvey, Chapter 7) or are actually hostile towards social and emotional learning (Humphrey, Lendrum, & Wigelsworth, 2010), or to evidence-based practice (Shute, 2012). Others lack confidence to work in new technologies or the social-emotional area, and desire more professional development (Askell-Williams & Lawson, 2013). Barnes and colleagues (Chapter 10) note that underprepared teachers may cherry-pick parts of programs with which they are most at ease, rather than those necessary to achieve student change.

Teachers need to be well-prepared, then, and both pre-service and in-service professional development opportunities have been identified by our authors. Professional development needs to be clear about mechanisms of change and the core components of programs that must be delivered with fidelity. The existence of helpful policies and resources of which staff may be unaware should also be covered (Astor et al., Chapter 15; Barnes et al., Chapter 10). Askell-Williams and Murray-Harvey (Chapter 7) have devised a model of the structural and functional components of teacher professional development on social-emotional learning, and highlight the importance of ensuring that teachers' pre-existing knowledge and expertise are embraced. Online training may be more cost-effective and flexible than face-to-face professional development (Barnes et al., Chapter 10), although a downside is that teachers particularly value opportunities for collaboration with colleagues (Askell-Williams & Murray-Harvey, Chapter 7). In some circumstances the need for teacher input can be minimised if students themselves can undertake a program online (Barnes et al., Chapter 10). However, great care must be taken that digital technologies are not used to relieve teachers and schools of responsibility for issues that are better addressed face to face – in particular, the temptation to adopt attractive but unevaluated ICT programs needs to be resisted, with many issues such as confidentiality needing much more attention (Richards & Hughes, Chapter 9).

Pre-service teacher education, too, has been raised, with a need identified for this to include training in communication skills for promoting partnerships with parents (Shute, Chapter 6), and a greater emphasis on evidence-based practice (Shute, 2012), which may lead to cultural change in the profession in the longer term. Nevertheless, Shute (Chapter 13) raises the possibility that some teachers may lack the necessary empathy or communication skills to deal with sensitive matters such as indirect bullying and suicidality, and students may be better served by receiving details of contact teachers who can help them with particular problems. Success in educating pre-service teachers in social-emotional literacy has been demonstrated by Astor et al. (Chapter 15) and these teachers have been snapped up by schools seeking such expertise.

The sheer numbers of programs available may overwhelm principals and teachers and, as several contributors have said, schools need to become more discerning. Policies that mandate evidence-based practice, and online lists of evidence-based programs can help. 'Boundary-spanners' are again important here, and a school psychologist, counsellor or a librarian with a suitable background could act as a knowledge broker to facilitate suitable matches between schools and available evidence-based programs.

Finally, teacher buy-in may be enhanced if, as Astor and colleagues suggest (Chapter 15), social-emotional data collection becomes a normal part of school.

They also believe that there may be much to learn from schools that have already, on their own account, incorporated social-emotional issues into the fabric of school life.

Hearing the voices of young people

What about student buy-in? Elsewhere (Shute & Slee, 2015, pp. 212–223), we have discussed several trends that are encouraging a greater inclusion of young people's voices in matters that concern them, including: the 'new sociology of childhood' and social constructivism; increasing views of children as actors in their own development; views of children as 'being' and not just as 'becoming'; increasing concern with children's rights and empowerment; and the digital age. Yet, one often gains a sense from the literature that mental health and wellbeing programs are something that is 'done to' students. Student voice comes through more strongly in this book in the ICT section, where the 'digital natives' are often more at home with the technology than are the teachers. Student voice was also incorporated into the evaluation of Australia's *KidsMatter* through focus groups and interviews (Slee *et al.*, 2009).

Education has shifted from teacher-centred dissemination of information towards student-centred inquiry methods, and a few examples exist of students being fully engaged in the research process (e.g., Kinash & Hoffman, 2008). We suggest that there may be value in increased partnership with students in the development and evaluation of mental health and wellbeing programs. The opinions of some young people from the United States about social-emotional learning can be found at *What Kids Can Do, Inc.* (n.d.).

What about gender?

There is little in this book about gender, though Cathy Richards and Jennifer Hughes (Chapter 9) point to how ICT can be tailored to meet the preferences of girls and boys. In general, there seems to be an assumption that a universal mental health program will be equally applicable to all, although the World Health Organization (2002) concludes that "[m]ental health policies and programmes should incorporate an understanding of gender issues in a given context". For example, Salwa Massad and Umaiyeh Khammash (Chapter 4) mention patriarchy as placing women and child refugees at risk. More broadly, as girls enter adolescence, they experience a fall in many measures of wellbeing, compared with stability or a slight drop in boys (e.g., Finch, Hargrave, Nichols, & van Vliet, 2014, in the UK; Skrzypiec, Askell-Williams, Slee, & Rudzinsky, 2014, in Australia). Historically, the bullying literature has tended to ignore gender issues, although girls in many countries experience or observe sexual bullying in schools on a daily basis (Duncan, 1999; Shute, Owens, & Slee, 2008). Girls' wellbeing is undermined by the practice of female genital mutilation and by sexual assault; almost half of

South African girls can expect to be raped at some stage in their lives (Wikipedia). Murderous attacks or kidnaps of girls seeking an education in some countries create headlines. While there are global and local initiatives to address some of these matters, the overall picture is very depressing and, in our view, constitutes a global emergency. As we have discussed elsewhere, while feminism has certainly influenced educational practice, it has hardly touched developmental psychology or clinical child psychology (Shute & Slee, 2015, pp. 192–211).In keeping with a systemic perspective, a wider understanding of, and willingness to address, patriarchy as undermining girls' mental health and wellbeing (as well as that of LGBTI young people) is sorely needed.

Revisiting ecology

As we observed earlier, holistic thinking has long been the norm for many Indigenous peoples, embracing the natural world as integral to wellbeing. Growing evidence shows that connection to nature promotes human beings' physical and psychological wellbeing. Recognising this, the President's Foundation for the Wellbeing of Society in Malta has as one of its core elements a National Hub for Ethnobotanical Research, linking wellbeing with the natural environment. The global context for such initiatives is unprecedented destruction of the natural world, and many children today have little contact with it. Dickinson (2013) has proposed that we need to move beyond a simplistic NDD ('Nature Deficit Disorder') metaphor to a more nuanced and complex understanding of children's alienation from nature. Kerret, Orkibi, and Ronan (2014) propose that 'positive schooling' (that promotes subjective wellbeing) and 'green schooling' (that adopts a whole-school approach to pro-environmental sustainability) could be united. They have put forward a new theoretical model that takes account of the psychological processes involved in green education, including a positive focus on 'environmental hope' rather than the guilt and privation often suggested by discourse about environmental sustainability. Such initiatives indicate an important direction for the future of mental health and wellbeing promotion through schools.

Acting wisely

Adaptive leadership is wise leadership, and this includes working to ensure that wellbeing initiatives are based on good evidence. However, what constitutes 'good' evidence may be contested (Beinecke, Chapter 2) and, unfortunately, as noted by various contributors, schools may be convinced by slick marketing to adopt unevaluated commercial programs, and some well-intentioned leaders have achieved widespread diffusion of programs lacking an evidence base. As described by Shin-ichi Ishikawa and colleagues (Chapter 14), in Japan, clinical psychologists may not understand, or may even resent, evidence-based practice, so leadership on this issue is especially challenging there. Leaders also need to monitor changes to the evidence base. For example, a novel meta-analysis by Yeager, Fong, Lee,

& Espelage (2015) indicates that anti-bullying programs are ineffective for older adolescents and may even *increase* bullying. A central role of adaptive leaders is therefore to advocate for the adoption of evidence-based programs and for policies that mandate their use.

Yeager *et al.* (2015) have cited the work of Gregory Walton (2014) on 'wise psychological interventions'. These are small changes, or 'nudges', based on good psychological theory, that act as levers to set in train positive events within complex systems. One example Walton gives is the provision to African American students, on college entry, the information that everyone takes time to adjust; compared with those whose induction omitted this detail, they showed much better academic attainment and better health three years later. The explanation is that they perceived difficulties as normal rather than as confirmation that they did not belong. Such brief interventions, Walton suggests, are better viewed not as snapshots, but as unfolding movies, where each subsequent experience helps to create a virtuous cycle. Wise interventions, then, can 'scale up' to produce surprisingly large effects, provided they target specific psychological processes, are sensitive to context (and adapted if necessary) and appropriately timed. They are necessary, but may not be sufficient, to create positive change: the context must be supportive of the desired outcome.

Conclusions

The challenges of promoting mental health through schools can seem over-whelming as we try to 'think big' and contemplate the range and complexity of the issues. We can take encouragement from the success of large-scale programs such as *KidsMatter* in Australia, the *WITS Programs* in Canada, and programs for military families in the United States. They have taken many years of effort, persistence and reiteration. It is also heartening that Astor *et al.* (Chapter 15) demonstrate the possibility of establishing social-emotional data collection as part of widespread regular practice, thus laying the foundations for greater systemic acceptance of initiatives; however, in some countries this process may not be so well accepted. As these authors point out, such data need to be used positively – a point well understood in Australia, where a new online system for the public presentation of schools' academic standards ('My School') has been used informally to build rankings of schools with no appreciation of their contexts.

Being aware of the big picture issues associated with the development and delivery of wellbeing programs, and our own limited place in them, need not lead to hopelessness, but can help us to see where we can best direct our efforts. This is in accord with Fullan's (2009) tri-level model of educational reform, whereby we focus on the level where we are employed (e.g., the school, province or country) but seek 'permeable connectivity' with the other levels (this takes us back to 'boundary-spanning'). Children affected by violent conflict, for example, may be helped at a macro level by appeals to bodies such as the United Nations to work towards conflict resolution, but in the meantime we can seek to create conditions on the ground that are conducive to the development of resilience. While our local efforts may sometimes seem like a small drop in an ocean of need, remarkable change is possible, provided our interventions are wise.

References

Askell-Williams, H., & Lawson, M., (2013). Teachers' knowledge and confidence for promoting positive mental health in primary school communities. *Asia-Pacific Journal of Teacher Education, 41*(2), 126–143.

Baylor, R. (2011). Review of Heifetz, R. A., Linsky, M., & Grashow, A. (2009). The practice of adaptive leadership: Tools and tactics for changing your organization and the world. Cambridge, MA: Harvard Business Press. Accessed 26.11.2015 at https://nclp.umd.edu/resources/bookreviews/BookReview-The_Practice_of_Adaptive_Leadership-Baylor-2011.pdf

Beinecke, R. H. (2009). Introduction: Leadership for wicked problems. *The Innovation Journal, 14*(1), 1–17.

Bell, M., & Palmer, C. (2015). Shaping a strengths-based approach to relational leadership. Ch. 11 in H. Askell-Williams, *Transforming the future of learning with educational research.* Hershey, PA: IGI Global, pp. 209–228.

Bronfenbrenner, U., & Morris, P. A. (1998). The ecology of developmental processes. Ch. 17 in R. M. Lerner (vol. ed.), *Handbook of child psychology: Theoretical models of human development* 5th edn. Vol. 1. New York: Wiley.

Bueren, E. M. van., Klijn, E-H., & Koppenjan, K. F. M. (2003). Dealing with wicked problems in networks: Analyzing an environmental debate from a network perspective. *Journal of Public Administration Research and Theory, 13*(2), 193–212.

Dalton, T. (2014). Class warfare. *Weekend Australian Magazine*, July 19–20 2014, 11–14.

Dickinson, E. (2013). The misdiagnosis: Rethinking 'Nature-deficit Disorder'. *Environmental Communication.* Accessed 28.02.2015 at http://dx.doi.org/10.1080/17524032.2013.802704

Dix, K. L., Slee, P. T., Lawson, M. J., & Keeves, J. P. (2011). Implementation quality of whole school mental health promotion and students' academic performance. *Child and Adolescent Mental Health, 17*(1), 45–51.

Duncan, N. (1999). *Sexual bullying.* London: Routledge.

Durlak, J. A., Weissberg, R. P., Dymnicki, A. B., Taylor, R. D., & Schellinger, K. (2011). The impact of enhancing students' social and emotional learning: A meta-analysis of school-based universal interventions. *Child Development, 82*, 474–501.

Finch, L., Hargrave, R., Nichols, J., & van Vliet, A. (2014). *Measure what you treasure: Well-being and young people, how it can be measured and what the data tell us.* New Philanthropy Capital. Accessed 28.05.2014 at http://www.thinknpc.org/publications/measure-what-you-treasure/

Fixsen, D. L., Naoom, S. F., Blase, K. A., Friedman, R. M., & Wallace, F. (2005). *Implementation research: A synthesis of the literature.* Tampa, FL: University of South Florida, Louis de la Parte Florida Mental Health Institute, The National Implementation Research Network (FMHI Publication #231).

Fullan, M. (Ed.) (2009). *The challenge of change,* second edn. Ontario: Corwin Press.

Grandin, R. (2011). School diversity disengagement: The impact of schooling on the wellbeing of students. In R. H. Shute (Ed) with P. T. Slee, R. Murray-Harvey, & K. Dix, *Mental health and wellbeing: Educational perspectives.* Adelaide: Shannon Research Press, pp. 227–236.

Hargreaves, A., & Goodson, I. (2006). Educational change over time? The sustainability and nonsustainability of three decades of secondary school change and continuity. *Educational Administration Quarterly, 42*, 3–41.

Heifetz, R. A., Linsky, M., & Grashow, A. (2009). The practice of adaptive leadership: Tools and tactics for changing your organization and the world. Cambridge, MA: Harvard Business Press.

Henggeler, S., Schoenwald, S. K., Borduin, C. N., Rowland, M., & Cunningham, P. B. (1998). *Multisystemic treatment of antisocial behavior in children and adolescents.* New York: Guilford.

Hughes, L. (2011). Integration of services requires collaborative working across professional and organisational boundaries. In R. H. Shute, P. T. Slee, R. Murray-Harvey, & K. Dix (Eds), *Mental health and wellbeing: Educational perspectives.* Adelaide: Shannon Research Press, pp. 285–296.

Humphrey, N., Lendrum, A., & Wigelsworth, M. (2010). *Social and emotional aspects of learning (SEAL) programme in secondary schools: National evaluation.* Manchester: Department for Education.

Intercamhs (2009). *International survey of principals concerning emotional and mental health and well-being.* Accessed 25.02.2015 at www.intercamhs.org/html/principals_survey.html

International Initiative for Mental Health Leadership. Accessed 27.11.2015 at http://www.iimhl.com/

International Mental Health Conference, 2015. *Mental health future for all.* Accessed 1.03.2015 at www.anzmh.asn.au/conference/

Jarvis, J. M. (2011). Promoting mental health through inclusive pedagogy. In R. H. Shute (Ed.), with P. T. Slee, R. Murray-Harvey, & K. Dix, *Mental health and wellbeing: Educational perspectives.* Adelaide: Shannon Research Press, pp. 237–248.

Kerret, D., Orkibi, H., & Ronan, T. (2014). Green perspective for a hopeful future: Explaining green schools' contribution to environmental subjective well-being. *Review of General Psychology, 18*, 82–88.

Kinash, S., & Hoffman, M. (2008). Child as researcher: Within and beyond the classroom. *Australian Journal of Teacher Education, 33*(6), Article 6, 75–93. Accessed 13.04.2015 at http://ro.ecu.edu.au/ajte/vol33/iss6/6

National Council for Curriculum Assessment, Ireland (2010). *Curriculum overload in primary schools: An overview of national and international experiences.* Accessed 28.02.2015 at www.ncca.ie/en/Publications/Reports/Curriculum_overload_in_Primary_Schools_An_overview_of_national_and_international_experiences.pdf

Page, S., & Clark, J. (2015). Modelling teachers' promotion of powerful positive affect in the primary mathematics classroom. In H. Askell-Williams, *Transforming the future of learning with educational research.* Hershey, PA: IGI Global, pp. 51–78.

Reinke, W., Stormont, M., Herman, K. C., Puri, R., & Goelet, N. (2011). Supporting children's mental health in schools: Teacher perceptions of needs, roles, and barriers. *School Psychology Quarterly, 26*, 1–13.

Sawyer, M. G., Pfeiffer, S., Spence, S. H., Bond, L., Graetz, B., Kay, D., Patton, G., & Sheffield, J. (2010). School-based prevention of depression: A randomised controlled study of the *beyondblue* schools research initiative. *The Journal of Child Psychology and Psychiatry, 51*(2), 199–209.

Scheftlein, J. (2012). *Lessons from the European Pact for Mental Health and Well-Being.* Brussels: European Commission.

Shonkoff, J. P. (2000). Science, policy, and practice: Three cultures in search of a shared mission. *Child Development, 71*, 181–187.

Shute, R. H. (1997). Multidisciplinary teams in child health care: Practical and theoretical issues. *Australian Psychologist, 32*, 106–113.

Shute, R. H. (2012). Promoting mental health through schools: Is this field of development an evidence-based practice? *The Psychologist, 25*(10), 752–755.

Shute, R. H., & Slee, P. T. (2015). *Child development: Theories and critical perspectives.* Hove: Routledge.

Shute, R., Owens, L., & Slee, P. (2008). Everyday victimization of adolescent girls by boys: Sexual harassment, bullying or aggression? *Sex Roles, 58,* 477–489.

Skrzypiec, G., Askell-Williams, H., Slee, P., & Rudzinsky, A. (2014). *IB middle years programme (MYP): Student social-emotional well-being and school success practices.* Adelaide: Flinders University Centre for Student Well-being and Prevention of Violence.

Slee, P. T., Lawson, M. J., Russell, A., Askell-Williams, H., Dix, K. L., Owens L., Skrzypiec, G., & Spears, B. (2009). *KidsMatter Primary Evaluation Final Report.* KidsMatter and the Centre for Analysis of Educational Futures. Accessed 18.05.2013 at http://www.kidsmatter.edu.au

Spears, B., Slee, P. T., & Huntley, J (2015) Cyberbullying, sexting and the law. A report for the South Australian Minister for Education and Child Development. Unpublished Report.

Srabstein, J. C. (2011). The prevention of bullying: A whole-school and community model. In R. H. Shute (Ed.) with P. T. Slee, R. Murray-Harvey, & K. Dix, *Mental health and wellbeing: Educational perspectives.* Adelaide: Shannon Research Press, pp. 297–305.

Stewart, S. L. (2008). Promoting Indigenous mental health: Cultural perspectives on healing from Native counsellors in Canada. *International Journal of Health Promotion and Education, 46*(2), 49–56.

Swan, P., & Raphael, B. (1995). Ways forward: National Aboriginal and Torres Strait Islander health information. National Consultancy Report. Canberra: AGPS.

Vostanis, P., Taylor, H., Day, C., Edwards, R., Street, C., Weare, K., & Wolpert, M. (2011). Child mental health practitioners' knowledge and experiences of children's educational needs and services. *Clinical Child Psychology and Psychiatry, 16*(3), 385–405.

Walton, G. M. (2014). The new science of wise psychological interventions. *Current Directions in Psychological Science, 23*(1), 73–82.

Weiner, B. J. (2009). A theory of organizational readiness for change. *Implementation Science.* Accessed 27.11.2015 at http://www.implementationscience.com/content/4/1/67

What Kids Can Do, Inc. (n.d.). Accessed 27.02.2015 at http://www.howyouthlearn.org/SEL_studentvoices.html

Wikipedia (n.d.). *Sexual violence in South Africa.* Accessed 1.03.2015 at https://en.wikipedia.org/wiki/Sexual_violence_in_South_Africa

World Health Organization (2000). Local action: Creating health-promoting schools. Geneva: WHO: Accessed 27.11.2015 at www.who.int/school_youth_health/media/en/88.pdf

World Health Organization (2002). *Gender and mental health.* Geneva: WHO. Accessed 16.03.2015 at www.who.int/gender/other_health/en/genderMH.pdf

Wyra, M., Lawson, M. J., & Askell-Williams, H. (2011). Teachers' wellbeing during schoolyard supervision: A photovoice study. In R. H. Shute (Ed) with, P. T. Slee, R. Murray-Harvey, & K. Dix, *Mental health and wellbeing: Educational perspectives.* Adelaide: Shannon Research Press, pp. 165–176.

Yeager, D. S., Fong, C. J., Lee, H. Y., & Espelage, D. L. (2015). Declines in efficacy of anti-bullying programs among older adolescents: Theory and a three-level meta-analysis. *Journal of Applied Developmental Psychology, 37,* 36–51.

INDEX